My Name Is Million

Books by W. S. Kuniczak

MY NAME IS MILLION
THE THOUSAND HOUR DAY
THE SEMPINSKI AFFAIR

Now my soul is incarnate in my country,
My body has swallowed her soul,
And I and my country are one.
My name is million, for I love and
    suffer for millions.

Adam Michiewicz, *The Great Improvisation*

AN ILLUSTRATED
HISTORY
OF THE POLES
IN AMERICA

HISTORY CONSULTANT
Dr. Eugene Kusielewicz
ARCHIVAL PICTURE RESEARCHERS
Ann Novotny and Rosemary Eakins
of *Research Reports*
PHOTOGRAPHY CONSULTANT
Frank Aleksandrowicz

My Name Is Million

By W.S. Kuniczak

DOUBLEDAY & COMPANY, INC.
GARDEN CITY, NEW YORK
1978

Library of Congress Cataloging in Publication Data

Kuniczak, W S   1930–
My name is million.

1. Polish Americans—History.   I. Title.
E184.P7K94   973'.04'9185
ISBN: 0-385-12228-4
Library of Congress Catalog Card Number 77–82954

For Elizabeth, Elizabeth, Stephanie, and Magda

The author wishes to express his special gratitude to Drs. Eugene Kusielewicz, Albert S. Juszczak, and Harry Dembkowski for their generous assistance in reviewing historical materials and suggesting additional research sources. Sincere thanks are also due to the staff of the Kosciuszko Foundation, and to the foundation's chairman of the board, Dr. Walter M. Golaski, for his initial encouragement. Their support was very much intangible, but it is appreciated. There must also be a way to acknowledge the contribution made by Max Gartenberg, the author's agent and lifelong friend, who conceived the idea for such a popular illustrated history as a service to the Polish community in America, and the professional skills and vision of Diane Matthews, then an associate editor at Doubleday & Company, whose final *imprimatur* gave publishable substance to an idea and a need.

In all respects, this book must be seen as a joint project of many persons of different skills and backgrounds who felt that it was time that the Polish story in America was told, in some fashion, to all their fellow-Americans in the English language. The analysis of the Polish-American cultural condition, and some of the views expressed as to its evolution, are the author's own and no one else may be held responsible for them. The physical limitations of this book can make that story no more than a survey, but the author hopes that it may encourage other American writers to pay some attention to historical truth in their treatment of Poland and the Poles in the United States.

W.S.K.

News of Columbus' epic voyage was quick to reach Poland which, at the dawn of the sixteenth century, neared the peak of her political, intellectual, and military influence in Europe. Such was the country's power, wealth, and reputation for tolerance and justice that members of its royal family were invited to rule in Hungary and Bohemia, while Polish scholars, philosophers, and artisans were welcomed in most Western European capitals, from Vienna to Madrid.

Stanislaus Polonus, a Polish publisher and printer in Spain, was among the first to spread the news of the discovery. Another Pole, a roving seaman named Franciszek Warnadowicz, who had settled in Cadiz under the name of Francisco Fernandez, was actually said to have made the voyage with the Genoese adventurer's polyglot crew. Not one scrap of parchment exists to support this story but, in its time, it helped to excite the imagination of an adventurous people.

Another Polish claim to kinship with the New World was that of Jan of Kolno (a town in the Polish province of Mazowsze), who was a navigator in the service of King Christian I of Denmark. Jan is said to have piloted a Danish flotilla in search of the old Norse colonies of East Greenland and also a new route to Asia. As the story goes, the fleet made landfall in Labrador in 1476 and then sailed down to the mouth of the Delaware River. Having found neither old Norse colonies nor new routes to Asia, the expedition supposedly sailed back to Denmark. Jan of Kolno, himself in part a product of legend, is said to have died on the

Jan of Kolno, a Polish navigator in the service of King Christian of Denmark, is said to have guided a Danish flotilla to the coasts of the New World in 1476, although no record exists of this accomplishment. Artur Szyk, the allegorical cartoonist who came to the United States almost five centuries later, painted this representation of what the legendary seafarer might have looked like in his own time. COURTESY OF MRS. ALICE BRACIE.

voyage home, and the entire tale dissolves in unsupported myth.

Legends may have been good for telling on a winter's evening, but the recorded work of scholars is based on solid ground.

This great age of exploration and adventure happened to coincide with the reign of

Poland's most brilliant dynasty, the Jagiellonians, whose Polish-Lithuanian Commonwealth formed one of the most successful federations in European history. The Jagiellonian University of Cracow, Poland's medieval capital, was a prime seat of European learning where, in the year before Columbus' little fleet sailed from Cadiz, the restless mind of Nicholas Copernicus had begun to revolutionize contemporary concepts of the solar system.

Polish scholars eagerly followed the news of the discoveries. By 1506, references to the *Novum Mundum* could be found in treatises published in Cracow, and the first fanciful map of America (complete with fabulous sea monsters) appeared at the Polish court in 1532. Some twenty years earlier, the new continent had already been engraved into the Jagiellonian golden globe in Cracow, and Copernicus himself—in the book that inaugurated modern astronomy in 1532—devoted an entire chapter to America. Discovery of the New World supported Copernicus' theory that "land together with water constitutes one globe," and helped to prove his heliocentric system.

Other scholars, poets, essayists, and travelers followed suit with enthusiastic and none too accurate accounts of the discovery. They made America appear as something real and attainable rather than a legend, and several groups of adventurous Poles set out for Spain and the New World. There is no record that any of them ever reached their destination.

Sixteenth- and seventeenth-century Poles were all in favor of colonization and foreign adventures, but the vast unpopulated steppes of Russia and the Ukraine were closer to home. Moreover, the sixteenth and seventeenth centuries brought no additional stimulus for would-be Polish immigrants to strike out into the unknown: No heretics were going up in flames in Poland. In an atmosphere of religious freedom unknown in other parts of Europe, the Reformation attracted the elite of the nation but didn't take deep root. Poland was entering its own brilliant Renaissance when the arts, literature, and humanist scholarship flourished along with a growing parliamentary system and the rudiments of wide political freedom. The Gothic altars carved by Wit Stwosz, or the first Polish-language writing in Mikolaj Rej seemed far more interesting to the Renaissance man of the Polish Commonwealth than feathered Americans. Not even lurid tales of Spanish gold could compete for attention with the works of Jan Kochanowski, the greatest pre-Romantic writer in the Slavonic world, whose surviving manuscripts include 16,700 poems in Polish and 7,000 in Latin. These were the years when Andrzej Frycz Modrzewski was writing his monumental *Reform of the Republic,* and Stanislaw Cardinal Hozjusz was about to invite the Jesuits and their Counter-Reformation to Poland.

Above all, for those who might have craved conquests and adventure, there were always the Muscovites and Tartars to be taught still another lesson in the eastern wilderness. And there were always the Turks rampaging just south of Poland's borders.

Yet only a year after the settlement of Jamestown, Virginia, in 1608, a contingent of Polish glassblowers, pitchmakers, and potash workers (and some Pomeranian Germans who had worked along with the Poles) came to the new colony in the *Mary and Margaret,* the first supply ship to make the voyage. This was no coincidence. Captain John Smith, one of the early governors of the colony, had spent some years in Poland, had fought beside the Poles against the Turks in Hungary, and had had an opportunity to observe the work of these artisans, whose craftsmanship had given Poland a near monopoly in the glass and naval supply trades. The London Company had hired them to bring their industries to America.

The Jamestown glasshouse, and the pitch and potash burners set up by the Poles, were the first export industries on the American continent outside Spanish

Settlers clear the land and build the first crude houses of Jamestown, Virginia, in this unsigned early sketch, which supposedly represents the earliest arrivals. Skilled Polish artisans arrived in the colony on the first supply ship to start the first industries in 1608. CREDIT: LIBRARY OF CONGRESS, PRINTS AND PHOTOGRAPHS DIVISION.

hands. Captain John Smith was delighted with his Polish workmen and gave them full credit in published accounts. To begin with, they were just about the only colonists who were willing to work. The original group that landed in Jamestown included only twelve workmen among ninety-two "gentlemen" who had never done a day's work in the Old World and didn't intend to do much in the New. By the time the Poles and Germans disembarked among them, only fifty-three of these gentlemen were still on their feet.

The Poles immediately set about digging wells, building better shelter, clearing the land for cultivation, and felling timber for wood manufactures. They built their glass furnace on a tract of land about a mile from the crude fort, and set up workshops for the manufacture of clapboard, resin, frankincense, and potash. These skilled pioneers proved such an asset to the English colony that more of their fellow countrymen were invited to settle in Jamestown and, within a few years, fifty Poles were living and working in the colony.

In his *Map of Virginia,* published in 1612, Governor Smith related how his

"Dutchmen" (Germans) had conspired with the Algonquin Chief Powhatan to kill him, and had stolen arms from the Jamestown arsenal. Smith also told how two Polish glassmakers had rescued him from ambush and helped to capture the Indian Chief Paspahegh, "a most Stout Salavage." Later, in 1619, during Governor Yeardley's first administration, "Robert, a Polonian," was noted as having distinguished himself in an expedition against hostile Indians.

But as to the kind and quality of the greenish-colored glass shipped from the colony to England, there is no contemporary clue. English archaeologists have found windowpanes and small drinking vessels that were probably made in the Jamestown glasshouse, but, as a profit-making venture, glassmaking soon gave way to tobacco in Virginia.

Little mention is made of the Polish glassmen after Smith's recorded fight and rescue near the glasshouse. It's possible they were among the victims of the "starving winter" of 1609–10 when "dogges, Catts, Ratts and myce were eaten . . ." and when one hungry English gentleman even killed his wife, salted her down, and devoured her. Scarcely able to keep body and soul together, the few colonial artisans who survived the famine, disease, and Indian attacks shipped little to the company's directors in London, and the glasshouse was abandoned. A second glassmaking enterprise was tried in 1621 with Italian workmen and fared no better.

The colonists had neither time nor energy to expend on complex industry that required skilled foreign artisans until the Virginia wilderness was tamed. But the two glassmaking ventures did not fall completely short of their goals. They taught valuable lessons for future manufactures in English America, among them the need to care for workmen.

As John Smith wrote to his London stockholders: "As for the hiring of the Poles and 'Dutch,' to make pitch, tarre, glasse, milles and soap ashes was necessarie and well. But to send them and sev-

entye more without victuall, to work, was not so well considered. . . ."

Two Poles of the original group of eight survived the famine, and by 1619 more had arrived to manufacture the pitch, tar, and resin without which England's "wooden walls," the ships of her navy, would have leaked like sieves. Ten years after the first Polish craftsmen landed in Virginia, more than fifty of them worked in and around Jamestown and were preparing to teach their English company directors yet another lesson.

In Europe, and in the giant Commonwealth where John Smith had met them and learned to value their courage and endurance, much had changed while the colony had struggled for its life. Poland and Lithuania had been joined under one King and one parliament, and free elections had inaugurated the era of Europe's first and only elective monarchy where every man above the trader class could cast an equal vote to elect his King, and every voter was considered equal.

In Virginia, Governor Sir George Yeardley issued the call for an assembly meeting in the Jamestown church on July 30, 1619, to organize the first representative legislative assembly in America and the beginning of the present system of legislative government in the United States. All native-born Englishmen were allowed to vote; all foreign-born Virginians were excluded.

The Polish settlers and their families, who felt they had contributed quite enough to the survival of the colony, demanded a right to vote and, when the governor refused it, staged the first strike for civil liberties in America. If their countrymen could elect the most powerful monarch in Europe, they told the astonished Yeardley, they could, surely, elect their representatives to the Virginia House of Burgesses.

They said: no vote, no work.

Such was their value to Virginia's economy that the company in London hastily ordered their enfranchisement and, on July

4

The Polish artisans who joined the Jamestown colony in 1608, and later staged the first strike for civil liberties in America, probably looked and dressed very much as they were painted by Artur Szyk in this decorative panel. COURTESY OF MRS. ALICE BRACIE.

21, 1619, just in time for the first assembly meeting, their demand was met.

"And because their skill in the makyng of pitche, tarre and soap ashes shall not die with them," the Court Book of the Virginia Company noted on that date, "It is agreed that some young men shall be put unto them to learn their skill, and knowledge therein, for the benefit of the country thereafter."

And so the Polish craftsmen not only helped to set up the first industrial experiment in the Colonies, and fought the first successful strike for civil rights, but also found themselves, unwittingly, the founders of the first American vocational school. It is a tragic and ironic note of history that in the year when Polish workmen won their right to life with dignity and freedom in English America, the first shipload of black slaves was landed in Virginia.

Among the Dutch of New Holland, where an entirely different breed of Poles had settled by invitation, they joined the ranks of the intellectual and political leaders of the colony. This Polish "Dutch Connection" with America, which was to last long past the War of Independence, produced the first classical Latin school in what would later be the city of New York, founded the city of Buffalo, New York, and established the only credit the fledgling United States would be able to find among European bankers for a long time after their struggle for independence.

The school's founder, and sole teacher, until other Poles were hired was Dr. Aleksander Karol Kurcjusz (Curtius), who was engaged by the Dutch West India Company in 1658 and who is also listed among the physicians and surgeons of New Amsterdam in 1659. His academy stood on Broad Street in Lower Manhattan, and he is named by John Shrady in *The Memorial History of the City of New York* as "the first physician of any prominence" in the city. Governor Peter Stuyvesant praised Curtius highly in reports to the company, upped his salary, and allowed him to begin a medical herbarium. Two other Poles, John Rutkowski and Casimir Butkiewicz, quickly followed Curtius as teachers in New Amsterdam.

But there were earlier well-known Polish settlers in canny Peter Stuyvesant's little colony who were almost as colorful as the peg-legged governor himself. They came from Holland, where a powerful community of Polish Protestants and religious reformers had established itself in the first quarter of the seventeenth century. These were astonishing men by any century's standards. Poland had seen no religious wars. It would not tolerate inquisitions; its Counter-Reformation was mild in comparison with the fiery persecutions throughout Western Europe. But a little bigotry goes a long way, and militant Catholicism, which had become identified with loyalty to the Com-

Fort Amsterdam, shown in this painting by Edward L. Henry, was built by Peter Stuyvesant on the site of the original Dutch fortification near Bowling Green, in lower Manhattan. It was said to have been commanded for a time by Captain Daniel Litscho (Liczko), a Polish officer who was one of Stuyvesant's most trusted aides and political allies. Litscho's daughter, Anna, later married an early mayor of English New York. COURTESY OF THE TITLE GUARANTEE COMPANY, NEW YORK.

monwealth during invasions by Protestant Swedes, helped to poison the intellectual atmosphere in which thoughtful men could flourish. Polish Protestants, who had been judged unpatriotic, were often expelled, and so the Arian Brotherhood, which had formed one of Poland's most extraordinary communities of thinkers and scholars, left their homeland to settle in Amsterdam.

From this community of philosophers, theologians, and educated nobles came men like Joannes a Lasco (Laskowski), the Polish social and religious reformer to whom Erasmus of Rotterdam sold his famous library; Krzysztof Arciszewski, who

rose to the rank of admiral in the Dutch Navy and who commanded the fleet that captured Brazil from the Portuguese; wealthy merchants and financiers like the Stadnicki family, who conducted Holland's profitable trade with Poland and Russia; and earlier political exiles like the Zborowski clan which had once rebelled against a Polish King.

It can be supposed that when Peter Stuyvesant asked the company in 1659 to encourage Polish settlement in New Amsterdam as a balance to the growing wealth and influence of New England, he didn't have pitchmakers or artisans in mind.

One of the earliest Polish settlers to make his home at the tip of Manhattan Island was Daniel Litscho, an officer in the Burgher Companies and a trusted aide of Stuyvesant in his struggle against the Dutch patroons. Litscho made himself conspicuous in Stuyvesant's conquest of New Sweden in 1655 and was one of the most influential men in the colony. His tavern at 125 Pearl Street was a political gathering place for Stuyvesant supporters, and his daughter, Anna, married Colonel William Peartree, who was mayor of New York City from 1703 to 1707.

Captain Marcin Krygier, a participant in Arciszewski's Brazilian conquest, was another Polish officer close to Stuyvesant. Krygier was elected co-burgomaster of New Amsterdam three times and commanded Fort Casimir, which defended the city. Fort Casimir, built by Stuyvesant in 1651, was supposedly named after King John Casimir, who ruled in Poland at that time. It was the first locality in the New World to bear a Polish name.

But the most colorful and, in time, the most distinguished of the Poles who came to New Holland was Olbracht Zaborowski,

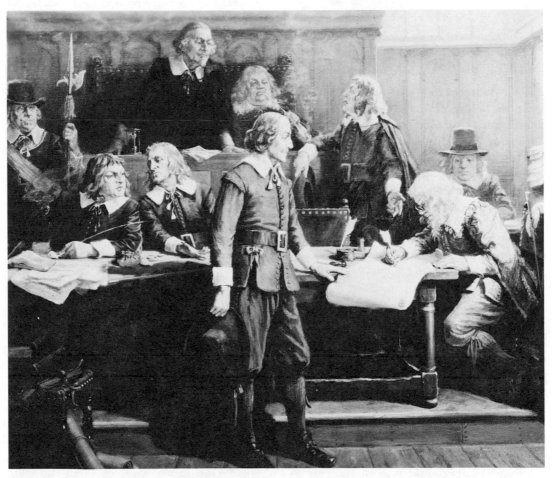

In this painting by John Ward Dunsmore, showing the signing of the first title deed recorded in New York, Polish Captain Marcin Krygier (Crieger, etc.) rises from the burgomaster's bench (in rear) to witness the signature. Krygier, a participant in Admiral Arciszewski's conquest of Brazil for the Dutch, was three times co-burgomaster of New Amsterdam and one of the Dutch colony's principal military commanders. COURTESY OF THE TITLE GUARANTEE CO., NEW YORK.

The most famous and best-remembered of the early Polish settlers in Peter Stuyvesant's Dutch colony in and about Manhattan was Olbracht Zabriskie (Zaborowski, etc.) shown here in an Artur Szyk cartoon. Zabriskie, a friend of the Indians along the Hackensack River, sent his son to live with the Algonquins so that the boy might learn their languages and customs. The boy, Jakob, later became a translator and negotiator between the Indians and the white colonists. COURTESY OF MRS. ALICE BRACIE.

who is said to have been a descendant of that Samuel Zborowski who had tried to overthrow a Polish King and lost his head in the process. The King's vengeance had pursued the family to Holland and, in 1662, Olbracht reached America. The family name suffered a variety of spellings before passing into American history and geography as Zabriskie.

Olbracht Zaborowski was an anomaly in his time. While others looked upon the American Indians only as subjects for exploitation, Zaborowski genuinely liked and respected his Algonquin neighbors, mastered their language, and became their friend. There is a story that Olbracht's son, Jakob, was kidnaped as a child by an In-

dian sachem, who then asked the boy's father to let him stay with Indians for a time so that he might learn their languages and customs and serve later as arbiter in their disputes with the colonial whites. The sun of the great Algonquin nation had not entirely set, but it was then only a matter of time; a friend in the whites' councils might delay the process of destruction.

One can imagine this sachem of doomed people and the exiled Polish nobleman, whose own nation had already passed the zenith of its power, as having more than buckskins and uncertainty in common. Olbracht apparently agreed to the sachem's plea. Whatever the facts of that meeting may have been, Jakob went to live with the Algonquins for seven years and, eventually, became the colony's foremost interpreter and negotiator between whites and Indians. His signature is still legible on early treaties and purchase agreements.

Olbracht Zabriskie became a landowner in what is now upper Bergen County in New Jersey and founded the Lutheran church in Hackensack. His Dutch- and English-speaking neighbors elected him their justice of the peace. His five sons married into the most prominent colonial families. A recently published history of the Zabriskies lists more than two thousand descendants in New York, New Jersey, Pennsylvania, Delaware, and Illinois, among the Astors, Jays, Bayards, Morrisons, Van Houtens, and in the family of Gouverneur Morris.

The American War of Independence saw Olbracht's grandchildren pitted against each other in what was truly a family tragedy of personal principles in conflict. As members of the colonial aristocracy, the Zabriskies had little to gain from joining a rabble-in-arms that only a historian could consider an army. Most of them did join, but one didn't.

Up to the day when musket fire rattled along the split fences of Lexington and Concord, John Zabriskie, head of the family as Olbracht's principal heir, had been a leader in the struggle for representation in England's parliament. He was a man of reason and believed in reason. As judge, member of the Bergen County Committee of Correspondence and colonel of militia, he had rallied the Patriot party of New Jersey to resist London's short-sighted colonial exploitation, but only to the verge of open rebellion. Like his extraordinary grandfather, John Zabriskie believed that only fools and scoundrels go to war. When the King's cause lost, with considerable assistance from some other Poles, Zabriskie didn't run to seek refuge and a pension in London, like so many other ruined loyalists. He remained in America, penniless and homeless, when his patriot neighbors gave his home to General Steuben. Washington's "Prussian" drillmaster (actually, von Steuben had been an unemployed Bavarian captain, not a Prussian general) had little feeling for principle but a high regard for appearances and order. He refused the gift knowing that, sooner or later, the victorious patriots of New Jersey would come to their senses and regret these precedents in expropriation. The family eventually regained its confiscated home. It is now a museum.

The spark of the American Revolution had not yet been struck in anyone's imagination when Polish names began to appear on the muster rolls of provincial levies for the French and Indian War and among the ranging frontiersmen of western Pennsylvania. Pennsylvania archives show that Polish immigrants had been part of the colony since the days of William Penn, and other Poles had settled in the Delaware Valley as early as 1650. Who they were and why they came here was never recorded. Their names were soon corrupted beyond recognition by backwoodsmen who would probably sooner tangle with a bear than with Polish pronunciation. But the best known of their names have survived mutilation and suggest that these lone, restless, fiercely independent hunters and explorers who pushed across the Alleghenies, down the Ohio, and into Kentucky and Tennessee, came from landed stock—

that turbulent, intractable, adventurous, and fearless Polish petty gentry that had been both the glory and the despair of the Commonwealth. Taught as children to "ride well, shoot straight, and tell the truth," resentful of authority other than their own, they seemed to have been fashioned by an ironic-minded providence to confront the western American wilderness. This was a breed of men that, as a class, was dying out in Europe, in whose thickly populated countries men's shrinking living space had reduced man's spirit; America's wilderness promised them those conditions of individual freedom that the gradual decline of their own vast country was making impossible as the seventeenth century drew to its end in Poland.

The Polish Commonwealth in the first half of the eighteenth century resembled a doomed and lethargic giant whose eastern provinces were dropping away like truncated limbs. At last, a hundred years later than in the crowded spaces of Western European countries, a motive and a stimulus for Polish colonization of America had appeared, and Poles began arriving in the American colonies not as skilled artisans, nor as an intellectual additive to the colonial life of others, but as colonists in their own right.

There was no "Warsaw Company" to supply and support them—as there never would be any kind of overseas government crutch to help in their settlement and development in America. Most of them came in small family groups with enough money of their own to buy their first few hundred Pennsylvania acres from Quakers and Swedes. And so the name of Anthony Sadowski, soon to enter American geography as Sandusky, first appeared on a title deed to four hundred acres of good land along the Schuylkill River, which he bought from a Philadelphia speculator in 1712.

There is no contemporary portrait of Sadowski—such men would lack the vanity to sit for a portrait—but his kind of Pole had become practically a stereotype from the Lower Dnieper in the Ukraine to the walls of Vienna: tall, lean, and rangy,

Explorer, hunter, and contemporary of the legendary Daniel Boone was Jacob Sadowski, who was the first white man to make the descent on the Mississippi River from the English colonies to the site of New Orleans and thus effectively open up the West. He is shown here in an allegorical portrait by Artur Szyk.
COURTESY OF MRS. ALICE BRACIE.

slightly stooped from years in the saddle, high-browed and -cheekboned, and with eyes seemingly borrowed from those cruel Tartar faces that had been so much a part of Poland's reality.

He would be fluent in Latin, the *lingua franca* of the Polish gentry, a variety of European languages and dialects learned for either warfare or commerce, and possibly the grunting speech of Tartars, whose semantic roots are so startlingly similar to the basic forms of the Algonquin language.

Where the Sadowskis came from in Poland is a properly irrelevant mystery. Some Polish-American historians have unearthed the roots of the Sadowski clan in the rich, cultivated plains of western Poland, in the Poznan region—which has also allowed a German-American historian to claim Sadowski for his fatherland. Wherever Sa-

dowski came from, he seems to have arrived with nine children, according to his living descendants in Kentucky, but if he spent more than token time on his pleasant Pennsylvania acres, there is no record of it. Governor Patrick Gordon used Sadowski as his envoy to various hinterland Indian tribes, and that *is* a matter of record.

In 1735, Sadowski left his lands in Pennsylvania and pushed alone beyond the Alleghenies into the northwestern wilderness that would become Ohio, and then—according to the family tradition—down the Ohio River to Kentucky and northern Tennessee, anticipating systematic white settlement of those regions within a hundred years. He did attempt to start a settlement along the clement shores of western Lake Erie and built a trading post near the site of today's industrialized Sandusky, Ohio—a name that may have derived from a mangled version of Sadowski's but was, most likely, a corruption of a Wyandot Indian phrase that described some geographical features of the region.

There is no doubt, however, that Sandusky Station in Kentucky derives its name from Anthony Sadowski's remarkable sons; archives of the state's historical societies attest to that.

At this point even an amateur historian, less interested in documented fact than in constructing a palatable legend, finds himself confused. History is never there to explain itself; at best it is a record of what might have been according to whoever observed an event. And so the story of Anthony Sadowski descends to the shadowed, speculative realms of folklore and legend. If he was not quite a precursor of Dan'l Boone, he does become a sort of Polish Paul Bunyan who seems to have been everywhere at the same time.

Part of the confusion is due to his name, which appears in various colonial documents in eleven variations that make sense only if a reader is skilled in Polish phonetics. One story has him marrying an Indian princess, a seemingly popular pastime in those days; another has him bringing his family ready-made from Poland. Perhaps he did both. There is no way to tell which of the later Sadowskis of Kentucky and Tennessee were his sons and which were his nephews. Even the where-and-why of his death are fabulous in confusion.

One of the legends that have sprung up about him says that he was killed in ambush in northern Virginia by a party of raiding Cherokees, as he hurried to the aid of some Algonquin chief who was his blood brother. Another sees him giving up his ghost in bed in Pennsylvania, the victim of respectability and old age.

Whatever or whoever ambushed Anthony Sadowski, who may or may not have been quite what historians make him, there is no doubt about his sons, James and Jacob, who carried various versions of his name into the western wilderness.

The two Sadowski brothers were members of Captain Thomas Bullit's surveying party that laid out the site of Louisville, Kentucky, in 1773 and joined James Harrod, the next year, in his expedition to make the first permanent settlement in that territory. They canoed down the Monongahela and Ohio rivers to the mouth of the Kentucky, then up that waterway to a creek called Landing Run. From there they cut their way through virgin forest to the Salt River and Fountain Bleau Spring to help lay out today's Harrodsburg, Kentucky.

Other Sadowski (or Sandusky) brothers —Anthony, Jr., and Jonathan—also pushed into the waterways and forests of Kentucky and founded the trading post of Sandusky Station in 1780. Two other Sanduskys, Emanuel and John, were pioneers in northern Tennessee. In 1775, a John Sanduske was one of the first settlers of Nashville, Tennessee, according to the records of the family.

But of all the Sadowskis or Sanduskys, who were as well known on the western frontier of their time as any of the picturesque long hunters, Indian fighters, bear wrestlers, and traders who have become so much a part of the American pioneer folklore, Anthony's son Jacob accomplished more with one perilous journey than all the lone legendary brawlers of the West.

When the Indians destroyed the first Harrodstown settlement in 1774, and James Harrod led his survivors back to what passed for civilization—not to return without heavy reinforcements for another year —Jacob Sadowski took his canoes down the Cumberland, Ohio, and Mississippi rivers to New Orleans in the first such descent made by a white man from the English colonies. The opening up of this waterway effectively opened up the West.

In those turbulent days, as sometimes in these, a Pole was a Pole in a crude and polyglot collection of "English" colonists, and what may have been true of one was often applied to another—they were rare and distinct enough for generalizations. And so the story of Anthony Sadowski's Indian marriage may have been lifted out of the remarkable life of yet another Polish explorer and envoy to the Indians who married not just one baptized Indian maiden but two of them in turn. This was the Reverend Christian Frederick Post, who had been born in Chojnice, Poland, in 1710, and who combined his missionary work, for the scattered brethren of the Polish Moravian Church in America with lone travels and diplomatic missions for the English. Most of his missionary travels were among the fierce Iroquois of northern New York and Connecticut in 1743, but he also described his life among western Indians in a sixty-seven-page pamphlet published in London in 1759. This *Second Journal of Christian Frederick Post on a Message to the Governor of Pennsylvania and the Indians of Ohio* was the basis of a later English alliance with the Iroquois, which forced the French to abandon Fort Duquesne.

But one name that should have entered American history, and might have had it sounded more like Lewis or Clark, is better known at the British Museum in London than in America. Captain Charles Blaskiewicz (or Blaszkowicz), a topographical en-

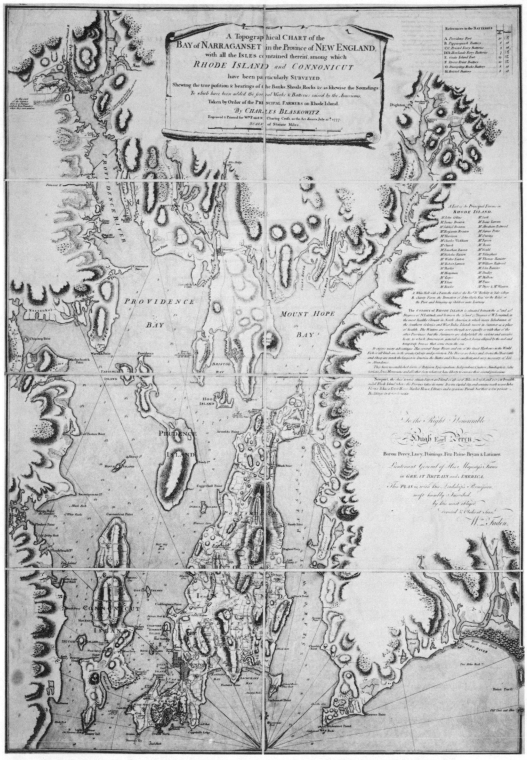

The earliest maps of the New England coast were drawn by Captain Karol Blaskiewicz, a Polish topological engineer in British service before the War of American Independence. This detailed drawing of Narragansett Bay, off the coast of Rhode Island, was printed in London, England, on July 4, 1772. It is believed to be the first map of that portion of America. CREDIT: LIBRARY OF CONGRESS, GEOGRAPHY AND MAPS DIVISION.

gineer in the British service before the Revolutionary War, made the first surveys of the New England coast, and charted the islands, bays and inlets, rivermouths, and natural harbors of Massachusetts, Connecticut, and Rhode Island in 1772—the year in which the troubled and dissension-ridden Polish Commonwealth was overthrown in Europe.

Poland's rapacious neighbors, Russia, Prussia, and Austria—whose precious Vienna had been saved by Poles from Turkish conquest in 1683—joined forces in the first of three partitions of the Commonwealth and carved away more than one third of her territories and one half of her population. Poland as a power, as an experiment in idealistic parliamentary systems (where all decisions had to be unanimous!), and as an architect of radical social and political thinking, had come to an end.

Dreams and illusions, the solace of the cruelly dispossessed, began to cloud the fine, clear prism of the Polish consciousness and mind, and some quixotic Poles looked beyond Europe for those vast, open spaces they had lost in the Ukraine and Russia.

A Polish colony in America was never really possible. But a project for such a colony, in which all sorts of libertarian notions were to be resurrected, did appear in Warsaw. Its author was Count Pawel Mostowski, the palatine (governor) of Mazowsze, whose geopolitical fantasies might have rivaled those of Ludwig of Bavaria in the century to come. His New Poland, seen as a combination of classical Athens and the Roman Republic, was to appear somewhere in the area of today's Florida and Alabama. The English were not at all averse to such an idea, as a way to challenge Spain beyond the Mississippi.

Nothing came of Mostowski's dream, as nothing could. History was moving even faster than the doomed, desperate Poles were able to imagine. Before anything substantial could be done about Mostowski's project, the young and vigorous American colonies were suddenly reborn as a new and independent nation, and Poland—

aged, weary, and powerless to defend herself—began her descent into more than one hundred years of virtual slavery.

A fittingly absurd footnote to Mostowski's grandiloquent sense of timing was the tonic he offered to George Washington's embattled colonials: "A Balme, with which the wounded soldiers can readily cure themselves without the aid of surgery, in the course of six or seven days, and in this short space of time be ready to return to the battle."

A Polish political thinker of considerably more importance to the future American republic than the impractical Mostowski was Wawrzyniec Goslicki, the author of a book first published in Venice in 1568. He was a doctor of philosophy and laws from the Jagiellonian University and the universities of Padua and Bologna; the title of his book was *De Optimo Senatore* (The Perfect Senator), which immediately stood monarchical Europe on its absolutist ear. The book had nothing to do with senators, perfect or imperfect, but everything to do with human rights of citizens under a just and responsible government. Its author demanded limitation of royal authority, equality of all citizens under law, and equal opportunity for all based purely on merit.

The first two Latin editions of this revolutionary work spread like wildfire throughout Western Europe and, like all other heresies, were burned at the stake in every capital west of Polish borders. Even in England, where a few copies were taken for safety, Elizabeth Tudor ordered them destroyed. New editions, subversively translated as *The Counsellor*, kept reappearing throughout Stuart Britain, and were burned as quickly as they could be found. But Goslicki's fame was such that absolute destruction of his work was never possible. As chancellor to three successive Polish Kings, he had respectful access to all the courts of Europe despite his appallingly humanistic views. According to the late Professor Ivor Golancz of Cambridge Uni-

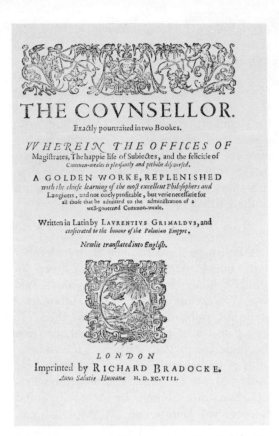

The title page of Wawrzyniec Goslicki's De Optimo Senatore, *as it appeared in its original English translation under the title of* The Counsellor, *with a Latinized version of Goslicki's name. Goslicki's sociopolitical treatise formed the basis for the U. S. Bill of Rights and the philosophical premise behind the U. S. Constitution.* BY PERMISSION OF THE FOLGER SHAKESPEARE LIBRARY.

versity, Goslicki met William Shakespeare at the English court, and the dramatist was so taken with his views that he modeled Hamlet's "Polonius" after him and lifted several passages from *The Counsellor* for two of his plays. Goslicki was revered by Robert Cardinal Bellarmine and by Bellarmine's disciple Algernon Sydney.

The last English translation of *The Perfect Senator,* made in 1733 by William Oldisworth in London, remained a standard text on democratic government for eighteenth-century social revolutionaries and reformers. One of these eager students, whose vision could encompass the sweep of monumental change through social justice and equality, was Thomas Jefferson, an intellectual follower of the egalitarian Sydney. When he sat down in 1776 to pen his own best-known literary effort, Jefferson wrote an almost word-for-word transcription of this translated sixteenth-century Polish political treatise, beginning with Goslicki's most unnerving line: "*We hold these truths to be self-evident that all men are created equal . . .*" He then restated each of Goslicki's political premises, including the right of the people to change their form of government should it no longer serve their interests.

Goslicki's soaring vision, the culmination of four centuries of Polish political thought, found expression not only in the Declaration of Independence but, later, as the philosophical basis for the American Constitution and the Bill of Rights.

On May 3, 1884, Harper's Weekly *featured this wood engraving, which
supposedly pictured a Polish marketplace in Manhattan's Lower East Side,
where many of the new peasant immigrants found their first American homes.*
COURTESY OF THE NEW-YORK HISTORICAL SOCIETY, NEW YORK CITY.

*Polish peasants, freed from serfdom by
Tsar Alexander in the 1860s, began
arriving in the United States during the
next ten years. Largely illiterate and
unskilled, they were soon objects of
American derision. This scene from a
popular American weekly of 1881
supposedly shows Polish immigrants
resisting attempts to inoculate them against
smallpox on their arrival in New York.*
CREDIT: LIBRARY OF CONGRESS, PRINTS
AND PHOTOGRAPHS DIVISION.

Piotr Rostenkowski, who would become a leader of the Polish-American community, posed as a young man in this pseudo-Polish military uniform in Stevens Point, Wisconsin, in the early 1880s. COURTESY OF POLISH MUSEUM OF AMERICA, CHICAGO.

Stanislaw Slonimski, a pioneer of Polish immigration, poses outside his store, where he sold and manufactured banners, badges, and religious articles, in Chicago in 1872. COURTESY OF POLISH MUSEUM OF AMERICA, CHICAGO.

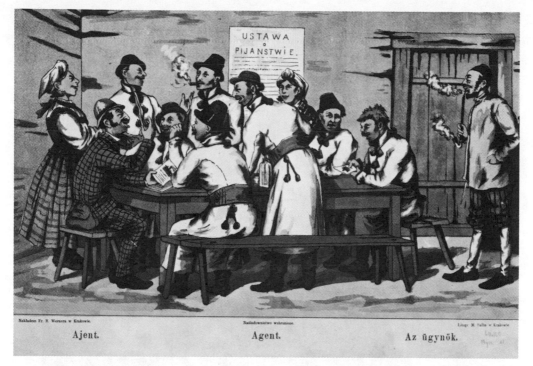

Ajent.   Agent.   Az ügynök.

Landowners in partitioned Poland bitterly resisted the peasant emigration that reduced their supply of cheap labor. In these two Austrian prints of the 1870s, Polish peasants of the Cracow region are shown as "falling into the hands of Jews." First an agent of a shipping line gets them drunk in a Jewish tavern, then they are cheated of their possessions and shipped off to an uncertain American future. Despite such propaganda, more than one hundred thousand Polish immigrants sailed for America each year between 1880 and the outbreak of the First World War. CREDIT: LIBRARY OF CONGRESS, PRINTS AND PHOTOGRAPHS DIVISION.

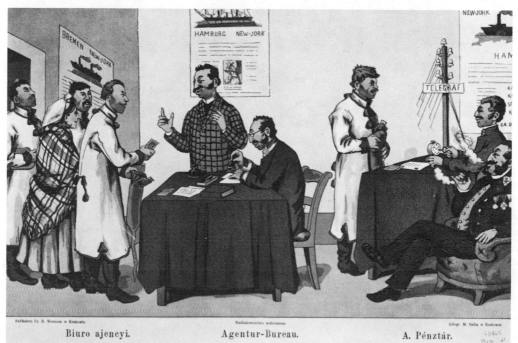

Biuro ajencyi.   Agentur-Bureau.   A. Pénztár.

Cultured and educated Poles continued to arrive in the United States in the peasants' time and tried to imbue these bewildered masses with a sense of national identity and consciousness. In this commemorative poster, printed in Chicago in 1891 on the one hundredth anniversary of Poland's first liberal constitution, Polish saints, martyrs, Kings, and historical heroes were enlisted in the cause of stirring Polish national awareness among peasant immigrants, few of whom even shared a common regional dialect. CREDIT: LIBRARY OF CONGRESS, PRINTS AND PHOTOGRAPHS DIVISION.

The Alliance of Poles was an early organization of Polish-Americans dedicated to the fostering of Polish national ideals in America. In this group portrait of an AOP company in ceremonial dress, which prominently features the traditional Polish square-topped lancers' caps, can be seen several men who were to be important in Polish-American life. CREDIT: WESTERN RESERVE HISTORICAL SOCIETY.

Words may inflame men's minds and prod humanity along its evolutionary paths, but living men and women are required to make a revolution and to win a war, and the New World was lacking in seasoned military leaders capable of fighting a major European power. One of the tasks of Benjamin Franklin in Paris was to find such leaders and enlist them in America's cause. In 1777, he scored a great success in this regard by winning over Casimir Pulaski, the most renowned cavalryman in Europe, who was a penniless exile in Turkey and France after the first partition of Poland. On May 29 of that year, Franklin wrote to Washington: "Count Pulaski, an officer famous throughout Europe for his bravery and conduct in the defence of the liberties of his country against three invading powers of Russia, Austria and Prussia, will have the honor of delivering this into Your Excellency's hands. The court here have encouraged and promoted his voyage, from an opinion that he may be highly useful to our service. Mr. [Silas] Deane has written so fully about him, that I need not enlarge; and I only add my wishes, that he may find in our armies under Your Excellency, occasions of distinguishing himself."

There may have been another reason why the gallant, polished young aristocrat (he was only thirty when he landed in Boston in July 1777), was Franklin's choice to become "The Father of the American Cavalry." When the British first began searching for mercenary armies to put down the American rebellion, they turned not to the German princelings of Hesse and Brunswick but to the mighty Empress Catherine II of Russia. They even made a formal offer of seven pounds sterling per man for twenty thousand of her veteran infantry. The Earl of Suffolk sarcastically consoled William Eden with the hope that "twenty thousand Russians will soon be charming visitors at New York and civilize that part of America wonderfully." The Revolutionary documents of 1776 and 1777 repeatedly mention this English hope and American fear of the Russian expeditionary corps. And Pulaski had won all his laurels in fighting the Russians.

Pulaski didn't find George Washington in Boston. The American commander's headquarters were constantly on the move. That summer, as for many difficult months to come, the war seemed to present an endless, wearying perspective of dubious battles with comparatively little hope of ultimate success—a feeling with which the young Polish volunteer was dreadfully familiar.

The countryside through which he rattled in a rented carriage in search of his general was drained of livestock and spirit but full of gloomy men who wondered how much longer Washington's militias could stand their defeats. The British, under General Howe, were preparing to march on Philadelphia, and another bloody battle was a certainty. Pulaski knew by experience that Washington's citizen levies had to be preserved as a fighting force, no matter what the cost. Once totally dispersed, an irregular army could never become an army again. As Pulaski traveled south, he drafted a plan for a mounted corps of vol-

A marble bust by Polish sculptor H. D. Saunders (Dmochowski) represents Count Casimir Pulaski in the rotunda of the Capitol in Washington, D.C. Pulaski's legion, a body of cavalry and light infantry raised largely at his own expense, gained him the name of the Father of the American Cavalry. He was Washington's most skilled cavalry commander. CREDIT: LIBRARY OF CONGRESS, PRINTS AND PHOTOGRAPHS DIVISION.

Brigadier General Count Casimir Pulaski, a Polish patriot who became Washington's chief of cavalry, was killed during the Franco-American attack on Savannah, Georgia, in 1779, when he attempted to rally dispirited French columns during an assault. His glamorous death has tended to obscure the more lasting services that he had rendered to the American cause. CREDIT: LIBRARY OF CONGRESS, PRINTS AND PHOTOGRAPHS DIVISION.

unteers who would act as Washington's eyes on the march and protect his retreats.

He tracked down the harassed Washington in Neshaminy Falls, Pennsylvania, and on August 27 the general wrote to John Hancock suggesting that Pulaski be placed in command of all the cavalry. The letter was sent only a few days before the start of Howe's march on Philadelphia.

The Americans moved out to meet Howe on the Brandywine. In this confused battle, which British officers called "a colonial turkey-shoot," Washington's crude and undisciplined army simply fell apart. Outflanked, outmaneuvered, and finally outfought, the colonials came within an inch of annihilation. Toward the end of the chaotic shootout, when Washington had lost control of his army, and skilled British maneuvering was threatening his rear, Pulaski asked for thirty men of the American commander's bodyguard and led them in a long sweep of the British line, which finally showed Washington what his enemies had been doing to him. Riding within a pistol's range of the British columns, Pulaski spotted the wide flanking movement with which the enemy had all but encircled the Americans and threatened Washington's baggage train and line of retreat.

As the day drew toward its end, with the battle lost, Pulaski galloped into the crude encampment where, among panicked stragglers and riderless horses, Washington's staff were urging their commander to ride for his life. Washington, according to contemporary accounts, seemed frozen in indecision, determined not to face his enemies in the Congress with the unpalatable fact of another defeat. Pulaski reported the dangerous British movement which, if completed, would have meant the end of Washington's army and career; Pulaski then laid out a possible line of march that could still extricate the Americans from their difficulties.

His commission from the Congress had not yet arrived, and Pulaski had no authority to command anyone, but Washington immediately ordered him to gather as

many stragglers as he could—with whatever American horsemen could still be found on the battlefield—and use them according to his judgment to cover a retreat. In a series of swift hit-and-run ambushes and one dashing charge—which the Redcoats could hardly have expected—Pulaski halted the flanking British columns, leading his pickup task-force from one end of the battlefield to another until the main body of the American army could escape.

Praise for Pulaski was fervent and immediate. Two days after the battle, James Lowell wrote to General Whipple that the young Polish volunteer had "greatly signallized himself, fully sustaining by his conduct and courage, the reputation for which the world had given him credit." The Congress immediately rewarded Pulaski with a commission as brigadier general in command of all American cavalry which, on September 15, 1777 (the date of his commission), meant the four scattered regiments of Colonels Bland, Baylor, Moyland, and Sheldon and which totaled fewer than three hundred men.

In the difficult defensive campaign that followed Brandywine, Pulaski vainly tried to unite the cavalry into a single corps with which to raid and disrupt the enemy rear. Instead, his troopers fought in scattered detachments, protecting retreats and scouting British movements, so that Pulaski seldom had more than a quarter of his men at hand. This was a bitter blow to the young cavalry commander, who found his best officers and men detached for courier, escort, and ceremonial duties while the actual work of the cavalry went undone. But he did all he could. In a letter to George Washington later in the year, Pulaski warned that "the weak state of the corps I command, renders it impossible to perform every service required. . . . Yet I cannot avoid hazarding everything that is valuable in life."

In the running fight on the Lancaster Road near Philadelphia, and in covering the retreat of Greene and Stephen after the Battle of Germantown, Pulaski finally won the confidence of Washington for the one branch of the service that the American commander didn't fully understand. When Washington marched his battered remnants into winter quarters at Valley Forge, all American cavalrymen rode behind Pulaski. At last he could begin fashioning a unified mounted force.

Sometime in December 1777 Pulaski took his cavalry to Trenton, where forage for the horses was easier to find, and there set about training and reorganizing this underprivileged arm of the American service. The one commodity he had in plentiful supply was, as he wrote to Congress, "a dearth and scarcity of everything I need." But this was scarcely news to the Congress in this difficult period in the war, and Pulaski was left largely to his own devices.

He spent the winter drilling and reorganizing his dragoons, much to the displeasure of their American colonels whose deficiencies as skilled cavalrymen were all too apparent, formed a detachment of lancers (whom he knew to be effective against infantry), supplied his cavalry with their first set of service regulations, and tried to inspire them with discipline and *esprit de corps*. In the process, he is supposed to have laid out sixteen thousand dollars from his own pocket for needed equipment, although his great fortune in Poland was long lost to him.

His biographer, Jared Sparks, was to write later that "his soldiers adhered to him as to a brother, and willingly endured fatigues and encountered perils, the most appalling, when encouraged by his approbation or led by his example. He possessed in a remarkable degree the power of winning and controlling men. . . ."

If that were true for soldiers, it was not so for his subordinate American officers, who disliked taking orders from a foreigner, however distinguished. Perhaps they also missed the easy days of ceremonial escort duty, when each had been his own independent cavalry commander. Pulaski, according to Sparks, was "amiable, gentle, concilliating, candid, sincere, generous to his enemies and devoted to his friends," but in Trenton he also found himself extremely confused. Apparently he had not realized the gulf that existed between America's native-born and foreign officers, nor the reasons for it. The few European officers who had come to America so early in the war treated American militia "colonels" with uniform contempt, often with good reason, and the Americans grew to resent the foreigners, who seemed to be monopolizing many higher ranks. While Pulaski was turning his troops into real cavalrymen, his colonels kept a sullen silence. News of their intrigues against him, however, were reaching congressional ears.

In February 1778, when the supply problems at Valley Forge threatened to force Washington to disband his army, Pulaski took his newly trained and orderly dragoons on a long raid against British provisioning detachments that were devastating the country around Philadelphia. The raid netted several British depots and a supply train, which Pulaski sent directly to Washington's relief, and drove Colonel Tarleton's Loyalist dragoons back into New Jersey. Pulaski then joined Anthony Wayne's column before Haddonfield, near Camden, and their combined forces won a much-needed American victory. Pulaski also won the hostility of Wayne, who disliked sharing credit for a victory with a foreigner. Wayne also thought that the supplies Pulaski had sent to Valley Forge should first have come to him.

In March, Pulaski gave way before the intrigues and hostility around him, which were demoralizing his cavalry and making command virtually ineffective, and asked to be relieved. Instead, he asked Washington to allow him to form, train, and equip a corps of foreign troopers who would not resent his European origin to the detriment of the American cause.

Washington, who knew all about subordinates' intrigues, and who knew the temper of his American officers better than most of them supposed, agreed with Pulaski, asked Congress to authorize the new corps of lancers and light infantry, and wrote on March 14 to Governor Livingston of New Jersey: "I am pleased with the favorable account which you give to Count Pulaski's conduct while at Trenton. He is a gentleman of great activity and unquestionable bravery and only wants a fuller knowledge of our language and customs to make him a better officer."

Congress acceded to Washington's request and resolved on March 28, 1778, that Pulaski should keep his rank as brigadier general in the Army of the United States and raise his mixed corps, which was to be modeled along the lines of a Roman legion. On April 13, 1778, a recruiting station for the Pulaski Legion was opened at Mrs. Ross's (no relation to the famous seamstress) house in Baltimore, and in July the legion was complete. Its officers were Frenchmen, Poles, and Germans; its lancers and riflemen were mostly German Americans from Pennsylvania and Maryland.

The one shortage of which Pulaski couldn't complain—and his voluminous correspondence with Washington and the Congress begins to take a rather petulant tone at this time—was the matter of recruits. Men were so eager to serve under him that they began to leave the regular Maryland line to join his legion, causing General Smallwood to protest to Washington, who ordered Pulaski on June 13 to send these men back.

Among the many Americans who served in the Pulaski legion—and there were many, because Pulaski's corps was used as a training ground for the later legions of Armand and Lee—was "Light Horse" Harry Lee, father of Robert E. Lee. Best known of the thirteen Polish officers on Pulaski's rolls was Major August C. G. Elholm, a native of Olsztyn, Poland, who had served under Pulaski's father in his native country and who went on to become cofounder of the short-lived state of Franklin in northern Tennessee. Jonathan Sadowski is also listed there—not as Sandusky this time, but with his name correctly spelled in Polish.

On July 29, the three troops of the legion's lancers and three companies of riflemen went through their paces for the bemused citizens of Baltimore, and Washington accepted them for service. Nothing quite so martial had been seen among Americans since the war began, according to the Maryland *Journal* and Baltimore *Advertiser* of August 4. But the best assessment of Pulaski's men was to come later from Major F. Skelly, brigade major of the English forces before Charleston, who called them simply "the best damned cavalry the rebels ever had."

Creating an American cavalry cost money and a lot of it. Congress had none to spare, despite the sacrifices of another arrival from Poland, the patriotic Haym Salomon, whom the Russians had barred from his native country for his wholehearted support of Polish independence. The legion's paymaster, a Captain Baldeski, noted that Pulaski spent more than fifty thousand dollars of his own money to equip his legion, but where that money could have come from is a mystery. Pulaski came to Boston on funds borrowed from Silas Deane in Paris, being quite penniless at the time. Some money came to Pulaski from Europe. When pressed by John Hancock for vouchers lost by his officers during the marches and campaigns of his legion later in the year, Pulaski said that he expected one hundred thousand livres from friends in Europe and would be glad to repay every farthing that Congress would advance to his troops. Pulaski's best bet for European credit would have been the heroic Haym Salomon, and that is the source of the legion's funding generally accepted by historians.

But if Pulaski had no money, at least he had a banner. On Maundy Thursday (April 16, 1778) the good nuns of the Moravian Church in Bethlehem, Pennsylvania, assembled in the Old Church for a reading of the tragedy of Gethsemane, and were astonished to see two distinguished officers enter the chapel, seat themselves reverently, and follow the sermon with close attention. The officers were Pulaski and his Colonel Kobatsch. The service was the beginning of a long association between the legionnaires and the Moravian

The banner of the Pulaski legion, shown in this reproduction, was embroidered for the gallant Polish soldier by the Moravian nuns of Bethlehem, Pennsylvania, where the legion was organized and trained. Officered by Poles and Frenchmen, the legion was composed largely of German-American settlers from Maryland and Pennsylvania, and included a troop of Polish lancers who were described by the British as "the best damn cavalry the rebels ever had." CREDIT: NATIONAL ARCHIVES (U. S. SIGNAL CORPS PHOTO).

nuns of Bethlehem. Pulaski's men guarded the convent whenever other troops were passing through town; the nuns sewed them a brilliant banner.

Reviews, parades, and martial exercises were all very well, but Pulaski fretted at inactivity. On September 17, he appeared before Congress and begged for some action. Washington ordered him to northern New Jersey to fight Indians and Tories. The legion's first action proved nearly disastrous. Surprised by four hundred English regulars under Captain Ferguson at Egg Harbor, the legion's infantry took a bad mauling, and its commander, the Polish Baron de Botzen, was among those killed. Pulaski's arrival with the cavalry saved the day, the British retreated, and Egg Harbor

remained in American hands. But Pulaski's reputation—and his even temper—suffered from this bad beginning.

He spent the winter of 1778–79—his last winter, as it was to prove—in the hard, thankless, and unglamorous work of ambushing Tory raiders and avenging Indian massacres in Cherry Valley and around Minisink on the Delaware River, complaining that he had "nothing but bears to fight." His letters to Washington grew despondent and fretful. Pulaski even started hinting about returning to Europe. A strange change came over this normally genial and enthusiatic young man. It was as if he had some intimation that his service—along with his life—would not last much longer, and he wanted one more brilliant chance to distinguish himself.

Washington wrote him kind and flattering letters until a suitable field of operations could be found for his legion and, on February 2, 1779, Pulaski was sent to reinforce General Lincoln in South Carolina. Lincoln was still far from Charleston, and the British under General Provost were hurrying toward it when Pulaski rode into the city at the head of his legion on May 8, the last American troops to reach it before the British.

The siege began three days after Pulaski's arrival. The town was surrounded. No one knew Lincoln's whereabouts or whether he was really on his way. General William Moultrie, Charleston's American commander, judged his situation hopeless, while the governor and Council met to agree on the British terms of capitulation.

The French Colonel Bentalou, who was there with Pulaski, and William Gordon, writing in London in 1788 from eyewitness accounts (*The History of the Rise, Progress and Establishment of the Independence of the United States*), paint a dramatic picture of Pulaski, racked by swamp fever and worn out by his forced march from the Delaware Valley, appearing before the Council.

"Already had the Governor and Council agreed on the terms of the capitulation, not the most honorable, when General Pulaski, accompanied by the brave Colonel Laurens, repaired to the Council chamber to protest against that precipitate measure, declaring that, as a Continental officer, he would defend the city for the United States," if Moultrie wouldn't defend it for South Carolina.

Provost was informed of that determination, judged it to be based on some news of Lincoln's imminent arrival, and began wrapping up his siege. To speed him along, and to revive the drooping spirits of the Charlestonian garrison, Pulaski led his legion in a sally. His infantry "from an eagerness to engage" showed itself too soon to surprise the British. "Pulaski, however, by discovering the greatest intrepidity, and by successful personal encounters with individuals of the British cavalry, had considerable influence in dispelling the general panic and introducing military sentiments into the minds of the citizens." This show of unexpected strength was enough for Provost, who turned back to Savannah. Pulaski's legion followed the British step-by-step, harassing them all the way to their refuge on James' Island, where he couldn't reach them because he had no boats.

The long campaign through low and swampy ground wrecked Pulaski's health, and he returned to Charleston. But he was up again in September to lead the cavalry screen for Lincoln's march on Savannah. It was to be Pulaski's last action.

On September 16, Lincoln's Southern Army joined up with the French corps of Count d'Estaing in what was to become a long and tedious siege, in which the climate and disease were doing far more damage to the besieging allies than British bombardments. Savannah was cut off from help on land and blockaded by the French fleet at sea; time alone may have sufficed to drop it into Lincoln's lap. But time called for patience, which d'Estaing didn't have. Disease was decimating his soldiers, and the lazy drift of hot and humid days was demoralizing them. He forced Lincoln to consider an all-out assault on the British bastion so that, at least, "the spirits of his men might be revived by an activity."

Pulaski's legionnaires had not had the sleepy leisure for demoralization. Their days and nights had been spent in scouting British fortifications, harassing their pickets, and foraging in the countryside for the army's food. D'Estaing had also placed all French cavalry under Pulaski's command since several of d'Estaing's officers were Polish, and his Frenchmen knew Pulaski's reputation.

Ironically, the young Polish brigadier general, who had had to resign his American command because American officers resented his European origin, found himself in command of French professionals who had such contempt for American officers that they would barely speak to them, far less take their orders. He tried to talk d'Estaing out of the assault, knowing at first hand the strength of the fortifications and the marshy broken ground through which the attacking French and American columns would have to reach their goal. He urged further patience; the British could not supply themselves through the French blockade and would soon have to surrender. But Pulaski's eloquence failed, and the assault went forward.

It was a disaster even before it started. An American deserter had betrayed the plan to the British, and the Redcoats were waiting. One version of what happened even states that General Lincoln knew he had been betrayed, but that d'Estaing, himself ill with fever, had become so committed to the idea of charging the city that he would not listen to reason.

Lost and stumbling in the swamps, tripping over huge gnarled roots of sunken trees that overturned cannon, floundering in the water traps prepared by the British, the French troops on the right flank and the Americans on the left walked into the calm, measured musketry and cannon of British regulars. D'Estaing fell with two wounds and was carried off the field. The French corps milled in chaos. Waiting in the rear with the cavalry and unable to see what was happening on the battlefield, Pulaski called Bentalou to follow him and rode into the smoke. Told by panicking

French soldiers that d'Estaing had fallen, Pulaski galloped into the swamp to rally the corps and lead it forward.

He was easy to see in his resplendent hussar-style uniform, plume waving and saber in hand, and his calm, practiced French (learned when he was a page to the Polish crown prince, and in the finest schools for Polish nobility) soon restored order, and the French corps followed him again.

The British also saw him. A gunner took aim. A charge from a swivel gun struck him in the thigh. He fell off his horse. The French, disheartened once again, retreated to the swamp. Some of the men from Pulaski's legion rushed forward to help him, and a Lieutenant Sitkowski carried him from the field. The wound was not mortal in itself, but gangrene set in and, two days later, Pulaski was dead.

He died aboard the American brig *Wasp*, which carried his body to Charleston for a hero's funeral, but this could have been only a commemorative service, because his grave has never been found. He is thought to have been buried at sea.

General Lincoln sent the mournful news to Congress which, on November 29, 1779, appointed a committee to plan a monument to the gallant young Pole. It was the first of many monuments to Pulaski raised by Americans, who also named several towns and townships after him, long before the Polish-American descendants of later peasant immigrations felt impelled to decorate their drab and dismal lives with a hero's mantle.

Pulaski was the most spectacular of the Poles who came to fight for American independence—a romantic embodiment of the flashing saber, the waving plume, and the thin crystal notes of trumpets summoning to the charge—and that is the way in which history has received him. The larger-than-life glamor of his death has obscured his steadier, quieter, lasting services in the drudgery of forging together a disciplined American cavalry that could shadow and report on the advancing British, in his unglamorous long-distance forage raids to feed and clothe the shivering scarecrows in the crude winter huts of Valley Forge, and in the bitter hit-and-run rearguard actions in which his small mounted corps covered Washington's retreats, slowed the pursuit of the victorious British and, time and again, saved the reeling Continentals from disintegration.

Explaining to Washington the reasons for his coming to America at a time when few European volunteers were anxious to join what seemed a lost cause, he wrote in one letter: "As to that, wherever men can fight for liberty, that is also our fight and our place."

In time, his fame in America would be eclipsed by a far more modest and unassuming hero, but only in the sense that a star's brilliance is made pale by sunlight. Like this other Polish soldier-idealist, whose name would become a symbol of freedom throughout Europe, Pulaski had expected nothing for himself. If seeking one's sense of being in a cause greater than oneself is romanticism, then Pulaski was the Great Romantic of the American Revolution, which legend has made him. But self-submersion of men in ideals was the coldly reasoned logic of the Poland from which Pulaski came; a Poland that was beginning to find its ancient vitality and valor once again, inspired by men like the young brigadier general.

Jean-Jacques Rousseau mourned him in Paris, writing: "He saved his unhappy fatherland, for he redeemed the glorious name of Poland and restored her moral forces." But his best epitaph might have been written by Poland's King, Stanislaw August Poniatowski (whose earlier subservience to the Russians Pulaski had opposed). Hearing of Pulaski's death, he remarked sadly to his ministers:

"Pulaski has died as he had lived—a hero. But an enemy of kings."

A partial scanning of Continental and militia regimental muster rolls shows the names of 110 Polish volunteers, including 3 Zabriskies and 5 Sadowskis. One, Captain Feliks Miklaszewicz, made a swashbuckling name for himself as a privateer, sailing the barque *Scotch Trick* and the 12-gun schooner *Prince Radziwill* under a congressional letter of marque, which he bought for $20,000. There were Polish officers in the French contingents under Rochambeau, mostly cavalry and technical troop commanders, and in de Lauzun's 1,200-man, polyglot *Volontaires Etrangers de la Marine,* whose Captain Jan Kwirin Mieszkowski distinguished himself in the siege of Yorktown.

But the most illustrious and self-effacing of America's Polish volunteers was Thaddeus Kosciuszko, a cheerful, thoughtful young man of such untimely modesty that he declined promotion time and time again, refusing to believe that, he had done anything extraordinary. Yet without his services as engineer and, in effect, chief of staff of various American armies, the course of the Revolutionary War might have been quite different.

Thaddeus Kosciuszko, the first major foreign volunteer who came here when there was no reason to expect success, and who served without pay until the last accidental skirmish of the war, was largely responsible for the stunning American victory at Saratoga in October 1777; the victory that turned the tide of the war in the colonists' favor. His fortification of Philadelphia thwarted the city's capture while Washington's beaten army retreated from New York. Kosciuszko's planning and building of West Point's defenses rendered that most crucial American strategic position impregnable to anything short of treachery. And it was his inventive genius and mastery of logistics that repeatedly prevented the British from capturing a retreating American army in the South.

Unlike Pulaski, scion to one of the most aristocratic families in Europe and heir to 14 towns and 108 villages, Kosciuszko was the son of an impoverished small landholder in Polish Lithuania and grew up in a village. No peasant lad by any definition, he ran through boyhood among country people: sly peasants, tricky peddlers, pom-

Brigadier General Thaddeus Kosciuszko, whose engineering skills helped to effect the first great American victory at Saratoga, is shown in this 1829 engraving by A. Oleszczynski. A hero of two continents, Kosciuszko won the admiration and friendship of Revolutionary America for his native Poland. He willed his American estates to the freeing and education of black slaves, causing Thomas Jefferson to call him "the truest son of liberty I have ever known." CREDIT: LIBRARY OF CONGRESS, PRINTS AND PHOTOGRAPHS DIVISION.

pous petty nobles, clodhopping dances, thatched roofs: a turbulent microcosm of sempiternal innocence, humor, pathos, fanaticism, superstition, generosity, kindness, decency, and madness. His atmosphere of childhood, peopled by every kind and condition of bucolic man, would later make him at home in America, which he loved from the beginning and would consider as "his second country" until his death. Brought up among Poles, Ruthenians, Lithuanians, Jews, Uniats, DisUniats, Dissidents, Greek Orthodox, Roman Catholics, Polish Tartars, Lithuanian Cossacks, Armenians, and every other racial or religious fragment that added up to the Eastern

28

Poland of his day, he seemed designed for the American experience. Yet, like all Poles no matter what their origin or religion, he was raised with a love of country and the ideal of its independence. His favorite hero of antiquity had been the Greek Timoleon because "he was able to restore his country's freedom, taking nothing for himself." Material things were simply immaterial to Kosciuszko.

When he landed in Philadelphia in the summer of 1776, his military qualifications stood out like a lighthouse. He had been first King's cadet at the royal military academy in Warsaw and a top graduate of the military engineering and artillery school in Mézières, France. He was, in short, the only trained staff officer Washington was to have until the French arrived—but he would prove to be far more than a staff man.

One of the legends that have grown up around him has him reporting dramatically to Washington's headquarters, on the day of his arrival, and saying "Try me," when Washington supposedly asked what he could do.

The truth is less romantic though no less dramatic. Washington was occupied in New York that summer. A sea-land pincer was closing on the Continental Army. Badly beaten in the Battle of New York, and driven north to White Plains, the Americans were falling back across New Jersey to Philadelphia, with Lord Cornwallis relentless on their heels. Out in the Atlantic, off the Delaware capes, an English fleet and transports under Admiral Howe made ready to take Philadelphia from the sea.

Kosciuszko had no sooner presented himself to the Board of War in the uneasy city when he was asked to devise some defense against this expected amphibious assault on the seat of government of an embattled young nation that had no navy at all. He was commissioned by Congress on October 18, 1776, as colonel of engineers (at a pay of sixty dollars a month which he would receive twenty-one years later) but he was at work, armed only with congres-

sional authority to "do what he could," several months before that.

Throughout that summer and autumn he designed and built sea forts on Billingsport Island, whose batteries controlled both riverbanks and the waterway itself. The Delaware River had been corked; the British pincers could not close. Washington had apparently not been told very much about this. Falling back across the Delaware just above Trenton, with his back to the wall, he ordered the Philadelphians to build fortifications in preparation for a last-ditch siege. It must have been with a sense of enormous relief that he learned that the rear of his army, and the government itself, had already been protected by Kosciuszko's work.

The rest is sheer drama: a Christmas night, Washington recrossing the Delaware, the Hessians struck at Trenton, and then the blow at Princeton, which sent Cornwallis reeling back to New Brunswick. Down in the Delaware Bay, Admiral Howe stood out to sea after evaluating the high cost of taking the Kosciuszko forts.

In the spring, Washington cast about for a man who might put up a wall against another expected British avalanche, coming down, this time, on Fort Ticonderoga, which guarded the main water route south from Canada, on the southern shores of Lake Champlain. "There is one in Philadelphia," he wrote, "but I do not know his name." In Philadelphia, the name of the young Polish engineer was known well enough, and Kosciuszko was immediately posted to the Northern Army and its commanding officer, General Horatio Gates.

Kosciuszko's plan for the defense of the vital fort was sheer military innovation. Rather than strengthening existing bulwarks, which defended the garrison itself, he called for a series of separate forts, on neighboring heights of land, whose interlocking cannon fire would protect far more than the forts themselves. None of the three armies that had garrisoned Ticonderoga in the past—French, British, and American—had done anything like that. Gates agreed, impressed by Kosciuszko.

The entrance to the "Place d'Armes," Fort Ticonderoga, which Kosciuszko tried to fortify against the advancing army of General John Burgoyne early in the American War of Independence. Kosciuszko's advice was not followed, and the British took the American fortress by placing batteries on Mount Defiance, where Kosciuszko had wanted to construct new American fortifications.
CREDIT: NATIONAL PARK SERVICE.

The plan rested on a battery of guns that were to be planted on nearby Sugar Loaf Hill (also called Mount Defiance), which overlooked not only Ticonderoga but also the fortifications on Mount Independence and the boat bridge that connected them. Mount Defiance was eight hundred feet tall, steep and difficult, but Kosciuszko believed that a road could be cut and the top leveled for his battery. Before work could start, Gates was replaced as Northern Army commander by his archrival, General Philip Schuyler of New York, who promptly put an end to the experiment and ordered a mere strengthening of existing works.

A month after Schuyler's arrival in Ticonderoga, the British were also there. Marching south from Canada with a well-equipped army of seventy-seven hundred regulars and twenty-five hundred Canadian, Hessian, and Indian auxiliaries, General John Burgoyne was ready to face Schuyler's twenty-five hundred colonials on June 30, 1777. Five days later the Americans could see "Gentlemen Johnnie's" troopers hauling cannon to the top of Sugar Loaf Hill, and Ticonderoga was as good as lost. That night the Americans abandoned the fort, leaving behind mounds of precious supplies and artillery.

"Badly armed . . . half-naked, sickly and destitute of comforts," as one American officer was to recall later, the Americans began a long and desperate retreat, with Burgoyne on their heels. There was no doubt that sooner or later the Redcoats and their Indians would catch up with what was left of the Northern Army and destroy it.

Kosciuszko was put to work obstructing Burgoyne's headlong pursuit so that the weary Americans could escape, regroup, and make a stand elsewhere. Trees were felled across trails and creeks, bridges cut, streams flooded, entanglements of topped pine and sharpened stakes were set up in ambush, and trenches were dug to turn the swampy country into a quagmire in which cannon drowned along with animals and men. Burgoyne's rush became a crawl of less than a mile a day, then it stopped altogether. With his supply lines from Montreal stretched to the limit, his men exhausted in the effort of removing Kosciuszko's ingenious obstacles, Gentleman Johnnie looked anxiously for help from New York.

The British plan, based on the fall of Ticonderoga, would have had Burgoyne marching on Albany, where he could join forces with a British army advancing up the Hudson from New York City, thus severing communications between the trading northern states and the food-supplying middle states and the rural South. Rebellion in the North could then be starved into submission and the South reduced in comparative leisure. That this didn't happen is due to many causes, not the least of which was the sacking of the incompetent Schuyler and restoration of Gates to the command of the Northern Army. Somewhat rested and reinforced while Burgoyne's troops floundered in traps and quagmires, the American army was put on the move north toward the enemy. Everyone knew that the battle against Burgoyne would be vitally important. If won, the Americans could turn against the British in New York or secure the crucial Hudson Valley. If lost, the British columns would probably connect, and their plan could prove successful in that autumn of "despondency and terror."

Kosciuszko was sent ahead of the army to find and prepare the battlefield where the Americans could hope to make a stand against Burgoyne's regulars. Kosciuszko settled on a place about twenty miles north of Albany and halfway between Gates' base at Stillwater and Saratoga. His brilliant engineering turned innocuous countryside into a fortress and a trap for Burgoyne. He found a little mound that controlled the narrow road between it and the river and crowned it with artillery. The mound was carefully chosen; it lay just below Mill Creek, which flowed into the Hudson, and placed a water barrier against the famous and expected Redcoat bayonet assault on the American right flank. Moreover, Mill Creek's four tributaries had formed deep ravines, which made natural breastworks for the American center and would make an infantry attack against it virtually impossible. Directing one thousand working soldiers, Kosciuszko laid out redoubts and entrenchments on a series of terraces and slopes on the one flank he wanted Burgoyne to attack—a place called Beamis Heights, which commanded both the river and all the ravines. There he placed and sighted the heaviest concentration of American cannon. As Gates himself noted after the American victory: "Let us be honest. . . . The great tacticians of the campaign, were hills and forests which a young Polish Engineer was skillful enough to select for my encampment." Burgoyne assaulted the impregnable American position on September 19, and again on October 7, both times repulsed with staggering losses, and on October 17, surrounded by an army that had grown to three times the size of his own, he surrendered his entire force to Gates.

Saratoga, the first great American victory of the war, had a decisive bearing on America's fortunes. It won the open support of the French, who had been sending money and supplies largely as an annoyance to their hereditary English enemy, and who had allowed some unemployed French and German officers to go to America. Burgoyne's surrender suddenly made "the impossible" appear probable: The Americans stood a chance of winning their war; a fleet of French battleships could make all the difference.

American historians pass over Kosciuszko in favor of such picturesque revolutionary stalwarts as Benedict Arnold and Morgan's Pennsylvania riflemen as the true architects of the Saratoga victory. They did the fighting. Arnold's gallantry is beyond dispute. Gates himself is downgraded to the role of a rather indecisive, slow-moving "old woman." But Kosciuszko's revolutionary comrades-in-arms knew whom they had to thank for their much-needed victory, and even Washington recommended him for promotion despite Kosciuszko's close personal ties to. Gates, who was Washington's rival. Writing to Congress concerning the promotion of some French officers, for the good effect this might have in France, Washington added: "I have been well informed, that the Engineer in the Northern Army (Cosieski, I think his name is) is a Gentleman of science and merit. From the character I have had of him, he is deserving of notice too."

Kosciuszko didn't think so. Unlike Pulaski, whose upbringing in the rarefied atmosphere of royal courts had given him a sense of fitness to lead and command—and an innocence concerning the feelings of others—Kosciuszko was all too aware of the resentment, among American officers, of the wholesale political promotions of French adventurers no more qualified or deserving than they. To a friend in Gates' camp he wrote: "If you see that my promotion will make a great many Jealous, tell the General that I will not accept of one because I prefere Peace more than the greatest Rank in the World."

Kosciuszko's attitude must have puzzled everyone around him in a time when all clamored or intrigued for rank and distinctions. But personal gain had little meaning for Kosciuszko. When Gates again wanted to get Kosciuszko a general's star in 1780, after his transformation of West Point into "America's Gibraltar," he again refused. "For my part," he wrote in his convoluted English, "nether Confidence I have enough to thyng [think] I deserve it, nor resolution

to ask . . . [although I am] extremely obliged to you for your kind offers." Only when the war was over, and Nathanael Greene insisted that he seek an adjustment of his rank as reward for his services to Greene's Southern Army, did Kosciuszko make a halfhearted attempt on his own behalf and wouldn't press the matter.

But history is an ironic and whimsical mistress. He who demands attention eventually gets little; he who asks for nothing, ignoring today's fortune and tomorrow's fame, receives a monument that time itself is unable to destroy. Kosciuszko's monument in America is West Point itself. It was a barely inhabited wilderness when Kosciuszko got there early in March 1778; two and a half years later, when he turned over his completed fortress to its new American commander, Benedict Arnold, hero of Saratoga, it was a bastion that only treachery could take.

The need to make West Point impregnable to British assault was obvious to everyone. Washington considered it "the key to America." It dominated the Hudson River —which was a private waterway for the British fleet—from a high cliff above a double right-angled bend, and could be approached only with difficulty on the land side. The ease with which the British had taken the nearby forts at Bear Mountain, during their autumn drive for Albany, made it essential that West Point become the barrier that would keep them bottled up in New York City. A French engineer, Lieutenant Colonel Louis de la Radière, had made a start at planning some orthodox defenses (which, if completed, would have taken most of the Continental Army for their garrison), but little had been done. Shortly after Kosciuszko arrived and began to work, de la Radière was sent packing at the request of the senior officers at West Point. "Mr. Kosciousko," wrote General Alexander McDougall to Washington, offering yet another mangled spelling of Kosciuszko's name, "is esteemed by those who have attended the works at West Point to have more practice than Col. Delaradière, and his manner of treating

Known as the Father of the American Artillery, for his indirect services in the War of 1812, Kosciuszko might have been more aptly called the Father of West Point. His fortification of this highland outpost in the War of American Independence denied the Hudson Valley to the British and made the American colonies safe from invasion from the North. CREDIT: WEST POINT MUSEUM COLLECTION, UNITED STATES MILITARY ACADEMY.

the people is more acceptable than that of the latter."

Given a free hand to do what he would, though neither the men, materials, nor supplies with which to do it, Kosciuszko set about effecting a defensive system rather than a standard eighteenth-century fort, as he had wished to do at Ticonderoga. He based it on a network of interrelated batteries and forts whose guns would protect each other and the river, and a similar system of forts and redoubts that protected West Point on land from the south. A small garrison could hold such works indefinitely if properly supplied. He also designed a great 60-ton chain, each link weighing 140 pounds, which was stretched across the Hudson between two of the forts, and the river was barred.

Work went on from five in the morning until sunset, under the most trying conditions, in steep and rocky country, with Kos-

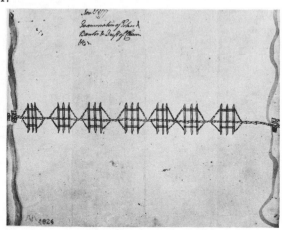

One of the defenses planned for the Hudson River by Thaddeus Kosciuszko was a gigantic chain, which blocked the waterway against British shipping. This early sketch of the Great Chain and Boom was supposedly drawn under Kosciuszko's direction. CREDIT: WEST POINT MUSEUM COLLECTION, UNITED STATES MILITARY ACADEMY.

ciuszko attending to every detail concerning his men, their food and clothing, fodder for the animals and teams, equipment and supplies, as well as bending late into the night over his drafting table, planning new redoubts and masked batteries, improving on what he had already constructed, only to be up before sunrise with his theodolite to measure the surrounding mountains.

Incidents that occurred during Kosciuszko's tour of duty at West Point afford some insight into his character. One story has it that he slept with a string tied to his toe so that the last sentry before dawn could pull it and wake him without disturbing any other officers with whom he sometimes had to share a bed in the crowded log cabin that had been given to him. Contemporary letters attest to the fact that he shared his meager rations with unfed English prisoners of war.

Washington came to inspect West Point late in the summer with his chief engineer, the French General Duportail, who pro-

nounced the works "almost impregnable" even at that time. It was then that Kosciuszko astonished everyone. With stunning candor, he pointed out some minor shortcomings in his own designs and showed how he would correct them to make the fortress impregnable indeed. From that moment, Washington knew he had an extraordinary human being under his command; he began to rely on Kosciuszko's honesty and judgment and took care not to misspell his name again . . . although no other contemporary American ever got it absolutely right.

The British were loath to give up their control of the Hudson highlands. They planned some sort of assault on West Point in the summer and fall of 1779, and massed troops in the area, but when they faced the engineering feats accomplished there ("these magazines completely filled, the numerous artillery one sees in various different fortresses"), the British generals ordered their troops withdrawn and never attempted to turn "the key to America"

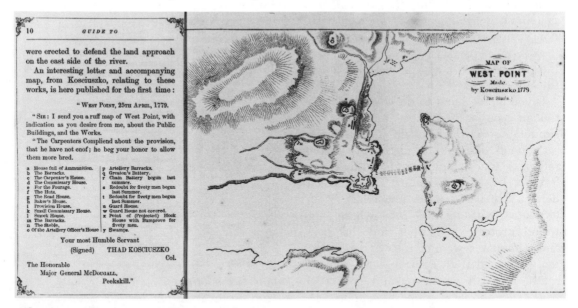

This facsimile of a map of West Point, drawn by Kosciuszko in 1779, shows the principal fortifications he designed and built. Kosciuszko sent this map to General McDougall, along with a letter, published in the official Guide to West Point and the Military Academy, *which appears at the side. Despite the convoluted English, Kosciuszko shows a concern about his men's welfare that made him one of the most popular officers in the Continental Army.*
COURTESY OF THE UNITED STATES MILITARY ACADEMY, WEST POINT.

West Point viewed from the North as it appeared at the Close of the War

Another contemporary sketch of Kosciuszko's West Point fortifications was made at the close of the War of American Independence by H. Livingston. Its accompanying legend identifies the Great Chain and Boom as "B," Fort Clinton as "C" and Fort Putnam as "D." COURTESY OF THE UNITED STATES MILITARY ACADEMY, WEST POINT.

again. For Kosciuszko, West Point was a greater triumph than Saratoga; it was a battle he won without a fight. He did it with a work force of eighty-two laborers, three masons, one stone cutter, and the skill of an inspired engineer.

The hard work, and occasional pleasant moments in the highland outpost, came to an end in August 1780. In the South, the war was going badly, and Gates was sent there in the hope that he could stem the tide of British successes, as he had done in the North at Saratoga. Told by Washington that he could expect few reinforcements from the Northern Army, he asked for only one: his engineer, Kosciuszko. Washington was reluctant to let Kosciuszko go. As he explained to Gates: "I have experienced great satisfaction from his general conduct, and particularly from the attention and zeal with which he prosecuted the Works committed to his charge at West Point." But Gates knew he would need Kosciuszko if there were to be another Saratoga in the South—and Washington knew it too. He gave his permission for Kosciuszko's transfer, and the young engineer set out for the South.

Some of the legends that have been spun around Kosciuszko make another de-tour at this point, but this time with the sound of truth. In his four years in America, Kosciuszko had not drawn one dollar of his pay, and owned only the one uniform coat that a Philadelphia tailor had sewed for him in 1776. He needed to equip himself for the southern campaign. As the story has it, he broke his journey in Philadelphia to see Haym Salomon, who had helped him before in a small way—as he did any American officer who needed assistance. But Salomon's fortune was practically gone. He had escaped from a British prison in New York with next to nothing, leaving even his family behind, and the demands for funds and credits by the impecunious Congress drained his resources as quickly as he could restore them. It would be in keeping with Salomon's character that he would share his supper with Kosciuszko in his Front Street house, join the patriotic young engineer in mourning the fallen Pulaski—whom both had admired—and that he would then pack a bas-

When Kosciuszko's fortress of West Point became the United States Military Academy, the cadets raised funds to erect a statue to the Polish engineer's memory. It was placed in what had been known as Kosciuszko's Garden, a shady spot overlooking the Hudson River, where this genuine hero of the American Revolution took moments of infrequent rest while building the fortress. CREDIT: WEST POINT MUSEUM COLLECTION, UNITED STATES MILITARY ACADEMY.

In this allegorical engraving by F. Girsch, entitled "The Leaders of the Revolution," Washington is shown at Valley Forge with his principal foreign officers. General Casimir Pulaski and Thaddeus Kosciuszko are pictured standing to the right of Washington, de Kalb, and Steuben, and to the left of Lafayette and Muhlenberg. Kosciuszko was the first major foreign officer to join the Revolution in 1776. LIBRARY OF CONGRESS, PRINTS AND PHOTOGRAPHS DIVISION.

ket of food for Kosciuszko's journey and give him his best blue coat. Supposedly they spent the evening talking about Poland, the country of their birth, planned ways to restore its independence in the light of their American experience, and it was then that Kosciuszko is said to have decided that he would return to Poland those egalitarian principles that Jefferson had penned into the American Declaration of Independence. True or not, no imaginative person can contemplate this scene without some emotion: the brilliant, patriotic Polish Jew who had become a devoted American patriot, and the unassuming, gentle Polish-American soldier who, in just a few years, would unite all of Poland's

fractious elements under a banner of universal freedom. Unable to love their country in its own territories, the two men loved it in exile. Then it was time to go. They parted, both spiritually restored, and never saw each other again.

Before Kosciuszko had time to reach the Southern Army, his friend Gates suffered a crushing defeat at Camden and was relieved of his command. The American cause in the South fell to its lowest ebb. The British countermarched through Georgia and the Carolinas at will. The first need of the shattered, scattered, and demoralized American army, which Nathanael Greene took over from Gates, was time to effect its own salvation. In the desperate winter of

1780, Kosciuszko explored the western wilderness of North Carolina, mapping the Catawba and Pedee rivers for use as transport waterways for men and supplies, and as possible highways for retreat to the North should Lord Cornwallis launch his columns against Greene before the Americans were ready. Then, while Greene set about rebuilding his army—in a camp that Kosciuszko found, fortified, and supplied for him—Kosciuszko offered him a weapon of new mobility that the roadbound British could not match. In a stroke of innovative genius, as novel as it was simple and effective, he conceived, designed, and built a fleet of flat-bottomed boats that could ride as wagons on swiftly detachable axles from river to river, then shed wheels and axles, take aboard their horses, men, guns, and supplies, and become river transports. With this one stroke, he freed Greene's Southern Army from dependence on roads, fords, and bridges, quadrupled its mobility, and introduced amphibious, wholly mobile warfare to the astonished British. When in January and February 1781 Cornwallis moved to crush Greene's unready patriots once and for all, Greene had the means to take his men to safety. In one of the most dramatic episodes of the Revolution, he led his barefoot, ragged army in a mad dash of two hundred miles across North Carolina, with Cornwallis breathing down his neck, to the patriots' fastness of Virginia. There Kosciuszko's boats carried his men to safety across the River Dan while Cornwallis, lacking boats and supplies, watched his sure prey escape him. The swift retreat saved the Southern Army, and in the months that followed, Greene and his generals drove the British from one outpost after another, and soon confined them to a few fortified coast towns. In October 1781, Cornwallis surrendered at Yorktown.

In the long, bitter campaign that lay between Greene's cross-country run and the Yorktown victory, Kosciuszko was always at the side of the American general, reconnoitering, choosing, and fortifying Greene's campsites and battle positions. He made, apparently, only one mistake, in the siege of the British outpost known as Ninety-six. He advised the breaching of British fortifications at their strongest point, a star-shaped redoubt that commanded all other British earthworks, and is said to have been lightly wounded "in the seat of honor" during a British sortie against his forward siege works.

After Yorktown the war was as good as won, although hostilities dragged on, in one form or another, through 1782, and in the tedious campaign of that year Kosciuszko fought more as a soldier than an engineer. He commanded Greene's advance guard near Charleston, raiding and harassing the British and effectively destroying their supply system. On November 14, 1782, he led a troop of fifty or sixty Americans against a British working party on James Island, where British infantry suddenly appeared. In the brisk skirmish, which turned out to be the last fight of the war, Kosciuszko's coat was pierced by four musket balls, but he escaped injury.

Then the war ended. America was free. Kosciuszko's thoughts turned once more to his homeland, which strove to save itself from foreign encroachments on its liberty. He was reluctant to leave America, having found here lasting and memorable friendships. To the high regard that Washington and Gates had for him there was now added the warm friendship and appreciation of Nathanel Greene. Kosciuszko was "among the most useful and agreeable of my companions in arms," Greene wrote to a friend in the spring of 1783, after Kosciuszko returned to the North. "Nothing could exceed his zeal for the Public Service, nor in our small but active warfare could anything be more useful than his attention, vigilance and industry. . . . [He was one] in a word whom no pleasure could seduce, no labor fatigue and no danger deter. What besides greatly distinguished him was an unparalleled modesty and entire unconsciousness of having done anything extraordinary."

The lawyers of the Congress found modesty suspicious; they were uncomfortable with a man who had declined promotions.

Fearful of setting a precedent while an entire army was clamoring to be paid, they palmed off Kosciuszko with a promise of payment of arrears at some unspecified future date and a grant of five hundred acres of public land, to which he was entitled as an officer. Kosciuszko's grant, located in the wilderness near what is now Columbus, Ohio, was inaccessible to him. As for promotion, Kosciuszko was breveted a brigadier general, along with every other officer who had not earned promotion in the war and was now advanced one step in rank.

This was too much for Washington, who insisted on a congressional resolution that would, at least, acknowledge "its high sense of his long and meritorius service." What surely must have meant far more to Kosciuszko than rank, pay, or politicians' comment was Washington's invitation to him to be present in the long room of Fraunce's Tavern in New York where, on December 4, 1783, Washington said farewell to the principal officers of his army.

All of Kosciuszko's American friends were there. Other than Lafayette and Steuben, he was the only foreigner invited. The officers of the Continental Army had formed the Order of the Cincinnati, and now Washington himself is said to have nominated Kosciuszko for membership. Then the austere Washington, a man of forbidding dignity and icy reserve, presented Kosciuszko with a sword thought to have been his own, suitably engraved. It was as though with this uncharacteristic gesture Washington were paraphrasing Gates' words after Saratoga on the larger scale of the whole war for American independence.

But Kosciuszko was not yet done with America, nor America with him. He sailed for France and Poland in July 1784, a troubled and uneasy man: Poland's affairs had not gone well during his eight years' service to America, and promised to go no better. The more the Poles did to revitalize their country, the more assiduously did their Russian and Prussian neighbors work (through bribery, corruption, kidnapings, and assassinations) to wreck their reforms.

Kosciuszko was heading once more into a grim and uncertain future, leaving behind friends and a country he had come to love, and a quality of life he had found inspiring. As he had written to Otho Williams from Charleston the year before: "O! how happy we think our Self when Conscious of our deeds, that we started from principle of rectitude, from conviction of the goodness of the thing itself, from motive of the good that will come to Human Kind." He was leaving the young American republic with regret, thinking himself "more than half a Yankee." America gave him much, in his intimation: a vision of his egalitarian ideal transformed into life. America, or rather his service to her Revolution, had taught him much that he would be able to use on Poland's behalf: tactics and the intricacies of practical warfare rather than textbook theory; strategy based on a poor country's limited resources; and, above all, a vision of how freedom and social justice might move badly armed, often ill-led and undisciplined men to victory over an imperial power and a regular army.

No one paid much attention to him on his return to Poland. Pulaski's glittering death was on the lips of all the angry young idealists; Kosciuszko's quieter services had not yet found an echo in his native country, which probably contented Kosciuszko well enough. First in seclusion, as a country squire, then (when his American fame had begun to spread among his countrymen) as a major general in the reformed and reorganized Polish National Army, Kosciuszko worked to imbue all classes of Poles, and all their ethnic and religious fractions, with a consciousness of national independence through social justice and personal freedom. The young, the cultured, and the civilized were quick to respond to his revolutionary message; the dispossessed could sense an intimation of dignity and freedom; the fat, complacent middle class was another story. Lacking the genius of an aristocracy or the honesty of peasants, they counted their pleasures a gold piece at a time, convinced that all was right with the world simply because the sky had not yet fallen. As he wrote to an inactive friend in 1789: "It is a sure fact that every citizen, even the most unimportant and least instructed, can contribute to the universal good, but he to whom the Almighty has given understanding of affairs greater than that of others sins when he ceases to be active. . . . We must all unite in one aim: to release our land from the domination of foreigners, from the abasement and destruction of the very name of Pole . . . and if we are covetous, [self-] interested, careless of our country, it is just that we shall have chains on our necks, and we shall be worthy of them."

In 1792 Kosciuszko helped to lead the army in gallant resistance to Russian invaders; his part in the struggle put him in the forefront of the nation's leaders. Known and respected—though many still feared his vision of a republican democracy, with its contempt for money privilege redolent of Jefferson and Paine—he became the leader to whom his country turned after the Second Partition of 1793, when Poland was robbed of half of her remaining territory and her government was terrorized into the role of a Russian puppet theater. Invested with absolute powers during The Emergency, he took the oath in the great square of Cracow in March 1794, swearing to fight to the end for Poland's liberty, integrity, and independence, and for the first time in Polish history called all classes and kinds of Polish citizens—not just the gentry—to bear arms. Peasant serfs turned their scythes into slashing pikes, the craftsmen and artisans of Warsaw formed peoples' battalions, and, in a move not seen in the world for four thousand years, the Jews of Poland raised, equipped, and manned a brigade of light cavalry for national service.

Poland was finally united under a national banner of freedom with justice, and all the social and military lessons that Kosciuszko had practiced and perfected in America were brought into play. In a series of stunning victories, the Poles smashed the Russians. Legend has tried to improve on truth by dressing Kosciuszko in a peasant coat instead of a commander's military uniform. The truth, however, is significant as Kosciuszko's dedication to American ideals. At the Battle of Raclawice, when Kosciuszko's scythemen charged and captured the Russians' artillery, Kosciuszko led them in his threadbare American uniform (it would be nice to think of it as Haym Salomon's old blue coat) and carried Washington's sword. That sword was in his hand, and that uniform (with the eagle badge of the Cincinnati) was on his back on October 10, 1794, when his army was finally overwhelmed by Russians and Prussians and, as an English poet wrote in retrospect, "Freedom shrieked as Kosciuszko fell." Slashed across the forehead by a Cossack saber, with part of his thigh shot away by a cannonball, he was bayoneted three times as he lay on the ground and left for dead on the field of Maciejowice. He was to spend two years in a Russian prison; then, after Catherine II had mercifully passed to her warm rewards, he was released, left Poland (which had ceased to exist as an independent nation), and never saw his country again.

Hailed by crowds and lionized by society in every capital through which he passed (including London, more than any other), he made his way to the United States again. Guns in the forts he had built to protect the city boomed in salute as his ship docked at Philadelphia on August 18, 1797, and a crowd of distinguished Americans went aboard the *Adriana* to carry him ashore (his wounds had never been properly treated; he couldn't walk unaided or even sit in comfort). Philadelphians harnessed themselves to his carriage and drew him, among cheering crowds, to the little house on Pine Street that friends had rented for him. Gates, Greene, and Thomas Jefferson (whom he had met in 1780 while on his way to join the Southern Army) called to renew their friendship. Washington wrote to welcome him: "I beg you to be assured that no one has a higher respect and veneration for your character than I have; and no one more seriously wished, during your arduous struggle in the cause of liberty and your country, that it might be crowned with success. But the ways of providence are inscrutable and mortals must submit. I pray you to believe that at all times and under any circumstances, it would make me happy to see you at my last retreat from which I never expect to be more than twenty miles again."

Congress had finally bestirred itself and settled his arrears of pay, plus interest, with a payment of fifteen thousand dollars, and he was making plans to buy a farm at Saratoga Springs, near the site of his great victory for America, but the ways of providence are inscrutable indeed, and he was to answer one more call in America's service.

Kosciuszko was now fifty-two years old, his hopes for mankind still intact although his health was shattered. Two friends were constantly with him. One was the Polish poet Julian Ursyn Niemcewicz, whose travels in America would produce the best contemporary account of Washington's private life and who would play a mysterious role in a strange and unacknowledged service that Kosciuszko was yet to render his adopted country. The other was Kosciusko's black servant, Agrippa Hull, who had hurried to him as soon as he had heard of his former master's return. Hull had been given to Kosciuszko as a slave at West Point, and Kosciuszko had immediately given him his freedom, finding the idea of slavery incomprehensible. Jefferson, then Vice President of the United States, was a frequent visitor to the house on Pine Street, and there, as the story has it, he asked Kosciuszko's help in ending the undeclared naval war with Napoleon's France, which drained American resources and threatened to destroy her much-needed years of growth in peace.

Kosciuszko was in an unusually strong position to influence Napoleon. Powerful Polish legions were forming under Napoleon's banners in hopes of regaining their country's freedom, and Kosciuszko's authority among them was greater than any. The story has him sailing to France under a false passport, secretly issued to him by Jefferson under the name of Thomas Kanberg (which is true enough) and then agreeing to Napoleon's further recruitment and encouragement of Poles in exchange for bringing the naval harassment of American shipping to an end. Certainly, in his absence, Niemcewicz traveled throughout America pretending that Kosciuszko was with him, so that no news of his sudden return to Europe would jeopardize the mission.

The idea of this selfless, honorable, and patriotic man trading on his countrymen's hopes for whatever cause simply does not ring true. The fact remains that he did nothing to discourage Poles from flocking to Napoleon, whose good faith in regard to Poland Kosciuszko never believed, while a month after the first of his several conferences with Napoleon the undeclared French war on American commerce came to a sudden end. Recent historical research has unearthed some reports from American diplomatic agents to Jefferson that seem to suggest that Kosciuszko was instrumental in ending French naval harassment of American shipping; apparently Napoleon never gave up his hope of using Kosciuszko and ended his undeclared war as a favor to the man whom he was trying to woo.

Before this final, secret departure to Europe, Kosciuszko drew up a will as though aware that he would never return to his "second country," as he could never hope to return to his enslaved homeland. The will directed Thomas Jefferson, as executor, to use all of Kosciuszko's American assets to free and educate black slaves and thus erase the last blot of inhumanity that marred the image of the America he loved. Though legal difficulties later invalidated this demand, Jefferson could still write of his Polish friend: "He is as pure a son of liberty as I have ever known, and of that liberty which is to go to all, not to the few or to the rich alone." In effect, among his other services born of love for America and the principles of freedom, Kosciuszko was the first important "American" to take a step toward the liberation and education of the blacks.

He retired in Switzerland, where he

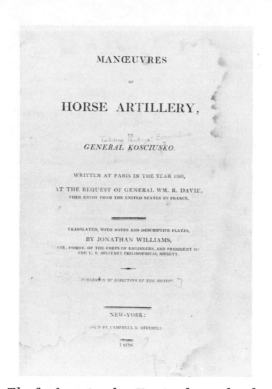

MANŒUVRES

OF

HORSE ARTILLERY,

BY

GENERAL KOSCIUSKO.

WRITTEN AT PARIS IN THE YEAR 1800,

AT THE REQUEST OF GENERAL WM. R. DAVIE,
THEN ENVOY FROM THE UNITED STATES TO FRANCE.

TRANSLATED, WITH NOTES AND DESCRIPTIVE PLATES,
BY JONATHAN WILLIAMS,
COL. COMDT. OF THE CORPS OF ENGINEERS, AND PRESIDENT OF
THE U. S. MILITARY PHILOSOPHICAL SOCIETY.

PUBLISHED BY DIRECTION OF THE SOCIETY.

NEW-YORK:
SOLD BY CAMPBELL & MITCHELL.
1808.

The final service that Kosciuszko rendered to his adopted country was a treatise on the use of field artillery, which he wrote in 1800 at the request of the U. S. Government. Entitled Manoeuvres of Horse Artillery, *the treatise was published in New York in 1808 and formed the basis for American artillery tactics in the War of 1812.* COURTESY OF THE UNITED STATES MILITARY ACADEMY, WEST POINT.

would render one more military service to America—writing, at the request of the American envoy, a treatise *Manoeuvres of Horse Artillery,* which the United States War Department adapted for use in the War of 1812, and which formed the basis of American artillery field service regulations until the dawn of the Civil War.

Kosciuszko died in Soleure, Switzerland, on October 15, 1817. He was seventy-one. His heart is buried in Switzerland at the request of the Swiss among whom he lived his last years of exile. His body was taken for funeral to Cracow where, in the royal crypt of the Wawel Castle, it lies among Kings. Outside the city, the people raised an artificial mountain in his honor, bring-

ing to it, in their caps and aprons, soil from every Polish battlefield on which he had fought. No soil came there from Saratoga, Ticonderoga, West Point, the Delaware Bay, and the countless swamps and rivers of the South where American independence had become reality, until Poland regained her independence in the twentieth century.

When Poland lost the terrible four-year war that ended in the First Partition of 1772, Kosciuszko, then a virtually unknown army captain, could remain in his country until the end of 1775, when the hopelessness of Poland's situation turned his thoughts westward. But Haym Salomon, who had already spent one fortune and all the energies of his idealistic youth in the cause of Polish independence, was driven from his home as soon as the Russians overcame the Poles. A young and vital man (he also was in his thirties when he arrived), Salomon came straight to America, the first of Poland's undaunted idealists to seize America's cause for his own.

Born in Lissa, Poland, into a Jewish merchant family that had come to Poland even before there was a Polish-Lithuanian Commonwealth (and long before Kosciuszko's Ruthenian-Lithuanian family could call itself Polish), Salomon landed in America as soon as the cannon cooled and the gibbets rose in the Poland that he would never see again. He became immediately involved in the patriots' conspiracy against British power.

Contemporaries have described him as "a quiet, thoughtful and dignified (young) man" who quickly established a reputation as a financier whose word was better than most men's signatures and seals. He had the same reputation among the bankers and credit brokers in Europe (the banking house of Peter Stadnicki in Amsterdam would accept his credit vouchers as currency)—a reputation that was to mean more to America's war effort than some of her generals.

Almost from his first moment in America

This rare sketch of Haym Salomon shows the financial hero of the American Revolution as he probably appeared after his dramatic escape from a British prison in New York. Salomon, a patriotic Polish Jew and friend of Kosciuszko, was the first of Poland's young idealists to reach America and raised the European credits without which the War of American Independence would have been impossible for the colonists to wage. He expended two fortunes on America's behalf. CREDIT: NATIONAL ARCHIVES.

he became one of the Sons of Liberty, at a time when most American money men tended to shy away from such unruly rabble. Salomon quickly won the trust of the Sons' Alexander McDougall (who would be Kosciuszko's commander at West Point), John Lamb, and Isaac Sears. With them, he formed the nerve center of the patriots' movement in New York.

When conspiracy became revolution and the war broke out, Salomon kept up the bankrupt American Government's credit in Europe almost single-handedly. His word was better among European bankers than

any bond the Congress could issue. Through the Polish "Dutch Connection" in Amsterdam, and the Jewish financial community in Germany and Austria, he negotiated war subsidies that kept the Continental Army in the field "on his own personal security, without the loss of a cent to the country and required a commission of only 1 quarter of 1 per cent for his invaluable services." Later, he would negotiate similar subsidies in France and become, in effect, paymaster to French armies in America.

As a U. S. Senate committee pointed out in 1850, Salomon also "gave great assistance by . . . advancing liberally of his means to sustain the men engaged in the struggle for independence at a time when the sinews of war were essential to success."

And success was by no means a foregone conclusion in 1776. It was no flight of accidental oratory that impelled John Hancock to urge his fellow members of the future Congress to "hang together" in their country's cause rather than be hanged one by one if that cause should fall, which seemed the likely prospect in a war against England.

During the British occupation of New York, Salomon was arrested, charged with conspiracy against the Crown, and escaped hanging only because the British thought he could be useful to them. Learning of his amazing knowledge of languages (he spoke ten fluently and knew at least four others), they paroled him as an interpreter among their foreign mercenaries. The Hessian General Heister made him his commissary superintendent and lived to regret it. Salomon not only used his position to aid in the escapes of captured Americans but also undermined Heister's command by propagandizing his mercenaries to join Washington. The bait he dangled before them was Washington's offer to one hundred acres of good land to each of the soil-hungry Hessian peasant soldiers who would turn against the British.

Salomon knew the risks of the deadly

game he played, but it was his only means to serve his adopted country while in British hands. On the night of August 5, 1778, he was dragged from his bed and thrown into the dreaded Provost Jail and again charged with treason.

The five counts of his indictment (each a capital crime under British military law) are witness to his courage and devotion to the Revolution. He was accused of using his home to assist the escape of American prisoners, of sheltering spies, of communicating with the Continental Army, of aiding in a plot to burn the King's fleet in New York Harbor, and of promoting wholesale Hessian desertions and treason. The evidence against him was overwhelming—as it should have been. He was found guilty and ordered to be hanged. By morning, Salomon and his Hessian guard had both disappeared.

One story has McDougall and the Sons of Liberty effecting his rescue in a daring raid that British contemporary sources mention in no account. It is more likely that he had hidden a roll of guineas in his clothing with which to bribe his guards. Whatever the truth may be, he left his wife and small son in New York and made his way to Philadelphia, where he asked the Congress for useful employment. But politicians' gratitude is even less dependable than the proverbial gratitude of princes; Salomon's application was turned down and he was left, suddenly impoverished, to his own devices.

Another man might have become embittered. Salomon turned for help to the Philadelphia Jews and again established himself as a broker and dealer in securities and exchange. Working out of a coffee house near his home on Front Street, he again managed to advance the revolutionary government more than six hundred thousand dollars, of which more than two hundred thousand dollars was in gold. To calculate the extent of Salomon's investment in America's freedom, there should be added advances of more than twenty thousand dollars "to pay the salaries of men holding government posts, in order to keep them in the service, and untold additional advances during the war to army officers, to foreign agents and for outfitting of soldiers."

Among those who received such "loans" from Salomon were James Madison, James Wilson, Joseph Reed, James Monroe, Kosciuszko and Pulaski, Edmund Randolph, Steuben, and General Mifflin. Writing to Randolph on September 30, 1782, when the state of Virginia could no longer afford to keep him in the Congress, Madison confessed himself to have been for some time "a pensioner on the favor of Haym Salomon."

"The kindness of our little friend in Front Street, near the coffee-house," he wrote, "is a fund which will preserve me from extremities, but I never resort to it without mortification, as he obstinately rejects all recompense. The price of money is so usurious that he thinks it ought to be extorted from none but those who aim at profitable speculation. To a necessitous delegate he gratuitously spares a supply out of his private stock."

Perhaps such faithful and generous service is less noticeable than the crash of cannon, although without it there would have been few cannon to fire. When the war ended, few of Salomon's "pensioners" remembered his kindness. Congress was even quicker to forget the larger moral debt. Salomon's sudden death in 1785, due largely to overwork, self-deprivation, and the ruin of his health while in British hands, left his wife and son practically penniless. The Congress owed his estate more than three hundred thousand dollars and never repaid it. Had British looters in the War of 1812 not burned every record related to revolutionary vouchers, the government's monetary debt to Salomon would have stood much higher. But by that time, as the new White House was going up in flames, Salomon's son, Haym M. Salomon, was doing his own patriotic duty: As a captain in the 115th Regiment, 10th Brigade, he was marching to battle against the British, and the family refused to press a claim against their government.

Peace came at last, bringing independence, and with it a struggle for survival that was hardly less desperate than that which could be settled on the battlefield. The triumphant but exhausted new American nation (its agriculture neglected, rudimentary industry in ruins, and commerce almost strangled by British blockades) strove to keep alive in the face of fiscal obligations that independence carries. The public debt was enormous, foreign loans exhausted, bonds not worth the paper promises that supported them, and—with Salomon dead—European credit was impossible to obtain. Yet without this credit, bankruptcy was inevitable, and any idea of peaceful development was an idle dream. As Hamilton warned those who urged default on the American war loans, America had to keep her credit in Europe if she wished to survive. President Washington's new U.S. bonds could be sold abroad to pay off the war debts, so that other American securities could finance recovery and growth, *if* a European banker could be found who'd take one more chance on the impoverished young United States. The trouble was that European financiers no longer viewed American credit with particular enthusiasm. Hamilton's sound fiscal theory—on which the undisputed credibility of U.S. bonds has rested to this day—seemed doomed before it could become a practical measure. By 1788 the United States stood on the brink of bankruptcy. England avoided buying American bonds, hoping to starve the new republic bank into the fold. France had her own worries. The Dutch grew cautious. Not even Thomas Jefferson's persuasions, as special emissary for U.S. bonds in Paris, could loosen European purse strings. Holland seemed like the last hope until American brokers there informed Washington that they could not sell the bonds allotted to them for 622,840 florins. But the future of the American nation, with its untouched resources, was assured if only financiers could develop the imagination to grasp this opportunity to make profitable loans. The first, and for a long time the only European

banker to do so, was Peter Stadnicki. With faith in the future of America, he had contributed to the American loan in 1780, when John Adams came to see him in Amsterdam. And eight years later, writing to Adams from Paris, Jefferson could make this comment: "A Mr. Stadnicki, one of our brokers, who holds 1,340,000 [dollars] of our domestic debt, offers, if we will pay him one year's interest of that debt, he will have the whole of the loan immediately filled up, he will procure the sum of 622,840 florins unsubscribed."

In another letter, to the commissioner of the Treasury, Jefferson could write later that "Mr. Stadnicki, our principal broker and holder of 1,340,000 dollars of certificates of our domestic debt—offers to have our loan of a million guldens immediately taken up . . ."

Once the icy reserve of European bankers was cracked by Stadnicki, other Dutch, French (and English!) financiers began to speculate in American securities.

In 1792, with three years of life remaining, Peter Stadnicki founded the Holland Land Company, which eventually owned five million acres of undeveloped land in western New York and Pennsylvania, opened up the southern shore of Lake Erie to mass settlement (not that too many settlers were anxious to go there) and founded today's city of Buffalo, New York. Stadnicki's son, John, started other settlements up to and beyond Erie, Pennsylvania, but by 1810 most of them had disappeared. Only the company's villages of New Amsterdam and Batavia prospered. They combined into Buffalo which, today, is one of the largest Polish population centers in America.

Then a brief hiatus occurred in the flow of Poles to the United States. The history of the Poles in America was always closely bound with developments in Europe, and during the Napoleonic wars patriotic Poles followed the charismatic military genius who called himself First Emperor of the French. They fought his battles on what

44

they believed was the road to an independent Poland. Few came to America while Napoleon was dazzling them with glittering promises. Fewer still believed that the Frenchman's plans for an independent Poland, restored to former territories and grandeur, existed only in the fever of their minds. They died for Polish independence, which was never even a remote possibility, while helping to impose French imperialism on the rest of Europe. From burning Moscow to the walls of Saragossa, Spain, from the Italian plain to Prussia, from the shadow of the Pyramids to the humid island of Santo Domingo (today's Dominican Republic and Haiti), the Polish legions died, crying "Poland is not yet lost" and "Vive l'Empéreur" as though the two had anything in common.

Even rational men like the philosopher-poet-statesman Julian Ursyn Niemcewicz were caught in the illusions of the Napoleonic dream. Niemcewicz, who came to Philadelphia with Kosciuszko in 1797, had been secretary to the Polish Senate and Kosciuszko's adjutant during the latter's insurrection in 1794; he had fallen beside his general on the bloody field of Maciejowice and had shared his imprisonment in Russia. A brilliant writer by any country's standards, he gave the world a detailed and perceptive picture of the American republic, its natural beauties and unnatural lack of civilization's polish, its social classes, customs, ways of thought, and values that grew out of the turbulent new environment. His *Short Story of the Life and Activities of General Washington* (published in Warsaw in 1803) remains the best biography of Washington as gentleman farmer. Niemcewicz was an honored guest at Mount Vernon as well as at Monticello. His account of the private lives of America's leaders is unique in fairness and perception. Jefferson made him a member of the American Philosophical Society, and Niemcewicz became an American citizen.

Writing to Niemcewicz, to disclose what were surely the contemporary sentiments of Americans for Poland, Washington declared: "That your country is not as happy as her efforts were patriotic and noble, is a misfortune which all lovers of sensible liberty and rights of men deplore; and, were my prayers during this hard struggle any good, you would be now 'under your own vine and fig-tree,' to quote the Bible, as happy in the enjoyments of these desirable blessings as the people of these United States enjoy theirs."

For the title of his monumental account of his travels in America, its personalities and conventions, geography and politics, morality and mores, Niemcewicz chose that biblical line quoted by Washington, and *Under Their Vine and Fig-tree* entered American literature.

Niemcewicz married the widowed Suzanna Kean and settled on a farm near Elizabeth, New Jersey, showing an unexpected talent for the management of the Kean and Livingston fortunes (which were Suzanna's and her son's, never his). But when Napoleon formed the rump Grand Duchy of Warsaw, invaded Russia, and summoned all Poles to his side in the name of their country's freedom, Niemcewicz felt "that it was my duty, as a Pole by birth, to go to the aid of my country at this important time."

Napoleon's doom, sealed in the Russian winter of 1812–13, did little to depress Polish patriotic frenzy. Niemcewicz moved to Paris among a flood of other Polish Napoleonic refugees to plot their country's independence, refusing to admit—as no Pole ever could—that their cause was lost for generations to come. Niemcewicz never managed to return to his American home and family. Another Polish uprising soon caught up with him. He died in Paris in 1841 to "the profound grief" of the American Philosophical Society.

Two more small wavelets of Polish immigrants reached America during the Napoleonic era but soon dissolved in the larger sea of this country's population. One was a remnant of the brigade and three battalions of Polish legionnaires whom Napoleon

Peter Stadnicki, a Polish financier settled in the Netherlands, was the first European banker to extend credit to the newly independent United States after the American War of Independence. His Holland Land Company opened up eastern Lake Erie to American settlement between 1801 and 1846, as is suggested by O. Turner in these four sketches showing the growth of Batavia, New York, which later expanded into the city of Buffalo. CREDIT: LIBRARY OF CONGRESS, PRINTS AND PHOTOGRAPHS DIVISION.

had sent to Santo Domingo to quell a slave revolt in 1802. The Poles had gone there under threat of imprisonment of all the Poles in Napoleon's legions, fought the blacks unwillingly, and were soon decimated by fevers and ambush. Some joined the blacks and settled among them. (One of their descendants, a Haitian black who spoke no word of Polish, astonished Polish officers during World War II by arriving in Scotland to enlist in the Polish Army; he had a tattered Polish patent of nobility, dating back to the seventeenth century, and a Polish name.) The British forced some into their own armies. Several hundred others reached Cuba; another remnant was shipwrecked in Florida and planned a short-lived colony there. The strongest group was a company of 240 men who were permitted to land in the United States where, in 1817, the Congress granted 92,000 acres in Alabama to French and Polish exiles of the Napoleonic wars. Another group of armed Polish and French veterans tried to set up a military colony west of Galveston in Texas, under Spanish rule, but gave up after eight months and dispersed in Louisiana.

It is probably accurate to say that most of this gallant Napoleonic debris found its way back to Europe in a year or two. For early nineteenth-century Poles there was only one justification for the agony of living: to fight, again and again, for Polish independence, and Europe was the obvious place for that. America was another world, a distant continent whose surrounding waters were less a geographic barrier than a gulf of vast historic, cultural, and philosophic differences. These could not be bridged with a clear conscience. To go to America was to abandon Europe, admitting in effect that Poland's cause was lost, which to the desperately patriotic mind was a peculiarly Polish definition of treason—"denationalization" (if such a word can exist in English) or becoming something other than a Pole.

For some Poles—priests—there was a higher loyalty. In the 1820s Polish members of the disbanded Society of Jesus began to arrive in Philadelphia at the solicitation of Bishop John Carroll. In a largely Catholic and Western-oriented Poland some erudite clergyman had played a major role in higher education; Bishop Carroll hoped that scholarly Polish Jesuits would do the same for Roman Catholic education in America. Most of these ecclesiastic immigrants left a heritage of a few scattered references in unimportant diaries, but one of them, the Reverend Francis Dzierozynski, must have exceeded the bishop's wildest hopes. According to contemporary churchmen, he saved the impoverished and demoralized American Jesuit movement from extinction, first as the superior of their Maryland mission in 1823, then as Jesuit provincial in Maryland, founding the College of St. John in Frederick, and accepting responsibility for Holy Cross University, which he staffed with able men.

The reputation for Poles and Poland that Kosciuszko, Pulaski, and Niemcewicz had created among the intellectual and political leadership of the United States, and among the humanists and libertarians of the American Enlightenment, acquired the final necessary touch of scholarship and practical education with Father Dzierozynski. It was soon to manifest itself in the first—and only—popular American support for yet another Polish immigration.

In 1815 the autocrats of Russia, Prussia, and the motley collection of restive peoples known as the Austrian Empire had banded together in a Holy Alliance dedicated to the crushing of all libertarian movements. But fifteen years later, hot winds of change were blowing across Europe; in Prussia the gendarmes had fired upon students; in Paris cannon sounded in the streets, and the people came out onto the barricades.

In November 1830, told that the Russians were sending them to Paris to put down that revolt, the Polish Army rebelled against its Russian overlords, and the bloodiest Polish uprising was soon under way. The revolt appealed dramatically to

America's sense of justice, as part of a broad intellectual and economic reaction to autocracy. Certain intellectual and liberal groups did try to aid the Polish cause. (Edgar Allan Poe wanted to enlist.) But denunciation of autocratic symbols by journalists and politicians seldom represents general American opinion. The embattled Poles and their émigré supporters in Paris had far less help and interest from America than has been claimed by some historians after research in political and editorial rhetoric.

A few distinguished Americans did throw themselves whole-heartedly into the Polish cause. Albert Gallatin, a close friend of Niemcewicz, tormented President Jackson for help for the Poles. James Fenimore Cooper, Ralph Waldo Emerson, and Samuel F. B. Morse joined the venerable Lafayette in Paris in forming an American Polish Committee to agitate and raise money on the Poles' behalf. Some American doctors went to serve with the Polish insurrectionist army. (Daniel Webster made another speech.) A gallant Boston philanthropist set off on a fantastic expedition to free insurgents who had been forced to cross Prussian borders and were interned in Danzig. A bad-tempered note from the Russian *chargé d'affaires*, protesting press support for the Polish rebels, resulted in his recall to St. Petersburg after the fight was over. But official American interest amounted to nothing. Jackson instructed his district attorneys to "throw cold water on our gallant youths." Even after the crushing of the insurrection in 1831, William C. Rives, American envoy in Paris, demanded the omission of a toast to Poland at a Fourth of July dinner for "Americans in Paris and their friends."

Official America came to the aid of the Poles only after their hopes were crushed, their country turned into a funeral pyre, and an embittered remnant of the gallant struggle began to land, as immigrants, on American shores. Between 1831 and 1835 America received 424 Polish immigrants, for most of whom arrival in the "Homeland of Liberty" was equal to surrender, since America opens her doors to the dispossessed with the understanding that they forget their foreign dreams and start to live in an American reality. The largest group of 234 defeated insurrectionists came here, like black slaves of an earlier era, below the decks of two Austrian frigates, which dumped them on the piers of New York in the summer of 1834. Their choice had been "voluntary" transport to America or delivery into Russian hands and certain execution.

Gallatin organized the first American Committee to Help the Poles in an atmosphere of retrospective sympathy and commiseration, a transitory sentiment that many Poles took for devotion to their cause. Other committees followed. Some ten thousand dollars was raised to help the immigrants to find a firm footing on American soil. The culmination of pro-Polish effort was the passage of a special bill, supported by such oratorical luminaries as John C. Calhoun, Henry Clay, and George Poindexter of Mississippi, providing for an Illinois land grant to Polish immigrants, the first and last American experiment in setting up a foreign colony in the United States. Nothing came of this "Little Poland" for reasons that had little to do with American good will. Dissension among the Poles, most of whom couldn't come to terms with the permanence of their new American home, trivial jealousies and quarrels over leadership, and finally the mechanics of survival in the East Coast cities, had sapped whatever pioneering energies they might have had at first. Legend has turned these valiant remnants of a lost cause into dynamic giants who shook America's conscience, undermined Jackson's good relations with Moscow, and went on to denounce slavery and oppression. But the standard of success and failure by which any immigration must be measured is its contribution to American life rather than the degree of its influence on governmental policies.

In this respect, the impact of the meager wavelet of the 1831–35 Polish immigration (and the ripples that followed it through the next decade) far exceeded its apparent means. In Polish-American history this is the period of the first Polish organizations in the United States, first Polish-language and English-language newspapers published by Poles, libraries, literary, dramatic, and political societies: a richness of community life that would never quite have that driving vitality again. These immigrants were part of the ten-thousand-person exodus of Polish intellectuals, poets, artists, military heroes, and *intelligentsia* that the destruction of their revolution had hurled into the world. During the 1830s they formed a committee to represent their interests in the United States. The Association of Poles in America was founded in 1842, and in 1852 they organized the Democratic Society of Polish Exiles, which denounced slavery. The intellectually vital atmosphere that they created for themselves would last beyond the Civil War, when the huge mass of Eastern Europe's illiterate peasantry rolled into America.

They did what all educated exiles have since learned to do: try everything, hope for a little less, and expect nothing at all. There is an ironic parallel between their early years in America and the later fate of the Russians who had driven them across the Atlantic: the taxi-driving Russian princes, the Tsarist guardsmen turned into Paris doormen, and the brutal Cossacks who would sing so beautifully as the Don Cossack choir. And so the first Polish newspapers in America began advertising the "Dance and Fence" academy of August Wegierski (a relative of a Polish poet who had toured the United States in 1783 under quite different circumstances), or describe the juggling and weight-lifting act of someone named Zajaczek, who opened at Peale's Museum in New York on February 11, 1834. Captains Rutkowski and Polkowski performed equestrian maneuvers on the same stage and taught young ladies of New York's society how not to fall off their horses in Battery Park. Fencing and dancing schools, riding academies, engineering classes, tutoring in mathematics and mod-

ern languages, as well as humble ditch-digging, gardening, and butlering in the homes of America's rich did what no propagandist could have managed in subduing their European dreams.

Some went a little haywire. In 1837 a muddled and misled Colonel Gustaw Szulc tried to show his new American patriotism by invading Canada in support of William Lyon Mackenzie. His "patriot army" beat off a few attacks by Canadian Mounties during the Upper Canada Rebellion of 1838 but, eventually, fell apart, and Colonel Szulc was hanged by the Canadians at Fort Henry.

Almost as though he wished to make amends for his compatriot's Canadian heroics, another Polish exile, Kazimierz Stanislaw Gzowski, took his new American wife to Ontario, became a pioneer of the Canadian railroad system, built the International Bridge over the Niagara—then considered a miracle of modern engineer-

This photograph of a painting on ivory shows Colonel Gustaw Szulc (also known as von Shultz), who led an unsuccessful invasion of Canada in support of William Lyon Mackenzie. Szulc was defeated and hanged at Fort Henry, Ontario, when Mackenzie's "American" cause failed.
CREDIT: ONTARIO ARCHIVES.

ing—and received a knighthood from Queen Victoria in 1890.

The activities of other Poles in America are bewilderingly eclectic. Captain Alexander Bielaski (who would die heroically in the American Civil War) made difficult surveys in Florida, then spent two years engineering kinks out of the Illinois Central Railroad; Captain Casimir Bielawski surveyed almost all the Spanish land grants in California and wound up with a mountain named after him in Santa Clara County. Edward Sobolewski composed *Mohega, Flower of the Forest,* an opera of the Revolutionary War (with Pulaski as its improbably romantic hero), which wrung

Sir Casimir S. Gzowski, a Polish insurrectionist of the 1831 immigration wave, was knighted by Queen Victoria after he helped to develop the Canadian railroad system and built the International Bridge over the Niagara River. He is shown here with his American wife and their large family in 1855. CREDIT: ONTARIO ARCHIVES.

The official portrait of Sir Casimir S. Gzowski, made shortly before his knighting by Queen Victoria. Gzowski's bridge over the Niagara River was considered a marvel of engineering in its time. He was also appointed an honorary colonel of a Canadian militia regiment. CREDIT: ONTARIO ARCHIVES.

tears from coast to coast until the Civil War. He also organized Milwaukee's first Symphonic Orchestra in 1861. In 1842, the first Polish monthly magazine appeared in English under the title of *Poland—Historical, Literary, Monumental and Picturesque,* edited by Paul Sobolewski, who also produced a massive study, *Napoleon and His Marshals,* and a volume, *Poets and Poetry of Poland,* in 1881. The first handbook of English for the Poles, entitled *Dialogues to Facilitate the Acquisition of the English Language by the Polish Emigrants,* had appeared in 1834, but Major Joseph Hordynski apparently didn't need it. A year earlier he had published in Boston his *History of the Late Polish Revolution* which, for a while, was a coffee-table must in sophisticated homes.

Henryk Dmochowski (Saunders) was the best-known American sculptor and miniaturist of his day; his monument at the grave of his daughter at Laurel Hill Cemetery, Philadelphia, was considered one of the finest sculptures of its kind in America;

Edward Sobolewski, who composed
Mohega, Flower of the Forest—*one of the*
earliest-known American operas (with
Pulaski as its romantic hero)—also
organized the first symphonic orchestra in
Milwaukee in 1861. NEW YORK PUBLIC
LIBRARY, LINCOLN CENTER.

his marble busts of Revolutionary heroes, among them Kosciuszko and Pulaski, decorate the rotunda of the Capitol in Washington, D.C., to this day. Dmochowski was killed by Russian troops in Poland, where he was on a visit during the last of the great Polish uprisings in 1863. Cyprian Norwid, one of the best known Polish poets of the preromantic period, settled in New York in 1851, but after three years of poverty and hardship made his way back to Europe. Stanislaw Hernisz, an interpreter for the American legation in China, published in 1854 what was surely the first English-Chinese dictionary. Dr. Louis Szpaczek, who had been personal physician to Hungarian hero Louis Kossuth, headed a clinic for New York City's poor until his death in 1859. Another Polish exile-physician, a Dr. Maszke, made pioneer studies of yellow fever in the South, and died of that disease contracted during research. About sixty exiles became teachers, among them Professor Leopold Julian Boeck, who founded the Polytechnic Institute of New York, Jozef Karge (who was to win fame as a Union cavalry commander during the Civil War), and John Joseph Lehmanowski, a Jewish-born, Polish veteran of the Napoleonic Wars who had become a Lutheran convert and was instrumental in founding seven Lutheran schools, a Lutheran seminary, and Hillsboro College in Illinois. The college was burdened, at first, with the name The Literary and Theological Institute of the Far West; it is now mercifully known as Illinois State University at Springfield. After the Civil War, Confederate Colonel Artur Grabowski became commandant of the Pennsylvania Military Academy and of the Worcester Highland Military Academy, superintendent of the Haskell Institute in Lawrence, Kansas, and president of Defiance College in Ohio—although not, one may hope, at the same time. Colonel Grabowski, supposedly, lived to be almost one hundred years old.

A strange and little-known personality, one Gaspard Tochman, emerged among the immigrants of 1831–35 and was to reappear a quarter of a century later among the Confederates of the Civil War. Tochman, a nephew of Poland's insurrectionist general Skrzynecki, and himself a decorated hero of that revolution, came to America in 1837, was naturalized in 1842, and two years later was already practicing law before the Supreme Court. Infuriated by a letter to a newspaper in which a reader dared to doubt the feasibility of Poland's restoration "any more than one can hope for the restoration of the Roman Empire," Tochman took to the hustings with seventy-two public lectures, including a harangue to the New York State Legislature, which hastily passed a resolution favoring the Polish cause. Something of a public figure among the new American Poles, Tochman organized the Polish-

Slavonian Association to promote Eastern European culture in the United States, then told bemused American audiences that Poland was "the morning star of toleration and conscience" which—in the sympathetic climate of the times—was probably believed.

Tiny though this group was in comparison with the later peasant avalanche—an avalanche, incidentally, that feared and distrusted them as "nobility"—they did more in two decades to improve the quality of American life than all the peasant millions could manage in two generations. They seemed to be everywhere at once, doing everything. Dr. Feliks Paul Wierzbicki, a restless physician, abandoned his rich practice to join a regiment of volunteers in the Mexican War and then, wandering through California, wrote the first book printed west of the Rocky Mountains. His *California as It Is, as It May Be, or Guide to the Gold Region* apparently drew another Polish Forty-niner there, one Aleksander Zakrzewski, a cartographer whose 1849 map of San Francisco is one of the few to have survived the city's famous earthquake and fire. Mount Radziminski in Kiowa County, Oklahoma, commemorates another Polish exile, who served on the boundary commission between Mexico and the United States after the Mexican War.

And in rebellious Texas, where everything seemed larger than life in less heroic regions, Lieutenant Feliks Andrzej Wardzinski had already gained his place in that republic's history when he appeared before General Sam Houston with a very valuable prisoner he had captured: the President and dictator of Mexico, General Santa Anna.

The Polish wavelet of 1831–35, soon to be joined by two more wavelets of their own highly idealistic kind, marks the true beginning of the history of the Poles in the United States by their commitment to American causes and involvement in purely American problems and ideas. The nature of the Polish immigration changes in that era from exiles who await the moment of return to immigrants for whom America becomes the reality that controls their lives. The two new small waves—or perhaps ripples in a weakened tide—came as an aftermath of two more Polish national disasters, which scattered educated Poles through all the continents. One was a moment of fratricidal horror, an Austrian-instigated peasant rebellion in the Austrian part of Poland (Galicia), where brutish peasants—mostly Ukrainians—massacred the gentry. (The Austrians paid a bounty for each severed head of a Polish noble and tens of thousands were murdered.) The other rising was one of the Poles against the Prussians in 1848, in that glorious democratic "Spring of the Nations," which rocked the autocrats' thrones while it lasted, and then became a long gray winter of oppression that fell upon demolished Polish hopes like a bar of shadow. Most of the flotsam of these two convulsions settled in France and England, still clinging to Europe, but some—perhaps the most energetic—sailed for America. By the mid-nineteenth century, with a terrible homemade American convulsion only a decade away, the Poles were an integral part of this country's intellectual, cultural, artistic, educational, and political life, as they were never to be again after the arrival of the peasant masses.

A satirical view of Polish miners' life in Pennsylvania, whose object was to show the "brutish" nature of the Polish laborers. This 1900 engraving in a local newspaper features straw and manure shoveled from a hovel into which a couple is moving in a rainstorm. Despite similar attacks, and living conditions that were not much better, Polish miners endured and overcame mine owners' exploitation and won a right to work with dignity and for a fair wage.
CREDIT: LIBRARY OF CONGRESS, PRINTS AND PHOTOGRAPHS DIVISION.

This scene is typical of the life of early Polish miners and their families in the anthracite coalfields of Pennsylvania. Here children pick scraps of coal off the slagheaps during the strike of 1902 in the Hazelton region. CREDIT: LIBRARY OF CONGRESS, PRINTS AND PHOTOGRAPHS DIVISION.

Nowhere in late nineteenth-century Poland did Polish peasants work as hard, or live under such conditions, as they were to find in the United States. This miner's shack near Scranton, Pennsylvania, was typical of the homes that the impoverished, unskilled Polish laborers built for themselves out of providential scraps in their spare time. Two entire families often shared one room, and unmarried young men often shared single quarters fourteen at a time. CREDIT: LIBRARY OF CONGRESS, PRINTS AND PHOTOGRAPHS DIVISION.

Immigrants' children, such as these youngsters, became Americans in their own Polish schools. In this 1913 photograph of a classroom in the Posen (Poznan) State Graded School, Thorp, Wisconsin, a Polish teacher taught American history and the language of the immigrants' new land. COURTESY OF DR. JOSEPH R. JEDRYCHOWSKI.

Everyone worked in the Polish peasant immigrant families, the youngest alongside the oldest. But after work, the children were sent to school. When they found that American public schools derided and humiliated their poorly dressed children, the immigrants built more than nine hundred schools of their own, such as this one in Thorp, Wisconsin, in 1910. COURTESY OF DR. JOSEPH R. JEDRYCHOWSKI.

Unskilled Polish laborers were, at first, herded to the coal pits to depress miners' wages, but soon became determined fighters for the rights of workingmen in the United States. During the Homestead Steel Strike in 1892, Polish laborers battled against Pinkerton guards and armed strikebreakers imported by the Carnegie Company. In this drawing by Charles Mente, strikers attack the Pinkerton men. Below: barges on fire outside the Carnegie mills. CREDIT: LIBRARY OF CONGRESS, PRINTS AND PHOTOGRAPHS DIVISION.

In July 1892, the Pinkertons gave up their attempts to subdue the strikers in the Homestead strike. This drawing by W. P. Snyder for Harper's Weekly *of July 16, 1892, shows the battered strikebreakers deciding to withdraw. Homestead was an early Polish settlement in the Pittsburgh, Pennsylvania, area. What contemporary journalists failed to mention was that more than one hundred Polish laborers were killed or maimed by armed strikebreakers in that struggle.*
CREDIT: LIBRARY OF CONGRESS, PRINTS AND PHOTOGRAPHS DIVISION.

The United States Army was sent against the strikers in the Homestead strike after the Pinkertons and armed strikebreakers failed to destroy this early effort of what would eventually become the powerful United Steelworkers union. In this drawing by T. de Thulstrup, for Harper's Weekly of August 6, 1892, the 18th Infantry Regiment arrives to quell the strikers. CREDIT: LIBRARY OF CONGRESS, PRINTS AND PHOTOGRAPHS DIVISION.

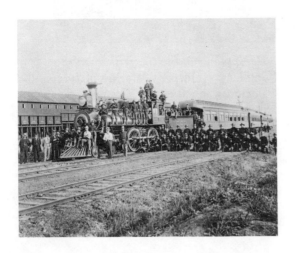

Unable to suppress the great railroad strike of 1894, railway owners once again called upon the Army. Here, a company of the 15th Infantry Regiment mans a special patrol train sent against the strikers at Blue Island, Illinois, an early center of Polish labor settlement. CREDIT: LIBRARY OF CONGRESS, PRINTS AND PHOTOGRAPHS DIVISION.

A typical shack in which Polish railroad workers, kept to unskilled manual occupations by the language barrier, lived during the great Pullman strike of 1894. Poles were, at first, used by entrenched manufacturers as strikebreakers but were quick to realize where their allegiance lay. Their thrift provided them with a cushion during the labor battles of the 1880s and 1890s and allowed a longer resistance than that of their Welsh and German predecessors. CREDIT: LIBRARY OF CONGRESS, PRINTS AND PHOTOGRAPHS DIVISION.

The greatest and most costly of the Polish workers' labor efforts in the United States came during the Shenandoah Valley battles that resulted in the founding of the United Mineworkers union in 1902. An estimated thirty thousand Polish and Lithuanian miners, a quarter of the labor force in the Shenandoah coalfields, finally won the strike despite official violence and intimidation. Here state militia pitch camp on the outskirts of a mining town. CREDIT: LIBRARY OF CONGRESS, PRINTS AND PHOTOGRAPHS DIVISION.

This Polish track layer in the Pennsylvania coalfields in 1909 is identified on various copies of this photograph as Slavic and Austrian. Immigrants from various regions of partitioned Poland were often listed by U.S. immigration officials as German, Austrian, or Russian, depending on which region of occupied Poland had been their home. PHOTO BY LEWIS W. HINE, INTERNATIONAL MUSEUM OF PHOTOGRAPHY AT GEORGE EASTMAN HOUSE.

In those last and rather splendid years of Polish participation in the full spectrum of American life—not as visiting foreigners but as welcomed equal members of the American intellectual leadership—two women, and one ascerbic count, won for themselves a place in this country's political and social history that few immigrants have equaled.

One of the women was Ernestine Louise S. Potowska-Rose, who battled for women's rights before many women knew that they had rights for which they might battle, and then immersed herself in the vanguard of the Abolitionist movement. The other was Dr. Maria Elizabeth Zakrzewska, whose anger at discrimination against women in medicine—and their frequently brutal treatment at the hands of male obstetricians—led to the founding of two hospitals for women staffed exclusively by women, the first American school for professional women nurses, and inauguration of the movement for children's urban playgrounds.

The count, an intractable and unpredictable radical agitator, whose European loyalties had turned and turned about with bewildering rapidity, was Adam Gurowski, an immensely influential Washington lobbyist known, in his time, as "Lincoln's gadfly" and as a tormentor of the President's conservative supporters. He made life miserable for anti-Abolitionists and even took on Daniel Webster for his backing of the first fugitive slave law. Supposedly, the "gadfly" was the only man of whom Lincoln was genuinely afraid; the President thought the pistol-toting count

was the only man capable of trying to kill him.

The first American petition for a married woman's property law reached the New York State legislature in 1836. It was the work of Ernestine Potowska, then married to an English silversmith named Rose, for whom the tragic social inequities of America—black slavery and the subjugation of women—seemed like personal affronts. The young republic to which she had come in 1836 offered its people some political freedoms, a sense of control over their own destinies, and a variety of rights that guaranteed the hegemony of a propertied middle class. In most other respects it didn't seem to differ from the autocracies and monarchies of Europe. American workmen could not strike nor organize a union, an entire black race had the rights of cattle, and married women—in total subjection to their husbands—ranked as incompetents at common law on a parity with lunatics and infants. A warm and articulate speaker (her critics found her foreign accent "charming"), Mrs. Rose spent twelve years of seemingly hopeless agitation among women—and their masters—to effect a law that would allow a married woman to keep what was her own.

"Some of the ladies said the gentlemen would laugh at them," she wrote to a friend, "others, that they had rights enough; and the men said the women had too many rights already. . . . I continued sending petitions with increased numbers of signatures until 1848 and 1849," when the New York State legislature enacted the first Married Women's Property Act in the United States.

Being a feminist organizer in the first decades of the nineteenth century was much like working for black voter registration in the Mississippi of the 1960s. It took physical courage, conviction, and a coldly reasoned grasp of the era's realities. At the twenty-fifth annual observance of Tom Paine's birthday (held on January 29, 1850, at the Chinese Museum on Broadway), William Allen rhapsodized over Mrs. Rose as "the morning glory of Poland; the lily of England; and she is the rose of America . . ." and suggested that she might well be admitted to that nebulous hall of American mythology that housed the uneasy spirits of Tom Paine, Jefferson, and Kosciuszko. To which the often-taunted and -abused veteran of feminist platforms replied, "Seven ancient cities contended for Homer dead" (having denied him a living while he was alive). And then she said: "Let us contend for the living. . . ."

She was the only leading American abolitionist who did not turn upon Frederick Douglass, the former slave, and later black orator and editor of a black-run abolitionist weekly. He had found tepid liberal white enthusiasms both patronizing and demeaning and urged blacks to seize control of their own liberation movement. In a speech to the American Anti-slavery Society in 1853, she asked, "What is it to be a slave?" And went on to say: "To work hard, to fare ill, to suffer hardship, that is not slavery; for many of us white men and women have worked hard; have fared ill; have had to suffer hardship and yet we are not slaves. Slavery is not to belong to yourself—to be robbed of yourself. . . . Not to be your own bodily, mentally, or morally—that is to be a slave."

She lectured also on free schools, religion, and the science of democratic government, pleading for better pay and working conditions for the exploited American wage-earner. After the Civil War she returned to England with her husband and died there in 1892, as embroiled as ever in feminist agitation.

Maria Zakrzewska's path to that necessary anger that topples prejudice was a little different. Daughter of a Polish midwife, who had herself wanted to be a physician —a near impossibility in the pompous *Mitteleuropaean* society of frock coats, soaring honorifics, and male supremacy in the consulting room—she had accompanied her mother on visits to patients and learned "all of life that it was possible for a human being to learn . . ."

"I saw nobleness in dens, and meanness in palaces," she was to write later. ". . . I learned to judge human nature correctly, to see goodness where the world could see nothing but faults. . . . The experience thus gained cost me the bloom of youth, yet I would not exchange it for a life of everlasting juvenescence."

At eighteen she was admitted to the college of midwifery in Berlin, where she eventually became a professor and chief

Dr. Maria Zakrzewska, who broke the barriers that hindered women in practicing medicine in the United States, founded hospitals for women in New York and Boston. She also pioneered the movement that opened the nursing profession to black women. COURTESY OF THE NEW YORK ACADEMY OF MEDICINE.

accoucheuse of the Charite Hospital. Hearing that in the United States women could become full doctors of medicine, Zakrzewska immigrated to America in 1853. Three years later she had graduated from the Western Reserve College of Medicine in Cleveland, Ohio, and set about revolutionizing American medical attitudes to women as doctors. She was determined to establish a women's hospital that would be staffed by women, and where a medical woman could get practical instruction. Several medical schools accepted a small quota of women as students, but there was no hospital in America that would take them as residents and' interns. Dr. Zakrzewska brought about the founding of the New York Infirmary for Women and Children (largely by browbeating funds and influence out of rich New York society wives) and became its first resident physician. In 1859 Dr. Zakrzewska organized a new hospital in Boston that would become The New England Hospital for Women and Children, where women doctors could care for women patients during the forty years that she was the hospital's director. Her hospital included the first American professional school for nurses, which she threw open to black women, in defiance of contemporary prejudice and usage, which almost cost her the school and her career.

Drawn strongly into the Abolition Movement (partly by the influence of Potowska-Rose, in part by white society's abuse of black women in the North), she demanded professional training for black women so that their lives could evolve "in usefulness, dignity and pride." The first black nurse in America graduated from Dr. Zakrzewska's school in 1879, and Dr. Caroline V. Still, one of the first black women to enter medicine, interned in her Boston hospital.

Dr. Zakrzewska was loved and admired, according to newspaper articles and contemporary letters about her; Potowska-Rose was admired and respected; but Adam Gurowski was feared, resented, and detested by almost everyone who came in contact with him—a state of affairs that he probably enjoyed. Love and respect are the trappings and also the tangible rewards of

This somewhat thoughtful portrait of Count Adam Gurowski suggests a far less violent character than that of the near-legendary radical who was known in America before the Civil War as "Lincoln's gadfly." Gurowski was a fanatical Abolitionist, demanding instant emancipation of black slaves and calling for a black army to fight in the Civil War. One of the most flamboyant characters of his time, he was the only man whom Abraham Lincoln suspected as capable of his assassination. CREDIT: THE NEW YORK PUBLIC LIBRARY, PRINTS DIVISION.

power; Gurowski held the puppeteer's strings that are power itself. What mattered to him was that influential men listened to his ideas, his unsolicited advice was seldom ignored, and few Washington politicians dared to stand in his way. Yet the only government position he ever held was as reader of foreign newspapers for the State Department.

In a way he really stands outside the history of the Poles in America: He was of them, by virtue of his Polish birth, but never one of them; he went his own way. Poles in America loathed him, wouldn't speak to him. He had deserted from their insurrectionist army in 1830 and later turned his back on their cause to become an apologist for Russia. "If all Gaul is divided in four parts," one of them wrote of him on his arrival in America in 1849, "then Gurowski must be four parts gall." Gurowski agreed. In later years he wrote of himself: "I must admit, I am impossible."

Furious contemporaries write of the way in which he marched into private offices in his stiff, semimilitary manner, sprawled on their desks, rummaged through desk drawers, openly thumbed through personal papers, broke into statesmen's conferences with unsolicited advice on every kind of matter, made or broke political and military careers with a vitriolic pen and an unbridled tongue, and got away with it all simply because no one knew what to do about him and almost everyone feared what this incalculable and unyielding radical might do.

A few weeks after his inauguration, with southern secession only a matter of time, President Lincoln was induced to give some thought to his personal safety. "Gurowski is the only man who has given me serious thought of a personal nature," he told his bodyguard, Ward Hill Lamon. "From the known disposition of this man, he is dangerous wherever he may be. I have sometimes thought that he might try to take my life. It would be just like him to do such a thing."

On that same soggy afternoon, a few blocks away on Pennsylvania Avenue, the somewhat ludicrous and improbable object of their fears was indulging in torrents of abuse against the President ("He is a beast!") and Secretary of State William H. Seward ("clever charlatan!") for the benefit of an open-mouthed young journalist who had known him earlier. They were standing in the middle of the street as a troop of cavalry approached at a trot. Battered blue goggles flashing (complete with side blinders), his broad-brimmed, bell-shaped hat askew on disheveled gray hair, a long black cloak of antique European cut

billowing in the wind, and huge boots stamping in the mud, the paunchy, bellowing Polish count was quite oblivious of the rearing horses and cursing troopers around him. His large round head with its bulging forehead and bushy sidewhiskers was shaking with rage as he denounced "the beast" and its "charlatan" for their delaying of his plans for an immediate black emancipation. Other radical Republicans would compromise their views in the emergency with Lincoln's conservative administration, but Gurowski remained the raging Puritan of radical politics no matter what could happen. Almost anything could happen with this self-appointed gadfly, and most of it did.

Like every other Pole who had come to America up to this moment of their history here, Gurowski was a member of the landed gentry. The title of count was given to his grandfather by the Prussians in exchange for a switch in allegiance during the First Partition of Poland, in 1772. His father tried to make up for that bit of family treachery by raising a battalion of infantry for Kosciuszko's insurrection in which he served as a private. Adam was born on one of the several Gurowski estates, near Kalisz in Great Poland, on September 10, 1805, and grew to early manhood in a dismembered Poland where resistance to established authority was a way of life. His upbringing seems typical of his class and time; at fifteen, he was studying philosophy under Hegel in Berlin, then more philosophy at Heidelberg, where Anton Friedrich Thibaut also taught him law and Friedrich Creuzer lectured in history. In 1825 Gurowski was back on the family estates, plotting revolution against the occupying Russians and making his first acquaintance with their jails.

Never a man for half measures, his plots included the kidnaping of Tsar Nicholas I when the autocrat of all the Russians arrived in Warsaw to have himself crowned King of Poland in the spring of 1830. (Nothing came of it; his fellow conspirators backed out.) When the insurrection broke out in November, Gurowski was the first and almost the only noble who freed all his peasant serfs who would take up arms—just as three decades later, in another world, he would demand the instant emancipation of American slaves and the organization of black armies for the Civil War. In either case, in America as in Poland, the conservative politicians in power were unready for such extreme social changes, nor could they cope with Gurowski's vitriolic attacks. In the Polish struggle, Gurowski started a newspaper in which he hurled charges of "incompetence, ineptness, lack of unity, lack of commitment to the war, indecision and private interest" at the insurrectional national government almost as though he were practicing his assaults on Lincoln's cabinet thirty years later. Gurowski served for a few months in the insurrectionist army, just long enough to learn how to use "a knapsack for a pillow, snow for mattress and blanket," but the tiny army's weakness drained him of optimism. (His young wife's illness might have contributed to his sense of futility and doom: she was to die in 1832.) He deserted from his regiment, went briefly into hiding, reappeared for a last short period in Warsaw's radical politics, and was next seen in Paris, where the intellectual flower of the Polish nation was assembling into what Polish history would call the Great Emigration. Great literature and music would come from them (Adam Mickiewicz's poetry, Frederick Chopin's music), and for the next three decades they would populate other peoples' causes which they would see as their own because, invariably, the enemy would be one of the autocracies that had dismembered Poland. But any energies they might have expended on their own behalf were dissipated in petty bickering and factional disputes, to which Gurowski contributed as much as any of them.

The refugee Polish national government finally challenged Gurowski to a duel, with its last Foreign Affairs Minister as their principal. In a gesture as flamboyant as it seemed suicidal, Gurowski chose the murderous Lepage dueling pistols at ten paces, which meant that neither contender could possibly survive. The .62-caliber soft-lead bullet of this portable cannon could blow a hole the size of a soup tureen in a man, and at that range it couldn't miss. But mist on a foggy morning, a miracle or some less divine interference with the powder charges, caused both pistols to misfire, and nobody was hurt. The implacable count's assaults on his fellow émigrés continued unabated. The controlling powers in Europe declared him the most dangerous radical on the Continent. When the Tsar offered an amnesty in 1832 to some of the exiled insurrectionists who wished to return, Gurowski's name was not on the list; he was condemned to death, the sentence to be carried out as soon as the Russians could get hold of him. This sentence intensified Gurowski's lobbying in Paris and London in behalf of Poland's national cause, but the French and British politicians limited themselves to denunciation of the Tsar's excesses in Poland and gave no practical help. Frustration came also to the count as he sat in the councils of non-Polish radicals in Paris. The only difference between them and exiled Polish radicals was that there were fewer of them to quarrel with each other.

Finally, the count was wholly isolated, pushed aside even by the Polish Democratic Society he had organized, and then, in 1834, he published a startling announcement in the Augsburg *Gazette:* He was, he wrote, no longer a Polish patriot but rather a member of the "Slavic race," which could fulfill its destiny only under the leadership of Russia. In his new view, Poland was unfit to be more than a Russian province—a view with which the Russians have always heartily agreed. From then on his writings in exile became such an unending assault on Poland that even Tsar Nicholas found it "difficult to believe such brutality." But the count persisted, writing his Panslavic panegyrics to persons who, he knew, would turn over his correspondence to the Tsar's informers; he even wrote one such letter to the director of police in Moscow.

"Strange thing," the Tsar commented to Ivan Paskevitch, his hangman-governor in Poland. "What does this man want? Direct that a letter be sent to him indicating that, to prove his sincerity, he appear at the border and surrender himself to our mercy. We shall see whether he will do this. We shall try [him out]."

Gurowski did as he was told. He returned to Poland and became the most devoted of the Tsar's collaborators there. His death sentence was set aside, but he received no other reward, nor did he ask for one; he had thrown himself as wholeheartedly into Russia's camp as he had formerly opposed it.

No biographer ever quite managed to explain the brilliant count's extremist leaps from one end of a political and emotional spectrum to another. His love-hate relationship with his countrymen, as with himself, doomed him to loneliness: a restless and resentful man without a country, always in touch with the extremities of life but never with its core. The Russians used him but eyed him with suspicion. To them he was always a former leader of the November Insurrection; his conversion to Russian Panslavism was incredible to them. Nor was he able to worm his way into their affections; his turbulent disposition seemed designed to create enemies. Distrusted by the Russians, hated by the Poles (his own brothers refused him hospitality), the count likened his life to a slow death in which no community or ideal could provide him with a cause greater than himself and offer him, in one climactic moment, a sense of purpose, identity, and justification. Then he fled both Poland and Russia, never to return.

One of the many stories that have sprung up about Gurowski in America has him arriving in New York by special invitation of the radical wing of the Republican Party, teaching at Harvard, and soon becoming so powerful that he could keep the writings of Karl Marx out of American newspapers. The truth about his early years in America is far more humble. He did expect to join the Harvard faculty and drove its president, Edward Everett, to distraction with his importunities, but the only teaching he did in Cambridge was an incomprehensible course of six lectures on Roman law given in his rooms. As for Karl Marx (who at that time was a European correspondent for Greeley's New York *Tribune,* where Gurowski also managed to anchor himself), his "writings" were a series of nine harmlessly objective articles on Russian Panslavism that didn't happen to follow Gurowski's pro-Russian line. The count mangled three of them with his atrocious English, and suppressed the remainder while the *Tribune*'s editor was away.

Far from receiving any invitations to cross the Atlantic, he had come here because he could no longer find a welcome or a cause in Europe. In the Polish uprising, he had rebelled against authority but had refused the evolutionary process among the insurrectionists. His turncoat years in Russia had brought no lasting satisfactions or continuing political faith, beyond a final rejection of authoritarian government. He had wandered through Europe in search of liberty at a time when democratic uprisings were crushed or betrayed. But America inspired and enchanted him. He applied for naturalization as soon as he could. The balance of liberty and authority was right, he reflected on looking eagerly around the American scene. Yet there was slavery, a blot and stain on his new country's conscience, a corrupting and demoralizing influence that was incompatible with the promise of American life.

For Gurowski, the fight against slavery could only be personal, uncompromising, and total. He threw himself into radical politics among the Abolitionists of New England, who were variously bemused, dismayed, or outraged by his violent assaults. "We all felt as if a huge gardenroller had gone over us," Henry Longfellow wrote after one meeting with Gurowski. "He drew me like a magnet," said John A. Andrews, the youthful governor of Massachusetts, who would later obey Gurowski's demands for black enlistment in the Union armies. Charles Sumner, the radical Republican leader, through whom Gurowski later manipulated military appointments, would remain the count's supporter for ten years (although, eventually, even the patient Sumner would order the persistent "gadfly" out of his apartments). Edward M. Stanton, who would become Lincoln's Secretary of War, also fell under the spell of Gurowski's violent energy.

Through such disciples—and a near infinite number of influential Americans among whom he pushed himself and his radical ideas—Gurowski found a job as European commentator for Greeley's *Tribune* and (later, after he was dismissed in 1857) as foreign press analyst in Seward's State Department where, he believed, his real job was "to keep Seward from making a fool of himself." Colorful, irresistible, unforgettable, the aging Polish count became the goad and conscience of Republican Washington during the Civil War. Everyone knew him, and most politicians feared him more than any imaginary devil. Thomas Nast cartooned him as Asmodeus in Blue Glasses after the king of demons, and it is this demonic energy that Gurowski turned upon anyone who seemed to hinder a swift destruction of slavery and the system that supported it.

By relentless pressure, agitation, propaganda, outright lies, and a sort of intellectual terrorism, Gurowski wrecked the Peace Convention in which conservative Republicans made a last attempt to placate the South. Because black emancipation wasn't a declared issue of the war, he launched a radical campaign to find and promote a Union general who would free the slaves on his own authority in southern territories under his control; several tried it, but Lincoln revoked their orders every time. Gurowski persisted, interviewing military commanders almost as though he were the Secretary of War, writing countless letters and reports to Stanton, and using his considerable propagandist skills to make or undermine military reputations. Generals McClellan, Halleck, Burnside, and Meade earned his wrath by their lukewarm attitudes toward blacks as soldiers; he engineered their removal, although his efforts were probably only part of a larger whole. "Fighting Joe" Hooker had his support for a while, but failed to follow Gurowski's plan for his army's reorganization swiftly enough to satisfy the count, and joined the other victims of his fury.

The count found the unorthodox and unusual commander for whom he had been searching in Ulysses S. Grant, whom he interviewed, approved, and pressed upon Stanton with such violence that Stanton wondered whether it was safer to face Gurowski's wrath or his enthusiasms. Gurowski also urged upon Stanton the creation of trained army staffs that would assist commanders, pointing out that even Napoleon couldn't lead huge armies without help. The "gadfly" then assaulted Lincoln with a barrage of letters urging the creation of a general staff on the Prussian model and of a chief of staff who would supervise all military operations. Lincoln apparently ignored these suggestions, including Gurowski's idea that the President himself should take command of the Army of the Potomac in the field.

But some of Gurowski's ideas were listened to in the War Department, although his part in them was never recognized. Huge Union battle losses, rather than any commitment to a principle, finally brought about enlistment of northern free blacks in their own regiments, as the count had demanded from the start.

As always with this extraordinary man, Gurowski's ideas went far beyond the point where his contemporaries dared to follow. Black soldiers occupied his vision as more than cannon fodder. He urged them upon Lincoln as a means of hastening the end of white prejudice and the widespread American belief, even among fervent Abolitionists, that blacks were biologically inferior. It was a belief he found "scientifically indefensible, morally incomprehensible." The blacks' skill and courage in the field, he argued, would be their best argument for equality, and ease their postwar integration into the fabric of

American life. He recognized that prejudice could leave black regiments unsupported on the battlefield, and urged the formation of black divisions and army corps that could stand against the enemy alone if they had to. He outlined a drill manual, regulations, and special equipment for a corps of black light infantry and cavalry to be raised from contrabands and runaways in the border states, where they would be a focus for southern black rebellions "like a ring of hot coals placed around a scorpion." He also petitioned both Lincoln and Stanton to appoint him colonel in a black regiment so that he might serve with free "Africo-Americans" (as he called them) in the field. Stanton did, eventually, agree to the organization of black light infantry (though nowhere near the one-hundred-thousand-man corps that Gurowski demanded), and Massachusetts' Adams, hypnotized by Gurowski's vision, recruited several black regiments in his state. As for Gurowski's colonelcy, it was put off, time and time again (probably because of the maniacal image he projected) until the war was over.

Some of Gurowski's ideas were so advanced that they were wholly beyond comprehension in his time. One of them was a formation of "flying infantry," which could be transported by balloons behind enemy lines to wreck communications, dynamite railroads and bridges, and foster black uprisings. It was probably this sweep of his imagination, coupled with the violence of his presentations, that made all his ideas suspect and hindered their acceptance. He was the first to recognize the fatal flaw of his own impatience with men whose vision was narrower or whose comprehension may have been less than his. But there was no other way for him to behave, nor did he try to change. Time was his enemy, he argued, draining his energies more quickly than he could create his ideas. The count was in the midst of mounting a campaign against President Andrew Johnson's "lack of determination" in completing the pledges of the black emancipation, when time caught up with him. He was sixty

when the South surrendered but seemed much older to his contemporaries, as though the end of violence had extinguished some vital spark within him. He died in 1866 in the home of Charles Eames in Washington, where he had come to supper several years earlier and never moved out. Walt Whitman, who watched him die, thought him surprisingly content. Senator Sumner, who had likened him in life to Barnum's whale ("who went around and around in his glass tank, blowing great spouts of air wherever he surfaced"), wept at his funeral. In his last moments, the radical count knew peace; his last great cause had prevailed, although not as completely as he would have wished, and that was enough.

Such immigrants as the Poles who came to America in the first half of the nineteenth century are rare in any country's history; such people seldom need to leave their own land; they are its mind and soul and often its heart. Only a great upheaval flings the flower of a nation to take root in foreign soil. No European people struggled more desperately than the Poles to remain in Europe in that era of libertarian hopes and cruel disenchantments. But once they were carried across the Atlantic, none left a greater imprint on American life. Although this Polish energy and imagination, with its curious dedication to abstract ideals, impressed itself on American history, the arts, education, and politics throughout the republic, it was in Texas—which had nothing to offer except geography—that a wholly different kind of Polish pioneer appeared.

The year was 1854, the place was Galveston, and the news of a strange sight drew vast crowds of gawkers to the dockside. There a battered sailing vessel had arrived and began to discharge a weary human cargo that seemed, to some, a circus; to others, a crusade. Nothing quite like it had been seen in Texas before. There was a robed Franciscan monk carrying an enormous cross, and behind him walked

A visionary of Polish settlement in America, Father Leopold Moczygemba, a Franciscan priest, led an entire village from Polish Silesia into the Texas wilderness in 1854 to found the first Polish settlement in Texas. The founding of the town of Panna Maria marks the beginning of the Polish peasant immigration, although it took several decades after the Civil War for a mass immigration movement to begin. COURTESY OF THE INSTITUTE OF TEXAN CULTURES.

In this allegorical panel by Artur Szyk, the Panna Maria colonists emplace the cross that Father Moczygemba carried from Silesia to the Texas wilderness in 1854. Their descendants still populate the prosperous town. COURTESY OF MRS. ALICE BRACIE.

some eight hundred men, women, and children who bore the entire contents of a Polish village on their backs. Carrying their plows, bedding, and cooking utensils, carved wooden chests and benches—and the cross of their church steeple from a Silesian hamlet—they had braved the terrors of an ocean crossing and now headed inland to build the first Polish settlement in the United States. Father Moczygemba, their leader, had been in Texas three years earlier and induced this entire village to transplant itself into what many of these immigrants believed, was a biblical land of milk and honey. What they found just two miles north of where the San Antonio River joined the Cibolo was a prairie full of rattlesnakes. L. B. Russell, who, as a boy,

witnessed their arrival, left this impression of their march through Texas:

"The arrival of the colony was one of the most picturesque scenes in my boyhood. The highway between Port Lavaca and San Antonio passed directly in front of our home. Up to that time, the people of Texas were entirely English speaking but for a few colonies from Germany. The consequence of this was, that simple frontier people like ourselves have never seen anything like the crowd which passed along the road that day. There were some eight or nine hundred of them. They wore the costumes of the old country. Many of the women had what, at that time, was regarded as very short skirts, showing their limbs two or three inches above the ankle.

St. Mary's Church, Panna Maria, Texas, built by Father Moczygemba and the Polish settlers he led from Silesia. Legend has it that these Polish immigrants, distressed by the wilderness in which they found themselves, tried to hang their Franciscan leader on the tree near which they later built the church. The first Mass was celebrated under the tree instead. PHOTO BY FRANK ALEKSANDROWICZ. COPYRIGHT © FRANK ALEKSANDROWICZ.

70

Some had on wooden shoes and, almost without exception, all wore broad-brimmed, low-crowned black felt hats, nothing like the hats that were worn in Texas. They also wore blue jackets of heavy woolen cloth, falling just below the waist and gathered into folds at the back with a band of the same material."

The scorched and barren prairie with its rattling reptiles seemed more like hell than the promised paradise to these exhausted marchers who followed Father Moczygemba's cross. According to a contemporary account, some of them wanted to hang the Franciscan from the nearest tree. But the nearest tree was barely visible on the far horizon, and the priest managed to get away. The settlers made their camp, cleared the land, built their homes and church and, later, their school. Then, more perhaps in hope of divine intervention than Old World nostalgia, they named their settlement Panna Maria (Polish for Virgin Mary). Many accounts of their difficulties with the land and its people have been preserved, including the Sunday custom of the cowboys to ride into their church and shoot out its windows. Panna Maria was soon followed by Polish settlements in San Antonio, Bandera, Yorktown, and St. Hedwig, and later still by Czestochowa, Kosciuszko, Falls City, and Polonia, all on Texas soil.

At about this same time the first Polish settlements began to appear in Wisconsin, Michigan, and Illinois, and a busy little community of Polish Forty-niners grew out of the Gold Rush in California and Oregon. One of those pioneering arrivals in "the country of the sun," an enormously energetic patriarch of a patriotic Polish-Jewish

One of the western pioneers who came from Poland in the period after the Polish insurrection of 1848 was Michael Goldwasser, a patriotic Jewish merchant, whose grandson, Senator Barry Goldwater, would be a candidate for the presidency of the United States. The Goldwassers settled first in Sonora, California, which was a center for Polish political exiles and adventurers. CREDIT: ARIZONA HISTORICAL FOUNDATION, COURTESY OF SENATOR BARRY GOLDWATER.

family named Michael Goldwasser, established a retail store in Sonora, California. Two generations later, his grandson Barry Goldwater stood for election as President of the United States.

Groups of Polish immigrants are moved aboard the New Rochelle, *one of the steamers that plied between the Baltic Sea and the United States up to the outbreak of the First World War.* CREDIT: NATIONAL ARCHIVES (PUBLIC HEALTH SERVICE PHOTO).

For many Polish villagers, the first step toward America was this bleak, cobbled courtyard outside the steerage passengers' compound in Danzig. The HIAS sign in the background stands for the Hebrew Immigrant Aid Society, which provided temporary quarters for Jewish emigrants only. CREDIT: NATIONAL ARCHIVES (PUBLIC HEALTH SERVICE PHOTO).

A group of young peasants from the Russian-held provinces of Poland arrives at Homestead, Pennsylvania, in 1909 to work in the steel mills. More than two million such young men, equipped with nothing but their hands and a capacity for back-breaking labor, had already come to America in the last twenty years of the nineteenth century. PHOTO BY LEWIS W. HINE, INTERNATIONAL MUSEUM OF PHOTOGRAPHY AT GEORGE EASTMAN HOUSE.

In Chicago, the center of Polish settlement in America, the stockyards were often the first place where Poles would be hired. Ironically, the Polish peasant immigrants' only skills were animal husbandry and knowledge of the land, which they were seldom to exploit in their new country. CREDIT: LIBRARY OF CONGRESS, PRINTS AND PHOTOGRAPHS.

The joys and sorrows of Ellis Island in 1905 are perfectly captured in this classic photograph of an immigrant family and its friends, variously listed as Slavic, Slovak, Polish, etc., by U.S. immigration officials, who took scant trouble to verify the immigrants' national origins. The immigrants themselves often did not know that they were Polish until they faced a violent American discrimination. CREDIT: LEWIS W. HINE, INTERNATIONAL MUSEUM OF PHOTOGRAPHY AT GEORGE EASTMAN HOUSE.

Immigrant laborers, such as these, scalded hogs before scraping at the Swift & Company packing house in Chicago in 1905. Thrift-conscious peasant workers accepted unsanitary and often dangerous working conditions, and pitiful wages, in order to obtain any work at all. CREDIT: LIBRARY OF CONGRESS, PRINTS AND PHOTOGRAPHS DIVISION.

And still they came, and still they kept on coming. Youthful immigrants join older workers in this 1912 group photograph of Polish miners near Scranton, Pennsylvania. The two "miners" seated on the ground are each fourteen years old. CREDIT: LIBRARY OF CONGRESS, PRINTS AND PHOTOGRAPHS DIVISION.

Carrying all his possessions in a home-made trunk, a youthful Polish worker in 1907 boards the President Grant *in Hamburg on his way to the United States.* CREDIT: LIBRARY OF CONGRESS, PRINTS AND PHOTOGRAPHS DIVISION.

The next step up from the stockyards for the unskilled laborer was, often, the primitive sausage industry in Chicago. In these photographs, Polish sausagemakers attempt to produce their village specialty. Similar home-made plants led many immigrants out of the ranks of poorly paid workers into businesses of their own. CREDIT: CHICAGO HISTORICAL SOCIETY.

One of the tales that shipping agents often told prospective peasant immigrants was that food was free in the United States. It was, on Ellis Island. Here immigrants, in quarantine at this famous gateway to America, do a little dance under a sign that tells in six languages, including Polish, that there is indeed no charge for meals here. PHOTO BY LEWIS W. HINE, INTERNATIONAL MUSEUM OF PHOTOGRAPHY AT GEORGE EASTMAN HOUSE.

Her shawl and skirts blown wide by the wind, a Polish peasant woman arrives in Chicago to join her three sons. Hard-working, thrifty village women were the backbone of the Polish peasant immigration to America. CREDIT: CHICAGO HISTORICAL SOCIETY.

This photograph taken in 1909 for the National Child Labor Committte shows a twelve-year-old Polish boy at his carding machine in the Quidnick Mills, near Providence, Rhode Island. Child-labor regulations were often ignored in the case of Polish children and young girls, who were thought to be able to endure better, and complain less, than those born in the United States. COURTESY OF THE EDWARD L. BAFFORD PHOTOGRAPHY COLLECTION, UNIVERSITY OF MARYLAND.

This classic 1912 photo by Lewis W. Hine shows the interior of a Polish working family's home near the cotton mills at Olneyville, Providence, Rhode Island. Brought up to care for children and to be mistresses of their own village households, young Polish peasant girls struggled to turn cheap hovels into clean and healthy homes. CREDIT: LIBRARY OF CONGRESS, PRINTS AND PHOTOGRAPHS DIVISION.

And this is how they came, lured by tales of wealth across the Atlantic, on crowded steamers that carried them directly to factories and coal pits from the fields and pastures of agrarian Poland. This rare photograph shows Polish village girls arriving in New York in the 1890s to join the young men who had preceded them and then sent for them to be their wives. CREDIT: MUSEUM OF THE CITY OF NEW YORK.

Thrift, self-reliance, and the labor of the entire family gradually allowed Polish peasant immigrants to return to the land. In this telling photograph by Jack Delano, a grandmother hires herself out to a Yankee farmer near Windsorville, Connecticut, to help to earn the money for her own family's farm. CREDIT: LIBRARY OF CONGRESS, PRINTS AND PHOTOGRAPHS DIVISION.

There were about 30,000 Poles in the United States when the seething ferment of discontent between North and South finally erupted upon the young republic. From the bombardment of Fort Sumter to the last tragic moments of Robert E. Lee's ride to Appomatox Courthouse, about 5,000 Polish immigrants fought to save the Union—167 of them as officers—while another 1,000 dressed in butternut gray to struggle for southern independence. One hundred years later, the wounds that had rent America in that bitter fratricidal conflict were still barely closing; it was only the advent of more immediately traumatic divisions among all kinds and classes of Americans that finally allowed the angry ghosts of the Civil War to subside in peace. This War Between the States (as the Southerners called it) remains the most profound single experience in America's history, when all the human passions—the graces and the virtues along with the seven deadly sins—engulfed the country's reason. New Americans, of whatever ethnic or religious background—sometimes understanding little of the real issues that had torn America in half—went to war with something close to joy. To many of them it was an opportunity to prove themselves more Yankee than a China Clipper or more southern than a Mississippi riverboat.

There was no Kosciuszko or Pulaski on either side this time; nor was there need for them. The dashing troopers of J. E. B. Stuart and Nathan Bedford Forrest learned from brilliant American-born commanders how to be the best light cavalry in the world, and generals such as Thomas, Jack-son, Sherman, Grant, and Lee were their own best strategists, tacticians, and field engineers. Three Polish immigrants did distinguish themselves as Union brigadier generals, 42 won battlefield commissions, and 20 others were captains in cavalry troops and artillery batteries they had raised themselves. Across the battle lines, 8 other Polish settlers became colonels for the South. All had been living in America for some time when the war began, and they fought for whichever side had become their country. They did neither more nor less than other skilled, courageous American soldiers in that most dreadful of all possible wars, although their partisans have elevated some of them into heroic legends, giving them victories they didn't win and even making one of them—the talented and undoubtedly deserving Wlodzimierz Krzyzanowski—the first American governor of Alaska. The truth is far more impressive in its humbler, understated clothing.

Krzyzanowski did hold the extreme left flank of the Union line for eight bitter hours on the first day of the Second Battle of Bull Run (and led two brigades in a gallant charge on the second day), and it was his brigade that held Cemetery Ridge during the second day at Gettysburg and undoubtedly decided the course of that battle. He did not, however, "save the Union Army, and therefore the Union." Nor did he get to be a brigadier general until the war had nearly run its course; nor did he ever hold high office in Alaska.

Lincoln recommended him to the Senate for promotion to general after Second Bull

Brigadier General Wlodzimierz Krzyzanowski was photographed in 1867 in the uniform he wore as colonel of the 58th New York Volunteer Infantry, known as the "Polish Legion," which he had organized and led during the Civil War. A gallant officer who distinguished himself at Bull Run, Chancellorsville, and Gettysburg, Krzyzanowski was twice passed over for promotion because no one in the U. S. Senate could pronounce his name. CREDIT: LIBRARY OF CONGRESS, PRINTS AND PHOTOGRAPHS DIVISION.

Run, and again after Chancellorsville, "but the Senate failed to confirm him," as his divisional commander, the veteran Carl Schurz, wrote after the war, "because—as was said—there was nobody there [in the Senate] who could pronounce his name." They could, apparently, pronounce the name of Schurz's other brigadier general, Schimmelpfennig.

Krzyzanowski came to America after the collapse of the 1848 Polish revolt against Prussia, along with the two other Polish patriots who would earn brigadier general's stars in the Civil War, and worked as

an engineer and surveyor in Virginia. Two days after Lincoln's call for volunteers, he enlisted as a private in Washington, D.C., and set about, on his own, recruiting a company of Polish immigrants. By July 1861 he had been raised to the rank of major and moved his company to New York, where there were more immigrants to choose from. His four-hundred-man battalion, christened by him the United States Rifles, formed the core of the 58th New York Volunteer Infantry, which is listed in the *Official Army Register of the Volunteer Forces of the United States* as the "Polish Legion."

There were at least as many Germans, Hungarians, Italians, Czechs, and Danes in that "Polish Legion"—all of them veterans of various European democratic uprisings —as there were Poles, although most of the officers appeared to be Polish. Perhaps more Poles would have joined Krzyzanowski if Jozef Karge hadn't been recruiting in New Jersey, and if other well-known veterans of European freedom wars, such as Colonel Joseph Smolinski, Colonel Emil Schoening (a Polish insurrectionist hero, despite his Teutonic-sounding name), Major Alexander Raszewski, and Captain Juliusz Krzywoszynski, had not been recruiting their own "Polish" regiments. (Colonel Smolinski's 1st United States Lancers became the 9th New York Volunteer Cavalry; Schoening's troops became the 52nd New York Volunteer Infantry, which the exile colonel commanded throughout the war; Raszewski's Polish companies became part of the 31st New York Infantry Regiment; and Krzywoszynski's cadre became the officers of the all-black 22nd United States Cavalry.) Many Polish veterans also served in the 1st and 4th New York Cavalry regiments and in the Independent New York Light Artillery Company of Captain Adalbert Morozowski. Krzyzanowski was one of the few men in that polyglot command who didn't have much practical military experience, but he was glad to stand in the shadow of such veteran freedom fighters as Schurz and Schimmelpfennig (both of whom had learned their military trade from the Polish revolutionary leader Mieroslawski), who taught him all they knew as soon as rhetoric had given way to cannon.

Krzyzanowski's 58th New York absorbed other picturesque volunteer companies such as the Humbolt Jaegers, the Gallatin Rifles (which had many Poles), and the little "Polish Legion" itself, which had become a part of the Morgan Rifles. This was the regiment Krzyzanowski led south as its colonel on November 7, 1861; it was eventually to become the backbone of the 2nd Brigade of Schurz's immigrant 3rd Division. What no American historian seems to realize is that most of these men either knew each other, or knew each others' reputations from various European independence movements, and that the war in America seemed to many of them only a logical extension of their national struggles in which, for the first time, they stood shoulder to shoulder whatever their nationality might have been. This gave them a cohesion and an *esprit de corps* that few American volunteer regiments had early in the war. Schurz joked that no Yankee would ever manage to pronounce Krzyzanowski's name (in his brigade he was known as "Kryz"), but it was a common kind of name in the immigrant regiments that marched on Richmond in that first disastrous campaign of the war.

The "Polish Legion," Smolinski's lancers, and Karge's New Jersey cavalry caused an amusing historical footnote when the Imperial Russian consul in New York sent a panicky telegram to St. Petersburg that "the Polish Revolutionaries are starting it again." The Tsar's government protested politely to Lincoln and was properly ignored.

Almost from the beginning of the wearying and unnerving game of hide-and-seek, with which the Confederates' Thomas "Stonewall" Jackson dazzled, confused, exhausted, and finally overwhelmed the Union armies of Fremont and Pope in the Shenandoah Valley, Krzyzanowski commanded more troops than his rank suggests, as he would do until the war's end.

At Cross Keys, Virginia, where Schurz's immigrant brigades checked Jackson's pursuit long enough for most of the wrecked northern army to escape, and then at Bull Run, Krzyzanowski fought as the 2nd Brigade's commander. He led five New York, Ohio, Wisconsin, and Pennsylvania regiments at Chancellorsville where, as the official Army history has recorded it, "the only real fighting which delayed Jackson's progress [in the wide flanking movement that trapped the Union army] . . . was done by foreign brigadiers Schimmelpfennig and Krzyzanowski of Schurz's Division and Buschbeck of Steinwehr's. . . ." At one point in that battle, although he probably didn't know it, Krzyzanowski parted his ranks for the cavalry of Karge and Smolinski, which would cover the retreat of Franz Sigel's corps. Schurz has written that he could always rely on the young Polish colonel to "rally broken men, lead a charge or hold a position."

Krzyzanowski was some miles distant from Gettysburg at the end of June 1863 when the sound of cannon put him on the march, with the rest of Sigel's immigrant corps some hours behind him. Krzyzanowski reached Gettysburg at noon on the first day of the battle, threw his three regiments into line across the road that led from Gettysburg and Chambersburg and held it, reinforced by Sigel as the other immigrant brigades arrived on the field. Pushed back by the Confederates, Krzyzanowski's men rallied on Cemetery Hill and held that until the corps of Hancock and Howard could come up in support. That night, Benjamin A. Willis, then a major on Krzyzanowski's staff, wrote him a letter of thanks on behalf of the brigade's officers. "Late in the evening," he wrote, "the enemy made a most desperate charge upon the battery supported by the 1st Division. They rushed forward with incredible fierceness and demanded a surrender. . . . Then you, seeing the critical position of affairs, and well knowing how soon the enemy would possess himself of the battery and the commanding heights if not forced back, called upon our regiment and the 58th New York Volunteers, also of your brigade, to fall in advance against them. . . ." General Howard of the XI Corps also singled out Krzyzanowski for praise and commendation.

At dawn the next morning, at the start of the day that historians have justly called the beginning of the end for Lee's splendid Army of Northern Virginia, Krzyzanowski's men were picked for the pivotal brigade that would face the main, and heaviest, Confederate assault on Cemetery Ridge. They held all day. Twice between noon and nightfall the Union line bent back and threatened to rupture; each time the 58th New York and neighboring regiments charged with the bayonet, led by Krzyzanowski. Other American commanders did as much on both sides on that day in which the balance of the war in the East would finally incline toward the Union. On the third and final day of that bloody battle, which broke Lee's invasion of the North and turned him back toward Virginia for good, Krzyzanowski positioned himself near the center of the Union line to face Pickett's charge. Not all of his brigade were with him when the gallant charge began; fewer still were with him on the bloody crest when the battle-worn Virginians under Armistead (some 150 of Pickett's 15,000 had survived the murderous Union guns) planted their Stars and Bars in the Union trenches—a lone moment of illusory success. Most of the 2nd Brigade were making their own stand in a field behind the cemetery, and possibly that is why Krzyzanowski's presence on the ridge has never been acknowledged. But that night's letters from the battlefield have identified him as the officer who rallied nearby Massachusetts, Maine, and Minnesota regiments and led them against Pickett's remnants. The doomed Virginians fought where they stood and, in the words of an observer, "fell where they chose to fight." Fewer than two dozen finally made their hushed and weary way back down the terrible slope they had climbed earlier in the day. It was a dreadful ending to the most spectacular, and ultimately most useless, act of mass heroism in the war.

Krzyzanowski never forgot that day. In later years he would say that he could still hear the crash of cannon and the cries of the stricken Southerners echoing in his ears, and, every time he would see smoke rising above wooded hills on a July evening, he would begin to talk about his three days at Gettysburg. He would never again go to Pennsylvania.

After Gettysburg, Krzyzanowski led his brigade in Sherman's late summer and fall campaigns in Tennessee, distinguished himself in the four-day battle of Chattanooga, in the relief of Knoxville, and in the November storming of Missionary Ridge—a sort of Pickett's Charge in blue, and a Union victory. Then, with one more brigade and a gunboat, he was left to cover Nashville, the Chattanooga Railroad, and the Tennessee River as far as Bridgeport, Alabama, while Sherman started on his march to the sea. It was then—while he was, in effect, commanding a division— that Lincoln finally breveted him a brigadier general. Whatever honors might have missed Krzyzanowski during the Civil War, he was remembered long after it by men who had served with and under him, and by his superiors. Old Carl Schurz came to speak at his funeral in 1887, as did other comrades. In 1938 his body was transferred to Arlington National Cemetery, where President Franklin Delano Roosevelt spoke at his reinterment. Eyewitnesses reported that the President had no difficulty with Krzyzanowski's name. With nearly seven million Polish-American voters as his radio audience, perhaps the President had practiced.

One of Krzyzanowski's acquaintances in the brief Polish revolt against the Prussians (although they were apparently never to meet again on American soil) was Jozef Karge, who holds an unusual distinction among American cavalrymen of the Civil War: He was the only Union officer to "get there fastest with the mostest" against Bed-

One of the most brilliant Union cavalry commanders in the Civil War was Brigadier General Jozef Karge, an immigrant from Poland, who distinguished himself during the famous Grierson's Raid in 1863 and who was the only Union cavalryman to defeat the South's legendary Nathan Bedford Forrest. Karge is shown in this photograph as colonel of the 2nd New Jersey Cavalry. CREDIT: LIBRARY OF CONGRESS, PRINTS AND PHOTOGRAPHS DIVISION.

ford Forrest and inflict on Forrest his only defeat. Like Krzyzanowski, Karge was always in command of larger forces than his rank would imply, often leading brigades (and once a division) and, according to William A. Packard, writing in New York in 1893, "he was assigned to the most dangerous and responsible positions" because he was invariably the most competent Union cavalry commander on the field. General G. D. Bayard, in his report to General Winfield Scott, called Karge "one of the ablest cavalry officers in the service. . . . Lieutenant-Colonel Karge I would particularly name, as always ready and valiant, and I would particularly ask that the General would notice him." But being noticed on the battlefield was the last thing Karge could have wanted.

Jozef Karge was a scholar, a classical historian, more at home with Caesar's *Commentaries* than with plumes and trumpets, who had learned contempt for military glories after a brief impressment into the Prussian Army. In the war, his contemporaries have written, "he fought like a tiger but only so that the battle might be ended sooner and fewer men be killed." Karge had received the best possible education at the universities of Breslau, Berlin, and Paris, and was preparing for a professorship at Cracow, when the "Spring of the Nations" swept him with the rest of his country's youth into revolution and then, inevitably, cast him abroad as an exile. He landed in New York in 1851, aged twenty-eight, at once declared his intention to be an American citizen, and began to teach. His first few years were spent in Danbury, Connecticut, where he taught literature and classical subjects; then he married the widow of a minister and, on her money, opened the private Classical and English School in New York City. In those days, his former Polish nationality was an asset that attracted the sons of New York's best families to his academy. Many of young Professor Karge's students responded instinctively to his firm but soft-spoken direction "as a cultivated European gentleman." One of them has described him as having "the courtesy of a courtier of Louis XIV. . . . His smile would charm Plato himself." He feared war as a disrupter of civilizations, but he was among the first to offer his services when Lincoln issued his call for seventy-five thousand volunteers to put down the southern insurrection. He did so, according to a contemporary account, because he saw many of his students preparing to go, and doubted their ability to pass through the trials of war without some serious damage to themselves. It would be several years after the war was over before he could return to his classrooms and students.

Professor Karge, now lieutenant colonel in the 1st New Jersey Cavalry, fought his first battle against politicians who were masquerading as officers in his regiment and against an unruly, enthusiastic mob of volunteers who resisted all attempts to turn them into soldiers. His smile might have been effective against Plato; it did nothing for New Jersey Governor Charles S. Olden, who saw all his political cronies thrown out of the regiment when they failed to qualify before the Examining Board in Washington. Slight in build, courteous, and soft-spoken, Karge also had a talent for imposing his authority with little visible effort; he led by example rather than direction and took no nonsense from anyone at all. The 1st New Jersey Cavalry capitulated before its commander, and Colonel Karge led them south in the fall of 1861. He left behind him disgruntled politicians who never forgave him and would oppose future recommendations for his promotion.

That fall and winter and through the next year at Strasburg, Harrisburg, Barnett's Ford, and then at Freedman's Ford and Cedar Mountain—in skirmishes, raids, reconnaissance patrols, as flank guard and screen for Union advances and as rear guard covering retreats—"he surprised and captured large bodies of enemy troops, extricating his own from the midst of superior forces by means of quick decisions and gallant leadership and desperate hand-to-hand conflicts," according to General Bayard's letters to Winfield Scott in Washington. At Strasburg his horse was blown to pieces under him; at Brandy Station, when Kilpatrick's 2nd New York Cavalry broke in a charge and opened up the center of the Union line, Karge turned his regiment in midgallop against the triumphant Confederates, ". . . emptied the chambers of his revolver into their ranks, and then throwing the weapon at their heads, dashed among them with his saber, followed by the men around him, the enemy giving way before his impetuous charge." At Aldie, Karge was within reach of a victory over the invincible Stuart, but an officer sent with a detachment against

Stuart's rear miscarried his orders. "Men began to retreat. Karge with his Adjutant charged unsupported upon a party of fifteen and drove them before him, but a bullet took effect in his leg. . . ." Still suffering from his wounds in October, Karge led his men on a raid to Warrenton, Virginia, and captured Confederate supplies. By December 22, 1862, Karge's wounds were still unhealed. (Then, as now, wounds didn't heal effectively on horseback.) Karge resigned from the service, and went home thinking that the war was over for him, but it was yet to begin.

The spring of 1863 was a time of rumor, panic, and fearful speculation as all the hitherto undefeated paladins of the Confederacy prepared to carry the war home to the North. New Union armies had gathered together under a new commander, but such armies had gathered time and time again, and few fearful politicians could suppose that General Meade would do better than his crushed predecessors against Lee, Stuart, Jackson, Longstreet, and the other victors of a dozen battles, all of them marching north together under one command. In May, in New Jersey, ex-Governor O. J. Parker (with some future political advantages in mind) gathered officials and citizens to petition the War Department for more New Jersey troops and asked that Lieutenant Colonel Karge be allowed to raise another cavalry regiment in the state. Governor Olden eventually endorsed this petition; Lincoln also endorsed it. Six days later, Karge was promoted to full colonel, named chief of all New Jersey militia, and ordered to raise the 2nd New Jersey Cavalry for service in the new emergency. By the Fourth of July the emergency was over; the smoke would hang for days above Cemetery Ridge, and fifty thousand fallen Americans made a bitter commentary on their country's birthday. But in the West the war raged more fiercely than ever, as the Confederates strove against the crushing weight of the Union armies to turn the tide of history itself. Karge was posted there in September 1863. A month later he was raiding the Confederate General Price in Mississippi, leading a brigade, and maneuvering for advantage against the West's undisputed ruler of cavalrymen—the ubiquitous and invincible Nathan Bedford Forrest. Seven long-ranging expeditions and a score of lesser sweeps, and skirmishes, from which he almost always emerged victorious, marked the milestones of Karge's first autumn west of the Mississippi. The names of his battlefields speak for themselves: the operation against Rienzi, the raid on Okolona and, in early May 1864, the staggering defeat of Forrest himself in the great cavalry fight at Bolivar.

"I cannot refrain from expressing my high appreciation of the valuable services rendered by that excellent and valuable officer, Colonel Joseph Karge, of the Second New Jersey Volunteers in his reconnaissance to Corinth," wrote General Samuel D. Sturgis in his report of the Mississippi campaign in June 1864, "and of his subsequent management of the rear guard during a part of the retreat, fighting and defending the rear during the whole afternoon and throughout the night following."

In December 1863, Karge had been picked for the most dramatic and memorable campaign of the cavalry war in the West, Grierson's Raid through the heart of Mississippi, and then the seven-hundred-mile dash to New Orleans.

"Sir," General H. B. Grierson wrote to the Secretary of War early in 1864, "I take occasion to bring to your notice Colonel Joseph Karge of the Second New Jersey Cavalry. He has been for the past year acting under my command, much of the time having charge of a brigade. He has particularly attracted my attention by his discipline in camp and in the field, and by his gallantry in action. During my late successful expedition against the Mobile and Ohio railroad, he bore a very conspicuous part, attacking the camp of the enemy at Verona [Station], which resulted in the capture and destruction of an immense amount of army supplies; and his promptness, energy and gallantry during the engagement, with the enemy, at Egypt, on the 28th day of December last, which came under my personal

One of the nine descendants of Olbracht Zabriskie (Zborowski) who fought for the Union in the Civil War was Colonel John Zabriskie, commander of the 9th New Jersey Cavalry, whose famous ancestor lent the family's name to several locations in the American Northeast. CREDIT: LIBRARY OF CONGRESS, PRINTS AND PHOTOGRAPHS DIVISION.

observation, cannot be too highly commended . . . and I cheerfully and earnestly recommended him for promotion to the rank of brigadier-general."

Lincoln nominated Karge a brigadier general by brevet in March 1865. The Senate, with one eye on New Jersey politics, didn't confirm the nomination for more than a year. It would be three more years before Karge could return to the East, on leave from the regular Army, for which the end of the Civil War meant only the beginning of a wearying and remorseless campaign against the finest light cavalry that Americans would ever encounter: the American Indian nations of the western plains. Karge's wise dealings with the frontier population and with the western tribes had helped to pacify those turbulent territories.

He returned to the classroom, first as an instructor in modern languages at Princeton, then as the university's professor of continental languages and literatures. The university's records show that he was the first incumbent of the Woodhull professorship in modern languages, founded in 1870. In 1871 he received an honorary doctorate from Rutgers and resigned his Army commission. Karge died suddenly, while on his way to a meeting in New York, on December 27, 1892. He is buried in Princeton Cemetery under a granite stone placed there by Princeton's faculty and students, which, in a stroke of bitter irony, names him "a native of Prussia."

The first and least known of the Union's Polish brigadier generals, Albin Francis Schoepf, had lived a youth of such romantic turbulence that few of his American friends could ever believe it. He had been born in 1822 on a prosperous estate across the Vistula River from Cracow, one of that generation of Polish idealists whose names would be known wherever an autocracy was threatened in Europe. His father was a thoroughly Polonized Austrian administrative official; his mother was a fervent Polish patriot who believed that Poland's independence could be restored only on the battlefield. She raised her son for a soldier's life, fed him heroic tales along with her milk; he knew the careers of Napoleon's marshals before he could walk. Young Schoepf received the best possible military education in Vienna. In keeping with his mother's Napoleonic dreams of destiny, he became an artillery lieutenant, rose swiftly in the Hapsburgs' service, and was the first foreigner to join the Hungarians when they rebelled against the Austrians in 1848. He enlisted as a gunner in one of the Polish legions that had come to Hungary to fight "for your freedom and ours," quickly became his own battery's commander and then a major on the staff of another famous Polish artillerist, General Jozef Bem who, next to Kossuth, is Hungary's greatest patriotic hero. The in-

surrection in Hungary failed and Schoepf followed Bem to Turkey, where the Polish independence movement would seethe for a decade. Bem shaved his head and became a Moslem and the Turkish governor of Aleppo; Schoepf became an artillery instructor to the Sultan's armies. But mercenary service lacked the idealism that had driven Schoepf. He sailed for America in 1851.

In his later years, General Schoepf would never talk about his early years in America, just as Krzyzanowski would angrily change the subject, and as Karge would smile and leave the room when asked about his. Friendless and penniless, Schoepf became a hotel porter in Washington, slept in a packing case in the hotel's basement, and ate kitchen leftovers. (A few hundred miles north, young Krzy-

The most unlucky of the Polish brigadiers fighting for the Union in the Civil War was Albin Francis Schoepf, a hero of the Polish and Hungarian revolutions of the 1840s, who was invalided out of active service to become a jailer of southern prisoners. His humane treatment of captured Southerners, as commander of the military prison at Fort Delaware, won him respect from his former enemies. CREDIT: LIBRARY OF CONGRESS, PRINTS AND PHOTOGRAPHS DIVISION.

zanowski was wandering about New York without a word of English, a friend, or a penny, none of which would be his until he married the beautiful daughter of a wealthy American hero of the Mexican War; in Danbury, young Professor Karge subsisted on language classes and searched for a job. Their stories were told in America before them, and would be told again as long as Polish exiles continued to arrive.) Schoepf's "gravity of demeanour and military bearing" attracted the attention of Joseph Holt, then the United States patent commissioner, who used to stop for an evening brandy at Willard's Hotel and chat with the porter. Learning that the young Polish officer (he was twenty-eight in 1851) was one of the heroes of Kossuth's Hungarian rebellion, a skilled artillerist, and military engineer, Holt found a job for Schoepf in the drafting room of the Patent Office, and when Holt became Buchanan's Secretary of War, he took Schoepf with him to the War Department.

Like Krzyzanowski, Schoepf worked on military surveys in Virginia just before the war. Unlike the other Polish future brigadier generals, he entered the Union Army with stars on his shoulders in 1861. From the beginning, he fought within the Army of the Ohio as the experienced right hand of General Henry Thomas in his battles against Zollicoffer and Crittendon in Kentucky, leading Union brigades and divisions at Lebanon and Somerset, and in the first decisive Union victory of the war at Mill Springs, where Crittendon was pushed back to the Cumberland. Thomas commended him heartily and used him to reorganize his Army of the Ohio into the West's most efficient military body, but Schoepf's insistence on European discipline among western volunteers gave him a martinet's reputation and led to intrigues against him. Wounded in the ill-fated campaign of General Don Carlos Buell against Bragg in the summer of 1862—a campaign that resulted in Buell's court-martial for incompetence—Schoepf became partially deaf and had to resign. He was particularly harassed by American newspaper reporters who hounded him, eavesdropped on his conferences, and undermined the workings of his staff.

Deaf, ill, and disgusted with the revelations of the Buell affair, Schoepf made ready to return to his old desk at the Patent Office. But history is an ironic mistress and a cruel one. The newspapermen whom he hated and chased from his camps had christened him a tyrant (with complex allusions to his service in the Sultan's army), and the Washington radicals, spurred by the violent Gurowski, were looking for a tyrant. Secretary Stanton had Schoepf recalled to duty three days after his resignation and ordered him to the command of the federal prison at Fort Delaware, where ten thousand Confederate prisoners were confined in the "Andersonville of the North." It was a ghastly place, by all accounts, the domain of a sadistic autocrat named Captain George Ahl, who had been placed there by Stanton himself as post adjutant and could not be dislodged. It was a bitter end to Shoepf's idealistic beginnings and to the tales of military virtue he had learned from his mother. Apparently he did what he could to improve quarters and to restore the prisoners' rations to survival level. One of his Confederate prisoners, Colonel Burton S. Harrison (who had been private secretary to Jefferson Davis), later named his son after Schoepf in gratitude for the disabled general's attempted generosity and kindness. Henry Kid Douglas, of "Stonewall" Jackson's staff, also wrote of Schoepf's courtesy and consideration to him while he was a prisoner at Fort Delaware. But these were drops of oil in a sea of gall. Schoepf's protests and recommendations went unheard and the strange Captain Ahl could not be restrained. Schoepf left the service as soon as he was legally allowed to do so in January 1866, and he spent the rest of his life within walking distance of his Patent Office. He never allowed his name to be used in any commemoration of the Civil War.

Perhaps he had one moment of pleasure during his tragic and disheartening months at Fort Delaware. His friends at the Patent

Office would occasionally send him blueprints of inventions to study and approve (he would eventually become the Patent Office's chief examiner). One of the young inventors whom Schoepf encouraged was a youthful lieutenant in the 2nd New York Cavalry, who had run away from home at sixteen and won his commission at Hatcher's Run in 1863. His name was Edmund L. G. Zalinski, a Polish-American born in Syracuse; his inventions would include a collapsible intrenching tool (familiar to every American infantryman of two World Wars and Korea), a ramrod-bayonet, telescopic sights for artillery and range-finding systems, and the pneumatic dynamite torpedo. John Kolinski, one of five other Polish Civil War inventors, had ridden behind Karge on Grierson's Raid, helping to wreck the Mobile and Ohio Railroad; he made amends by inventing railroad collision equipment.

One out of each five Polish immigrants, and sons of immigrants, who fought for the Union was either killed or disabled, according to the majority of available statistics. One of those lost, Captain Aleksander Bielaski, died with particular heroism during Grant's attack on Belmont, Missouri, when, "having dismounted from his horse, which had been several times wounded, [he] was shot down while advancing with the flag of his adopted country in his hand, and calling on the men in his rear to follow him," as General Logan reported to McClernand.

Of the four thousand Poles who lived to march behind Ulysses S. Grant down Pennsylvania Avenue in that vast parade of the Grand Army of the Republic, at least one other was a genuine American hero, after whose death, in 1910, Supreme Court Justice Oliver Wendell Holmes wrote a personal tribute. Gustav Magnitsky, born Gustaw Hagnicki in Wroclaw, Poland, on March 10, 1840, had enlisted as a private in Massachusetts' 20th Regiment, became a sergeant for his heroism in the Battle of Petersburg, Virginia, and was promoted to

Captain Aleksander Bielaski fought in the Polish insurrection against Russia, then came to the United States, where he helped to build the Illinois Central Railroad, surveyed the swamplands of Florida, and was killed heroically in the Civil War. CREDIT: NATIONAL PORTRAIT GALLERY, SMITHSONIAN INSTITUTION, WASHINGTON, D.C.

a captaincy for valor on Cemetery Ridge, where the Massachusetts regiments stood against Pickett's charge. Justice Holmes had been Magnitsky's company commander.

There were others, many others among the dedicated 167 officers who served as troop commanders, engineers, and signals specialists on the staffs of Sherman at Shiloh, Grant at Fort Donnelson, Thomas at Chickamagua, and on the stricken field at Chancellorsville, where Captain Joseph Gloskowski's signal company had been the first to warn the luckless General Hooker of Jackson's approach. Juliusz Krzywoszynski had also served in the infant signals branch of the U. S. Army (as well as in the artillery and the engineers) before his command of black cavalry. Artur Wrotnowski, another Polish commander of black Americans, was colonel of the 95th United States Colored Volunteer Infantry.

By an odd coincidence, the first man to fall and then die of his wounds, on each side in this war waged by Americans against Americans, was a Pole. Captain Konstantyn Blandowski, a professional soldier who had fought in the Italian and Hungarian struggles for independence, and then served in the French Foreign Legion in Algeria, had been living quietly in St. Louis for ten years before the war. He had come to America in 1851 in search of peace, but volunteered for the 3rd Missouri Regiment as soon as Lincoln's call was heard in St. Louis. Blandowski was mortally wounded during the siege of Camp Jackson on May 10, 1861, the first known Union casualty of the war. The first recorded Confederate casualty was eighteen-year-old private, Thaddeus A. Strawinski, Jr., son of a Polish ex-officer insurgent of 1830 (who also served as a private in the Confederate Army). Young Strawinski was born in Charleston, South Carolina, and was a first-year student at the University of South Carolina when the war began. He was shot accidentally when someone's revolver went off during horseplay in the Columbia Artillery's barracks, and died on January 27, 1861—a mute and foolish comment on the idiocy of war.

No parades marked the end of the war in the beaten South, where equally heroic Americans were taking off their tattered gray coats and making their sad way home. Legend would turn them all into unmitigated gallants, and many were just that— at least in the beginning. Somewhere along those dusty southern trails rode Colonel Valery Sulakowski, "the Louisiana Tiger," whose exploits are straight out of a romantic novel; the bitterly disillusioned figure of "General" Tochman might have been seen there, with the remnants of the Polish brigade he had raised for the South. And among the weary foot-soldiers trudging home were survivors of the rifle company from Panna Maria, the first major Polish settlement in Texas.

Most of these "Polish Confederates"
were a strangely idealistic and romantic band—in part dreamers of the absolute, in part confused crusaders for an absent cause—for whom the South's rebellion evoked memories of their own European insurrections. They found no difficulty in rising to resist invaders (as they would see the North) nor in defending the rights of their states against outside domination and control—as they had fought for generations for Poland's right to manage her affairs. The South had been a generous hostess to many of them. The surface ease of plantation life, the apparent leisure for gentlemanly pursuits, the ritualized chivalry and codes of honor that seemed to imbue the men and women south of the Potomac, had a dreamlike quality of something lost and dimly remembered for the transplanted officers of Napoleon's Polish legions and the exiled landed gentlemen of the 1830 and 1849 Polish insurrections who had settled in the South. The cultured French and Spanish influence in Louisiana and Alabama, with its emphasis on manners and form, had drawn many nostalgic Poles (for whom French would have been a second language anyway). They could love the South, and many of them did. Slavery may have seemed as appalling to them as it did to many other Southerners even then, but the war was never fought over slavery. The South rose in arms to be independent, and Polish citizens of the Confederacy were just as loyal to their new country's cause as were the Polish immigrants who fought for the Union.

There were about five thousand Poles living in the territories of the Confederacy, the greater part of their number in Louisiana, among whose picturesque Zouaves, Tigers, and Querillas their names were mostly found. Sixteen Poles were wealthy owners of plantations, including the cultivated Colonel Ignatius Szymanski. Most were in the professions, as teachers, engineers, and physicians; several were sea captains. If they had married, it was to southern ladies whose way of life had become their own. The magic names of Kosciuszko and Pulaski were invoked to call the South's Polish citizens to arms, and most of them complied without noting the irony. Among them was a lively colony of Polish Jews, who were indefatigable in the raising of a Polish legion.

What made the Poles in gray so different from the Poles in blue were some wildly romantic and utterly unreal plans and deeds—like an attempt to bring over thirty thousand Polish "volunteers" to save the Confederacy from disaster, a fantastic scheme to smuggle another Polish army from Mexico to Texas, and the frenetic "General" Tochman's attempt to make himself into a Kosciuszko of the Confederacy. Gaspard Tochman, one of the real heroes of the 1830 insurrection, had arrived in America in 1837, became naturalized five years later (which was as quickly as the law allowed), and set himself up as a propangandist-prophet, lecturer, and leader of his people. There were many like him among the exiled soldier-intellectuals of this Polish diaspora; unlike most of the others, Tochman couldn't make his peace with harsh American realities. As a contemporary critic has described him: "His body lived in America, running frenziedly in ever-narrowing circles; his head and his spirit were wandering in the stormy clouds of Poland." His Byronic stance made him more at home among the gentlemen of Virginia than elsewhere, and that's where he settled.

Major Tochman, to use his Polish insurrectionist rank, started out as an ardent supporter of Lincoln, tried to negotiate the differences between North and South, wholly misunderstood the question of slavery (for which the poisonous wit of Count Gurowski made him a laughingstock), and even asked Secretary Seward to send him to Paris to keep the French Government from intervening on the Southerners' behalf. Seward ignored him, and Lincoln wouldn't see him. On the surrender of Fort Sumter, and Lincoln's declaration of war on the seceded states, Tochman offered his flamboyant talents to Jefferson Davis "in the name of the cause for which I have striven all my life—the principle of self-determination."

The Poles who had settled in the North, and all the Polish Democratic Societies in America and Europe, repudiated him at once. On May 1, 1861, when war seemed a certainty, Tochman offered to raise ten or twenty companies of a "Polish brigade," on the understanding that he would command them. (That understanding proved to be his alone.) Six days later he had his permission from the War Department in Montgomery, and, on May 7, the New Orleans *Daily Crescent* reported as follows:

"At a meeting of our citizens of Polish birth, held Saturday evening last, Mr. J. Przedmoski was called to the chair and the following gentlemen were elected Vice Presidents: Messrs. H. Pajevsky, A. Kossovsky, L. Cedrowsky, J. Print, Clores, Jacobovitz, Morris Hager and Mr. Alexander. Mr. Solomon Silverstein was appointed secretary. The object of the meeting, namely the formation of a military corps to vindicate Southern Rights was explained by the President in eloquent and feeling terms. Mr. Silverstein, being called on, addressed the meeting eloquently, exhorting his brother citizens of Polish birth, to stand true and firm to the cause of liberty and right, in resisting the aggression of the North upon the South. . . ."

Tochman had set up his camp 50 miles north of New Orleans. He contributed most of his own money for his men's equipment, bought a battery of artillery for his brigade with $7,000 subscribed by his New Orleans supporters, and in fewer than 6 weeks had managed to enlist 1,415 foreigners and 285 Americans of foreign stock, including Zebulon York, a former citizen of Maine who had settled in Louisiana to practice law and plant cotton. On July 29, the *Daily Crescent* could report that "the first regiment of the Polish Brigade under Colonel Sulakowski left today for Virginia. The second regiment nearing completion will be in Virginia long before Lincoln, Scott and Company will decide upon their renewed march to have a dinner-date in

Legend persists that Brigadier General Zebulon York, the last military commander of the Confederacy, was the grandson of a Polish insurgent-immigrant from Maine. York had settled in Louisiana before the Civil War, enlisted in Colonel Valery Sulakowski's Confederate "Polish brigade," and rose to be the brigade's commander. CREDIT: LIBRARY OF CONGRESS, PRINTS AND PHOTOGRAPHS DIVISION.

Richmond, where General Tochman is preparing a menu which the Polish Brigade hopes to serve them." But Tochman would find himself in an entirely different stew.

With his brigade ready for battle as the 10th and 14th Louisiana Infantry Regiments (soon to be grouped in Virginia as the 7th Brigade under Sulakowski), "General" Tochman asked for his stars and was told that it had all been a mistake. The Confederate Secretary of War, Leroy Pope Walker, had apparently promised him such rank, but Jefferson Davis demurred; Louisiana had claimed the troops for itself, and all that the state offered Tochman was a colonelcy. Tochman protested, resigned from the service, tried to sue the Confederacy for his money back, and then

vanished from history, clearing the stage for the genuine larger-than-life appearance of "The Louisiana Tiger."

Valery Sulakowski was a civil engineer in New Orleans when the war began, but there is no record of what he might have built. At thirty-four he had a demonic energy and a reputation for violent and extreme solutions in matters of honor. Sir Walter Scott might have been his author, but only if Clausewitz and Jean Lafitte had been his editors. Sulakowski was the sternest disciplinarian in the Confederate Army, who would confront his unruly companies with a pistol in each hand and shoot any man who disobeyed his orders. Utterly fearless, merciless, and despotic, he cowed the most ferocious denizens of the bayous into the only Confederate military unit where an officer's order was obeyed without question. His 7th Brigade fought on every Virginia battlefield in 1861 and 1862 and was decimated during the Seven Days.

When Zebulon York, who had gone to war as a captain in Sulakowski's 14th Regiment (and rose to brigadier general in September 1864), took over the Polish brigade from Sulakowski, the "Louisiana Tiger" became chief engineer to Major General J. Bankhead Magruder. In that capacity, Sulakowski designed and built the Yorktown–Warwick line of field fortifications that stalled McClellan's peninsula campaign, built the defenses on the Teche River in Louisiana, and fortified Galveston. "Colonel V. Sulakowski, is an officer of the highest merit," Magruder wrote to the Army's general inspector in Richmond. "His service to our cause is irrevocable. If Galveston remains protected from the hands of the enemy—I expect it—it will be attributed to his untiresome work." By the end of summer 1863, Sulakowski had become a sort of flying engineer of the Confederacy, fortifying the Strait of Sabine, and the ports of Velasco and Quintana in Texas; and in October, Colonel A. Butchel, commander of the operations at Niblett's Bluff, Louisiana, urged Magruder "that by all means and immediately to send Sulakowski to him, at least for several hours, because the fortifications are weaker than he [Butchel] had judged."

In December 1863 Magruder asked Texas Governor Murrah to appoint Sulakowski brigadier general, writing: ". . . His abilities as an engineer have already been proved, and now that active operations are about to commence in the field, I would be glad to give him an important command with troops, knowing that his abilities as a strategist and tactician are equal to those which he has displayed as an engineer." Evidently nothing came of this recommendation, and Sulakowski remained a colonel until the war's end. But by that time the "Tiger" was already pondering one of the most daring yet feasible plans made in that era of desperate proposals for the South's salvation.

In Poland, the last of the great uprisings against Russia had collapsed by midsummer 1863. Partisan warfare would continue into the next spring, and long columns of shackled prisoners would be winding their way into Siberia for several years to come, but the "January Rising" was as good as crushed. Neither the peasants nor the great Jewish minority in Poland had supported that rising of the gentry—indeed, the peasants hunted the defeated insurrectionists in the forests on the Russians' behalf, and the Jews were glad to buy up the patriots' confiscated manors. The insurrection's aftermath was another outpouring of exiles into France and the Balkans. Sulakowski worked out a detailed plan to bring a corps of these seasoned Polish veterans to the Confederacy's assistance, although he knew that none of them would ever fight as mercenaries but only as new citizens of an adopted country. For all its knight-errant daring, the plan betrayed the ruthless logic of a cost-conscious engineer. It offered the Confederacy a bargain that the embattled Southerners simply couldn't resist. In effect, the Confederates would receive thirty thousand Polish officers and soldiers—recruited, armed, and equipped in Europe—and transported to a Southern port through Mexico—at a cost of eighty-seven dollars a man, payable in cotton. Magruder checked and approved the plan. His superior, General Kirby Smith, was enthusiastic about it, assured the "Tiger" that his Polish corps would be granted citizenship once they were sworn into the Confederacy's Army and that Sulakowski would become a general as soon as he had brought two or more Polish regiments to Texas. The Confederate Congress accepted the proposal, and Jefferson Davis was pleased to endorse it.

Eight months had passed from the moment when Sulakowski had submitted his plan to Magruder and, by March 1864, Sulakowski was ready to sail. The schooner *Dodge* was loaded with three thousand bales of cotton—bound, ostensibly, for Havana—and the "Tiger" went aboard to wait for good sailing weather which, in the face of a tight Union blockade of Confederate ports, meant the first available storm. More days went by. The Confederate Secret Service was sure that the voyage had not been betrayed, but few secrets could be kept from black stevedores, whose grapevine-telegraph had long since alerted the Union blockaders. The captain of the *Dodge* began to have misgivings about the long and dangerous voyage ahead, but Sulakowski threatened to shoot him and his entire crew (and set fire to the ship, according to the story) unless the *Dodge* sailed. On the night of April 3, a violent storm swept through the gulf, blowing Union cruisers out to sea, and the "Tiger" got his desperate venture under way. The *Dodge* raised anchor, slipped out of Galveston, and fought her way through the hurricane into the open sea. But the storm's contrary winds had slowed her progress. She had not put enough distance between herself and the blockaders' stations, and the voyage ended under the guns of the U.S.S. *Scioto*, which had fought through the hurricane to keep her station some twenty miles southwest of Galveston. Hailed to heave-to, with warning shots raising fountains off his port bow, the captain of the *Dodge* damned the "Tiger" and his brace of pistols and hauled down his sails. the *Dodge* sailed north with a

Union prize crew, and the shackled "Tiger" went into the American warship's hold. How he escaped has never been made clear (it could hardly have been through either charm or money, both of which had been in short supply aboard the luckless *Dodge*), but Sulakowski broke out of the ship's brig and jumped overboard off Matamoros, Mexico, where he swam ashore, still determined to carry out his plan. He set up the Mexican end of the operation, wrote to Magruder that he would try again to get to Europe (this time on a neutral ship), and was once more prepared to sail when he received news of Appomattox. With Lee's surrender, the hopes of the Confederacy joined the great lost causes of the world, and Sulakowski returned to New Orleans.

While he had been away, four other Poles—officers in the 1863 uprising—had arrived in Richmond with a plan much like his for the enlistment of a Polish army in Europe. The Polish volunteers were to come to Mexico under the guise of colonists and then use Sulakowski's pipeline to move into Texas. This time, Jefferson Davis instructed Judah Benjamin, his Secretary of the Treasury, to remit fifty thousand pounds of silver to Colin J. McRae, the Confederate Treasury agent in England, to cover the costs of shipping these new Polish immigrants to Mexico. The storm that delayed and, eventually, scuttled this plan was not one at sea but in Paris, where Polish exiled leaders denounced the negotiating quartet as opportunists and urged the ex-insurgents not to support the cause of slavery. Some Polish exiles did land in Mexico shortly afterward, but there is no record that any of them found their way to the Confederacy or the rebels' armies.

Confederate regimental muster rolls and histories have, for the most part, shared the fate of government papers that went up in flames with the fall of Richmond. Surviving ones offer clues and hints but little evidence of other Poles' participation in the South's doomed struggle. Colonel Ignatius Szymanski (planter and yachtsman in Louisiana) did try to hold the Mississippi

Delta against Admiral Farragut's attack in April 1862, and three other Poles rose from private to colonel in the Confederacy's service (mostly in engineering, commissary, and medical positions). But of the remainder, only two made a memorable name for themselves. The first was Hippolitus Oladowski, an artilleryman and ordnance specialist, who distinguished himself at Shiloh; the second—and one of the most unusual Louisianians of his time—was Leon Jastremski.

In July 1861, young Leon, aged seventeen, enlisted in Tochman's "Polish brigade" and went to war under Sulakowski in the 10th Louisiana Volunteer Infantry. At Yorktown Jastremski was promoted to staff sergeant for heroism in battle, then fought at Williamsburg, along the Chickahominy, at Seven Pines, and in the bloody Seven Days, where the "Polish brigade"

Perhaps one of the most colorful of the South's Polish defenders was Leon Jastremski, who rose from private in the "Polish brigade" to brigadier general in the Louisiana National Guard after the Civil War. He died during an apparently victorious campaign for governor of Louisiana in 1907. COURTESY LOUISIANA STATE LIBRARY.

was whittled down to the size of two small companies. The list of the battles in which Jastremski fought sounds like a calendar of the Civil War in Virginia: Second Bull Run, Chantilly, the siege of Harper's Ferry, and Strasburg. In the first Maryland campaign, he was promoted to a captaincy. Seriously wounded at Chancellorsville (where the Confederates' "Polish brigade" found itself, for some hours, fighting against Krzyzanowski's "Polish legion"), Jastremski was back in service to fight at Gettysburg. He was taken prisoner at Spottsylvania and imprisoned at the fort on Morris Island, from which he managed to escape in 1865. He smuggled himself into New York City, then set off for the South, where remnants of the Confederates' troops, under Zebulon York, were still fighting their final campaigns. But the war ended before Jastremski could take any further part.

After the war, Jastremski settled in Baton Rouge, became its mayor in 1876, and served for some time as the United States consul at Gallao, Peru. He wrote prolifically on a variety of subjects, from politics to practical medicine (his father, an ex-insurgent of 1830, had been a doctor in Paris before coming to America), became a brigadier general in the Louisiana National Guard, and swam in and out of that state's political shoals for the rest of his life. He died in November 1907 in the middle of a heated—and apparently vic-torious—campaign for the governorship of Louisiana. Jastremski's death can be taken as the final date in the rich and spirited eight decades of Polish participation in the mainstream of America's life.

The Poles who had come to the United States in the first half of the nineteenth century, represented the best element their old land could give to the new. Their personal qualities were such that they could swiftly take their place at the forefront of American social and intellectual movements. Most of them came here unencumbered with family and baggage; if they brought anything, it was a trunk full of books and papers. Their ideas were among the most progressive and liberal in the Europe (and America) of their times because they were not chained to centuries of ignorance and superstition. Their entry into America's life and their submergence in it were as total as they were immediate; no herd instinct, nor any artificial social or religious construction stood in the way of their complete assimilation and transformation into Americans. Above all, in making their contributions to American life, they knew what no future peasant immigrant could even imagine—that the trappings of material success were not commensurate with achievement, and that achievement was not a synonym for accomplishment. And by the time of Jastremski's death, a wholly different kind of Polish immigrant had settled in America.

John Kowalski, a marine enginemaker, built this airplane in his spare time, hoping to gain prestige for the Polish community in America. The plane got off the ground near Aspinwall, Pennsylvania, early in 1910. Then it crashed.
CREDIT: LIBRARY OF CONGRESS, PRINTS AND PHOTOGRAPHS DIVISION.

POLISH ARMY

At hall on this site on April 3, 1917, a speech by I. J. Paderewski to delegates at convention of the Polish Falcons began the movement to recruit a Polish army in U.S. to fight in Europe with Allies for creating an independent Poland.

PENNSYLVANIA HISTORICAL AND MUSEUM COMMISSION

In an attempt to gain official American sympathies for the cause of an independent Poland, Paderewski urged the creation of a Polish army in France even before the United States had entered the war. Known as the Falcon Army, after the gymnastic society that formed its core, this Polish-American contribution to the Allied cause helped to strip the immigrants of their leadership once the war was over.
© FRANK ALEKSANDROWICZ.

In an attempt to stir national consciousness among Poles in America, and to remind Americans of Poland's contributions to the independence of the United States, the Polish-American community, led by Ignacy Paderewski, raised these monuments to Thaddeus Kosciuszko and Casimir Pulaski in Washington, D.C., before the First World War. Paderewski won the sympathy of President Woodrow Wilson for the Polish cause. PHOTO BY FRANK ALEKSANDROWICZ. COPYRIGHT © FRANK ALEKSANDROWICZ.

Scenes such as this citizenship class in Cleveland took place throughout the United States as Polish immigrants flocked to take out their naturalization papers so that they might enlist in the United States Army for the First World War. WESTERN RESERVE HISTORICAL SOCIETY.

Even before Paderewski's call to arms, Polish Falcons formed training companies, such as this one photographed in Cleveland in 1913, for the coming struggle for the independence of Poland. All of the Polish-American community's awakened energies were marshaled in service of a Polish cause in Europe.
CREDIT: WESTERN RESERVE HISTORICAL SOCIETY.

Returning Polish veterans of the First World War found their leaderless community unable to cope with the country's rising economic problems. The advent of the Great Depression hastened the process of their Americanization. Here, Polish workmen attend a Sunday rally on behalf of the labor movement. CREDIT: ILLINOIS LABOR HISTORY SOCIETY.

ROBOTNICY I ROBOTNICE!

Wszyscy bezrobotni i częściowo pracujący przyjdzcie na

Demonstrację
w piątek, dnia 9-go września
o godzinie 1:30 popołudniu
przy Paulina i Dean ulic, blisko Milwaukee Avenue

Żądamy spełnienie następujących żądań:

1. $5.50 tygodniowo w gotówce dla wszystkich samotnych mężczyzn i kobiet.
2. Zapłacenie komornego, by wstrzymać wyrzucenie z mieszkania.
3. Zapłacenie rachunków za elektrykę i gaz, aby uniknąć zamknięcie mytrów.
4. Natychmiastowe wsparcie dla wszystkich nowych członków.
5. Dostarczenie ubrania i obuwia dla niepracujących familij i samotnych.
6. Natychmiastowe wsparcie wszystkim robotnikom, których niskie zarobki nie pokrywają wydatki codziennego życia.
7. Usunięcie złego traktowania na stacjach zapomogowych.

Biliony dolarów wydaje rząd na przygotowania wojenne i udziela kredyty bankom i kolejom, a ani centa dla bezrobotnych.

Wstępujcie do Rad Bezrobotnych i walczcie
o rządowe ubezpieczenie od bezrobocia.

Oddział No. 5 odbywa swoje posiedzenie w każdy czwartek o godzinie 2-iej popołudniu p. n. 1815 West Division ul., trzecie piętro.
Oddział No. 53 odbywa swoje posiedzenie w każdą środę o godz. 2-ej popołudniu p. n. 1359 W. Grand Ave.
Oddział samotnych odbywa swoje posiedzenie w każdy piątek o godzinie 2-ej popołudniu p. n. 1815 W. Division st.

A Polish-language handbill, calling for aid to the unemployed, as eight hundred thousand workers lost their jobs each month at the height of the Depression, attempted to mobilize Polish-Americans for protest demonstrations. The Depression wrecked the stability of Polish neighborhoods as strikes and demonstrations racked the major areas of Polish settlement in America. CREDIT: CHICAGO HISTORICAL SOCIETY.

Even in independent Poland, in the 1920s, impoverished Jews and Polish villagers continued to dream of a golden land across the Atlantic. Here, prospective immigrants apply for U.S. entry permits at the U.S. embassy in Warsaw. Racist quotas kept Polish immigration down to a token six thousand a year between the World Wars. CREDIT: NATIONAL ARCHIVES (PUBLIC HEALTH SERVICE PHOTO).

Looking far older than his twenty-six years, a Polish-American plant worker in New Britain, Connecticut, stands outside the factory where he has worked since his sixteenth birthday. Government statistics show that unemployment among Polish-Americans is the lowest of all ethnic groups in the United States. CREDIT: LIBRARY OF CONGRESS, PRINTS AND PHOTOGRAPHS DIVISION.

This 1938 Farm Security Administration photograph might have been taken yesterday in almost any Polish-American club, in any middle-sized industrial town. A hunter's trophy is flanked by portraits of Marshal Jozef Pilsudski, founder of independent Poland in 1918, and President Franklin Delano Roosevelt, whose social reforms gave a measure of dignity and security to American workingmen and -women. CREDIT: LIBRARY OF CONGRESS, PRINTS AND PHOTOGRAPHS DIVISION.

Even as late as 1938, Polish miners worked under conditions that would have appalled modern mine-safety inspectors. Here a Polish miner in the Shenandoah Valley sets dynamite for a blast in a tunnel of the Maple Hill mine. CREDIT: LIBRARY OF CONGRESS, PRINTS AND PHOTOGRAPHS DIVISION.

Homes such as these steelworkers' houses in Aliquippa, Pennsylvania, divided into "plans" by nationality, gave Polish-American workers a cohesiveness that has lasted to the present day. From such homes emerged an entire generation of American professional persons. CREDIT: LIBRARY OF CONGRESS, PRINTS AND PHOTOGRAPHS DIVISION.

Thousands of Polish workmen invested their savings into land that earlier farmers had abandoned as no longer fit for cultivation. Their labor resurrected much of the Connecticut tobacco industry, and the truck garden farming of New York and New Jersey. Here the wife of a successful Polish farmer near Hartford, Connecticut, puts away lard from a home-fed pig against a shelf full of pickles and preserves done in the old-country manner. CREDIT: LIBRARY OF CONGRESS, PRINTS AND PHOTOGRAPHS DIVISION.

The Polish immigrant "view from the hill" was often a vista such as this, a street in the mill district of an industrial city. Within one generation, university professors, priests, engineers, and Army officers were emerging from Pittsburgh's "Polish Hill" and similar areas across the country. CREDIT: LIBRARY OF CONGRESS, PRINTS AND PHOTOGRAPHS DIVISION.

A Polish farmer and his Yankee neighbor (right) harvest tobacco near
Hartford, Connecticut, while yet another Polish farmer's daughter (below)
tends to the one-horsepower farm machinery. The secret of the Polish farmers'
success in America was thrift, hard work, no credit, and total self-reliance.

Working conditions changed slowly for Polish miners in the Pennsylvania coalfields, but this young Shenandoah miner returns to a prosperous family dwelling after his day in the pits. CREDIT: LIBRARY OF CONGRESS, PRINTS AND PHOTOGRAPHS DIVISION.

A lifetime of work, patience, honesty, and kindness are etched into the features of this Polish woman, married to a farmer in New England. The endurance and the labor of Polish immigrant women such as this held the uneasy Polish community together in America and propelled its children into a better future. CREDIT: LIBRARY OF CONGRESS, PRINTS AND PHOTOGRAPHS DIVISION.

A group of Polish-American women who became nurses for the Polish National Aid Committee, an organization of immigrant workers who raised more than fifty million dollars in money and goods for the relief of devastated Poland during the First World War. CREDIT: WESTERN RESERVE HISTORICAL SOCIETY.

A group of Falcon volunteers for the Polish Army in France leaves from Monessen, Pennsylvania, in November 1917. They hold a sign that reads: "Goodbye America, we go to struggle with the despot Kaiser for your freedom and ours." CREDIT: WESTERN RESERVE HISTORICAL SOCIETY.

This classic study by Jack Delano of a Polish working family living in Mauch Chunk, Pennsylvania, in 1940, shows the emergence of a new American generation, which would struggle to take its place in the middle class. The conformist spirit of the Polish ghettos in America often hindered higher forms of children's education and retarded the community's progress. CREDIT: LIBRARY OF CONGRESS, PRINTS AND PHOTOGRAPHS DIVISION.

Sheer joy and perhaps a little disbelief are painted on the faces of this Polish farming couple in Connecticut as they are told that they finally own the land on which they have worked, partly as hired laborers, for the length of a generation.
CREDIT: LIBRARY OF CONGRESS, PRINTS AND PHOTOGRAPHS DIVISION.

They had begun to come here in the late 1870s, first in a slow, steady stream bound for the anthracite fields of Schuylkill County, Pennsylvania, then more rapidly (then torrentially!), shipload after shipload in the 1880s, driven by an illusion of wealth awaiting them across the ocean, hungry for land and money—so much human raw material for the blast furnaces, the forges, the quarries, and the coalpits that had transformed America's landscapes after the Civil War.

When Polish peasant immigrants landed in America, the United States was no longer a land of small farms, country towns, sprawling plantations, and rural pioneers; it had become a factory, a pit where men toiled in black tunnels deep under the earth, slept in the thunder of industrial cities under a sky made crimson by the glow of smelters. America's progress was no longer being measured in the genius of its individual men and women, but in so many miles of railroad and cables, so many tons of shipping, or iron ore and coal torn from the earth by the sweated labor of thirty million immigrants. And still they came, and still they kept on coming.

By the century's end, 2½ million Polish peasants had come, first from the western regions of the country, where German law made it impossible for a Polish peasant to own his own land, then from Russian Poland, and then from Galicia (the part of Poland occupied by Austria)—the poorest region of an exploited and impoverished country with no government of its own. Unlike their noble predecessors, they were totally unequipped for the American experience. They had no skills, no superior qualities, no language that anyone could understand. The Polish image in America became a faceless mass. Yet even in that mass these immigrants brought something so personally theirs as to make it seem an individual characteristic: a capacity for back-breaking labor, hardship, and endurance that could rival that of the slaves of the Old South. No slaver drove them into the crowded spaces between steerage decks, but poverty and hatred of oppression did what slavemasters couldn't. The immigrants went of their own will, lured by tales spun by agents of the shipping lines, having virtually sold themselves into indentured service to pay for their tickets, and it was only the possession of that will and of determination to better their fate that made them more than slaves.

The world in which these immigrants landed was not a better world for them than the one they had left. Their one qualification was knowledge of the land, but territory for homesteaders in the West had been staked, fought over, wiped out, and staked again. The sun had set on the last frontier, and the golden age of the individualist was gone, leaving an iron age of giant corporations. The majority of the landless peasants who stood stunned and dazed on American piers had come straight from the fields and villages of Poland with no industrial skills to offer. They were, for the most part, illiterate, with no notion of historical grandeur to sustain them. Their tradition had been one of labor, piety, and patience, with no privileges at all. (Serfdom had been abolished in Russian Poland only in the early 1860s). Many had little notion of their national identity; speaking regional rural dialects, they seldom even had a language in common. Ironically, most of them became "Polish" only in America, assuming their nationality as a shield against the insults and abuse born of a violent American prejudice against them.

Venal county sheriffs herded the new arrivals to the coalpits to depress miners' wages; insurgent miners shot them down in dozens to protect their own livelihoods. (In just a few years it would be Polish miners who would go down before the guns of deputies and strikebreakers in the great union battles of Lackawanna County.) No nineteenth-century peasant had ever worked as hard on any master's acres as these Polish immigrants did in the United States. Nowhere in nineteenth-century Poland did any villager live in such squalor as the unskilled Polish laborers in the anthracite fields of Pennsylvania, where every kind of prejudice denied them even the most menial jobs.

By the thousands, and then by the millions, these Polish peasants brought their calloused hands into the textile mills of New England, the railroads and lumber mills of the West, the slaughterhouses of Chicago, the steel mills of Youngstown and Akron, Ohio, and Gary, Indiana, into the copper, iron, and coal mines of Illinois, Michigan, Minnesota, Colorado, Arizona, Wyoming, Utah, and Montana; thousands of patient, unresentful pick-and-shovel men, dock hands, teamsters, the heavers and haulers of an industrial era that had neither machinery nor respect for human dignity. Willing to do the heaviest, dirtiest, and most poorly paid work, they won the bitterness and resentment of English-speaking workmen (the Irish and the Welsh who had, themselves, replaced native-born Americans in the coalpits). Beaten by jealous mineworkers, clubbed by corrupt constables, exorbitantly fined by justices of the peace, harassed and imprisoned by petty officials, these early Polish peasant immigrants had no one to turn to for help or advice. Most of them had emigrated from village economies that had reached a point of labor saturation and,

placed by mine-owners' greed in the anthracite and bituminous coalfields, or rented at the dockside for the heaviest labor in the mills and forges, they had neither the time, the means, nor the knowledge to look for work elsewhere.

Newspapers abused the immigrants, complaining of the "mixed populations with which we are afflicted." In stores they were cuffed and laughed at when they came to make their trivial purchases in broken and insufficient English. Security of person, property, and worship was not guaranteed to Poles. Their wages were not always paid, and their miserable lodgings were so exorbitantly priced that as many as fourteen of them would share a single room. And should a native American grocer condescend to feed them, they paid as much as five times the article's true price. Cheated of their wages and denied the rights of civilized human beings, they were driven to caves for shelter and housed in rickety shanties in which they, in Poland, would have refused to house cattle.

Few of them came with the idea of staying; all came to make money. But the opportunities for a better life in America eventually won them over and made a return to some landowner's Polish acres virtually impossible. The man came first, alone, then sent for his woman, or for a girl from his village who might want to marry him. Few of them could write a letter, but each community soon found its *pisennik* (professional scribe)—for whom the alphabet was not a mystery. A great many of these letters have survived, thanks to Russian censorship, which confiscated them and kept them in archives.

And this is what the immigrants wrote: ". . . If you complain so much about your miseries, sell everything and come to America with the children, because it isn't the work here that's so bad, but the loneliness. . . . I'm always a stranger among strangers here. . . . Dear Parents, always it will be better for you to live here than there . . . if you're to break your back on some master's land, do it here on your own. . . . God's truth, when I remember the misery at home my skin crawls. . . . Dear Sister, I'll send you a *shiffkarta* [one-way ticket], because back home you're serving others from childhood, and so it will be until your old age, but in America you can make something of yourself. . . . When I went on the ship, the water was coming through the chimneys [ventilators] and I thought we would drown, but we didn't. . . . There were 1800 of us on the ship, and four young children died, but eight more were born and so it evened out. . . . We are lonely here. . . . Here you hear only noise, thousands of people going here and there, and the factory whistles. Yes they have birds and flowers, but they are far away, in a garden, and who has the time to go and see them for nothing? Who will pay for that? . . . When people tell you that in America the gold lies in the streets, don't you believe it! Here everybody has to work, like there, in Siberia. . . . This is no Golden Land, but it is a new land; here you break your back for 12 hours a day, and back home they're thinking that they'll be filling their aprons with gold the minute they've come. . . . So they come, knowing nothing, like the blind. . . . They say all of Europe will be empty soon, with everybody here. . . . In America, you will spill more sweat in one day than in a week back home. . . . But I will not go back if someone was to give me the master's estate. . . . Once you have tasted America, there is no way to go back to those old miseries."

And this: "I have work, I'm not hungry, only I have not yet laughed since I came to America. . . . But come and see that here no one goes to bed on an empty stomach because one Pole will save another, if he can. . . . Here they pick out their workmen like cattle at the market, but you can make a life for yourself better than the landed gentleman back home. . . . Dear Brother, write to me, did the potatoes freeze this winter? . . . Dear Wife, write, did the storks come back this spring? Have you sold the wheat? Try for another half-acre and put down potatoes, I'll dig them up in autumn when I'm back with

you. . . . I work many hundreds of feet under the ground, don't see God's sun from morning to night for those two dollars they give me. . . . I will have 60 dollars saved for you this month, if I don't get ill. . . . Who can't make a life for himself in this country, will never do it anywhere else; I would like to marry Zoska, because the girls in America are lazy and let themselves go, so send me Zoska. . . . Dear Cousin, I'm happy that old Mrs. Kalinowska is bringing me a pretty girl, but maybe she can bring two? Because, you see, there's two of us bachelors here and we'd both like to marry. . . ."

The girls and the women began to arrive and immediately altered the nature of the peasant immigration from temporary to permanent, because where these lusty Polish women put down their bundles there were soon Polish children, and that meant roots and work for yet another generation. They took in boarders at $.15 a week to feed their families when the factories closed, and then wrote to their relatives in Poland: "In America only he is unhappy who will not work. . . . In winter, it is very hard when the factories stop. . . . In winter you can make so many debts that it will take you all summer to get out of them. . . . So don't come here right now, because two thousand souls join us every week and the work is scarce. . . ."

"Dear Mother," said the letters that the young girls dictated for their families in Poland, "Don't be angry with me because I married without you knowing about it, because you forbid me to get married in America. . . . But there is no joy in the old country, and he loves me and will always love me, so bless us both. . . . Dear Mother and Father, don't long for me, because I thank you with all my heart for sending me to America, and I have faith in God that I may yet see you before death divides us for ever. . . . I am really happy because I am healthy, and so are my children, and that I can help them get ahead and that I can still do everything that I must. . . ."

The earliest Polish peasant immigrant

lived on a hillside near his mine in a one-room hut built with his own hands from broken pit-props and discarded boards, which he had gathered along the highway in spare moments, and roofed with tin pressed out of empty powder cans; or in ramshackle company barracks that became furnaces in summer and iceboxes in winter; or crowded into single rooms in the poorest sections of industrial towns. Determined to survive, to earn money, to reach beyond the limits imposed upon him by his new American circumstances, he accepted low wages, dangerous and unsanitary working conditions, abuse, and exploitation. His hungers were not intellectual, his needs were immediate: survival in the present and into the future in its most primitive form. He had brought with him all the virtues of the Polish peasant and all of his vices. Clannish, suspicious, contemptuous of fine language, dour, and unforgiving when oppressed (or when he imagined that he had been cheated), the Polish peasant tried to live wholly in the present, unable to comprehend a life beyond his experience and hostile to everything that he didn't understand. He was given to smoldering hatreds, superstitions, and bursts of violence that could explode in alcoholic frenzy against his frustrations. He was also painfully honest, self-reliant, and he knew how to bide his time.

Perhaps the best clue to the nature of this strange folk, who came to an America that could not understand them, lies in the lessons taught by their folk tales, which they brought with them and taught to their children. Honesty, the tales teach, may be the better policy when you are dealing with your own kind, under conditions that you understand, but a devious road is often shorter than a straight one when you are facing the unfamiliar and unknown. The peasants' own self-image was one of strength, shrewdness, native wit, inventiveness, and cunning with which to overcome human cruelty and, if necessary, the devil himself. The devil, according to the folk tales, was not always as bad as he was painted (his power was unavailing before simple virtues) but, in the peasant folklore, the devil was always dressed in the "German" garb of influences foreign to the peasant: book learning and the glitter of sophistication. Poverty, hunger, the spite of a neighbor, a lost inheritance, or the greed of a cruel master were all seen as natural disasters, but miracles were readily available for anyone who would take the trouble to bring them about. Success was possible, the tales assured, but only if this miracle of success was of your own making. Humiliation must be borne with patience so that the tables may be turned upon the tormentor, at which point revenge became a waste of time; tradition had taught the peasant immigrants that each man's punishment was worse if it were self-inflicted.

Though maligned and abused by everyone with whom they came in contact, these early Polish immigrants clung to their new country, picked huckleberries on the mountains behind the pits, scratched gardens into the wasted soil, and raised their potatoes, cabbages, and onions. They kept pigs and chickens. They were deliberate and careful and watched what other people did. Priests were their natural leaders, if only priests would lead them. But at first there were few Polish priests among them, while American Catholic priests—Irish to the hilt—gave them only insult, contempt, and verbal violence. They had no help from earlier, settled Polish intellectual immigrants, whom they distrusted as "nobility" but who did try, over several years, to organize this mass of raw material into a variety of national associations. Slowly, laboriously, the Polish peasant immigrants put together a civilization of their own, pitting themselves against every obstacle and —somehow—breaking down the barriers that limited their opportunities. In that survival, which gradually transformed primitive human masses into a social force, in their ascent from every kind of impoverishment into the middle class—among educators and professional men and women—lies the miracle of their accomplishment. But that would take them more than half a century and, even so, it is only a beginning.

Held back by labor laws that favored English-speaking workmen, the Polish peasant-workers wrestled with the language of Shakespeare, as interpreted by *McGuffey's Reader*, with its injunction to "try and try again." Their ragged, ill-dressed children were scorned and jeered in the schools, but they were determined. Slowly the Poles found their way around the obstacles put up against their progress, and formed study groups and social and political clubs, which prepared them for naturalization examinations. (Their citizenship papers seemed magical to them, as both their exit visa from a dispossessed ethnic minority and an entry permit into the American nation). Then they began to organize to secure a living wage and working conditions fit for human beings; and suddenly Hamtramck, Michigan, Homestead, Pennsylvania, the railyards in Pittsburgh, and the mining communities of Lackawanna County, Shenandoah, Scranton, and Wilkes-Barre, where Poles, and other Slavic immigrants, had become three quarters of the labor force—were bloody union battlefields, and strife-torn antilabor citadels fell one by one.

In the large Polish families everybody worked; grandparents went to work at dawn beside their grandchildren, and tumbled into bed long after sunset. Children were the wealth of the Polish family: The larger the family, the more work it could do, and the more money it earned. Penny by penny and dollar by dollar, the money went into savings, and the savings bought land. Within ten years of their arrival in America, Polish immigrants were buying abandoned and depressed farms in New England and the Middle West—little hard patches of earth on the outskirts of the great industrial cities and soil that had been ruthlessly worked and abandoned as exhausted in Long Island, Connecticut, western Massachusetts, New Jersey, and New York. The miracle of hard work, no credit, thrift, and their own cheap labor transformed the rootless and anonymous Polish peasant immigrant into prosperous farmer and employer.

But for some of them—the vast majority of millions—this journey from a Polish village, through the purgatory of American mines and mills, to their independence, took all of a generation. Often it took two. In the process, they acquired an indelible identity. Discrimination threw them upon their own resources, limited though these were. For them, the American melting pot was a dismal failure. It rendered them fleshless in their own eyes, made them feel destitute of spirit and of pride. They fought against it with every memory they had brought from Poland, through their clubs and churches, in their own schools and customs, which suddenly acquired enormous importance. America taught them in one generation what a thousand years in Poland had, in many cases, failed to accomplish: They were Poles who could rely only on each other and themselves. Contemptuous American schoolteachers often taught their children that they, and their laboring parents, were little better than mere beasts of burden. So the peasant immigrants, whose knowledge of Polish history and culture seldom extended beyond dim memories of village life and customs, began to search for an acceptable human identity in history, legends, and the cloak of heroes. If America degraded and dehumanized them, they would build their own version of America in which their Polish origin could be a matter of pride.

This struggle for survival, for economic independence and for a sense of their own worth and value is what created a wholly different and non-European kind of Pole in the United States—one who is more conscious of his Polish heritage than many Poles in Poland and who insists today on total acceptance in American life. No public or private agency lifted a finger in their behalf; they built their own institutions, and around them they constructed their own, isolated lives, clinging together in their neighborhoods, resentful of intrusion. No other way of life was open to them in America; it would take their third generation to break out of this protective Polish ghetto which—like all ghettos—tended to create a self-centered, inward-looking culture and its own imprisoning bars.

There was nothing passive about the peasant laborers' acceptance of their exploitation. It took some time for them to find firm footing on American soil, to understand that their humility was harmful to other workingmen, and that there was something that they might do to improve their lot.

On New Year's Day 1888, the miners of the Shenandoah Valley went out on strike to protest an arbitrary cut in their miserable wages. The Poles and other Slavic workers joined the picket lines and soon became targets for police bullets and a violent assault by the hysterical local press. They were "different." They could not explain their grievances. They were accused of biting the hand that fed them when they stoned strikebreakers. On February 3, panicky deputies fired on eight hundred Polish miners in one colliery and, a few days later, on five hundred in another. Twelve picketing strikers were shot down, and the newspapers cheered. Welsh and Irish miners "rewarded" the Poles for their show of solidarity by forcing the passage of a Pennsylvania law that required English-language qualifications for work in the pits. The law made employment of Polish miners virtually impossible for five years.

In 1894, one out of ten protesting marchers in the ten-thousand-man "Coxey's Army" of the unemployed, who tried to force an unresponsive American Government into a program of public works, was Slavic, with the Poles as a heavy majority. Again, the results of this desperate labor effort were disillusionment, unemployment, and—this time—a blacklist. In the winter of 1894, Polish peasants in America were doing what they had never done in Europe: More than a hundred of them starved to death.

On August 12, 1897, a strike by Polish and Italian mule drivers at six collieries owned by the Lehigh and Wilkes-Barre Coal Company, in Pennsylvania, started a series of violent demonstrations that led, on September 6, to the Lattimer Massacre, when a hundred sheriff's deputies fired on a protest march of Polish, Lithuanian, and Slovakian workers, killing nineteen and wounding thirty-nine. Twenty-six of the casualties were Poles. The deputies' claim was that they had attempted to disarm a rebellious mob, but even the venal papers of the day reported that no arms of any kind were found among the strikers and that most of the dead and wounded had been shot in the back. An official inquiry exonerated all officials concerned. But the bloodiest union battles for the Polish workers were still to come . . . as were their union victories.

Once they had won the right to work in ways that gave them pride in labor, Poles moved into city sawmills and lumberyards, became bricklayers, blacksmiths, stevedores, carpenters, cabinetmakers, mechanics, and craftsmen. If they could manage to enter a business they became cigar- and cigarettemakers, bakers, butchers, and marketers of meat. They were truck-garden farmers, dairymen, bartenders, and saloonkeepers, textile and garment workers, wheelwrights and wagonmakers, high-steel men in the building trades, and operators of the murderous drop hammers that eviscerated workmen in the forges. They had come to this country to earn money, and money had liberated them from the pits and shanties. It would give them their own homes, gardens, businesses, and farms, buildings that might be repaired for renting to newer arrivals, stores and farm equipment. Money and what it could buy were their only goals. Immediate wages seemed better to them than unpaid apprentice labor or study that could lead to higher-paying jobs but that brought nothing in the months or years of training. No family could afford one idle pair of hands. The peasant's sense of vision was confined to what he could reach, or what instinct told him.

The bitter, debilitating struggle of the Polish peasant immigrant in America exacted a tragic price in creative and intellectual backwardness. Intelligent but untrained young minds were forced, by their parents' desire for security, to stay within such limits as the older generation was able to comprehend. The young were turned away from the higher forms of human intellectual and artistic development. To the Polish peasants struggling in America, a narrow middle-class horizon of material security and success seemed like the farthest imaginable edge of all possible human aspirations. Money had given them respectability; money, they thought, would buy them respect. Their American descendants would be doctors, lawyers, university professors, millionaires, industrialists, members of the Congress, and bishops of the Church, but they would not give to America one internationally important creative artist, or one wholly original intellectual mind. Such accomplishments would come only from Polish men and women born and educated in Europe, not descended from emigrating peasants.

But once again, the narrative anticipates events. Three quarters of a century would pass before five thousand immigrant grandchildren would hold doctorates from American universities, before college presidents, Army generals, surgeons, and engineers would emerge from the dark railroad flats of Brooklyn and Chicago, the squalid tenements of Manhattan's Lower East Side, out of three-decker Boston frame and clapboard houses, from "Polish Hill" in the teeming slums of Pittsburgh and the crowded, ill-shaded cottages of Detroit. Eking out a meager living for themselves, the peasant immigrants pushed their children into a wider and richer world than they could ever know. They drove their children as hard as they drove themselves and demanded that young hands be as calloused as the old. Having accepted their own dismal role as toilers and strugglers in an alien, Protestant, and money-motivated American world, they would not accept a lifetime of underprivileged hardship as their children's lot. Work was their ethic, pride was their sustenance, religion was their consolation, ignorance was their bane,

and education was the magic door beyond which lay mysterious opportunities. They saw to it that their children worked but also that they went to school every day.

Books had been alien to the Polish peasants; they lacked the scholarly tradition of the Polish Jew, and looked with suspicion (and a sort of shamed, incoherent hatred) at the fine ladies and gentlemen of their own Polish intelligentsia. (Even well-spoken, grammatical Polish was anathema to them; they created their own crude Polish-English jargon, which bore no traces of the "gentry" they had left behind in Europe.) Unobserved at home, as story after story relates, they handled their children's books with reverence and awe, half ashamed of their own ignorance, proud of whatever knowledge their child displayed, afraid to show their pride, and hiding their pleasure in artificial gruffness. They feared to lose their children's working hands, and looked uneasily into a future in which their children and grandchildren would soar above their own limited levels of comprehension and opportunity. But when they found that American schools humiliated their children, they built more than four hundred schools of their own. (Once grown, their children doubled that number, including eight institutions of higher learning.) But progress was slow, restrained by the peasants' own neighborhood traditions.

The peasant immigrant was so dependent on his neighbors' good will and approval, so conscious of being part of a self-contained, self-perpetuating whole, and so fearful of being thought "too good" for his peers ("stuck-up" was a term of particular damnation in the Polish ghettos) that he would sometimes cripple his children's future rather than step beyond conformity. Time and again the Polish parish priest, himself the son of peasant immigrants, would confront a mother who had worked her son's way through college and planned to spend another five years on her knees, scrubbing offices after a day at a factory bench so that the young man might go to graduate school. The priest would warn her that so much education would make the boy "different" from his neighbors, that four years of college was enough to get a good job, and he would ask whether the mother thought herself "better" than the other women of the neighborhood. It was a brave, determined mother who would close her ears to the official voice of the parish—but many of them did.

The Polish peasant immigrants built their social clubs, national homes, and meeting halls, and put up statues to Polish heroes, poets, soldiers, and statesmen whose ideas had been wholly different from their own. In fact, in their own inward-looking lives, these monument builders were the antitheses of the liberal and radical heroes they were honoring. And yet they ignored the true heroine of the Polish peasant immigration: the woman, worker, wife, and mother—living in subjugation to her husband—whose thrift, sobriety, immense fortitude, and self-denial held the community together and propelled its children into a better world. Women, who had been brought up to be mistresses of their own village households, trained to affection and authority and the practical management of family affairs, found themselves stripped of all identity on the wharves of Philadelphia and New York. Their pride was in their womanliness, their ability to care for children: the woman's quite unhumble role which, as they understood it, came to them in direct descent from the Mother of God. Many of them were to walk on foot from New York to Chicago, and beyond, and found themselves working in the core rooms of factories, in the dusty heat of twine mills, and in the slicing rooms of tin-can factories where unsafe machinery scarred their faces and severed hands and fingers.

In St. Louis, Missouri, Polish women worked in nut and tobacco factories, spending ten hours a day on four-legged stools picking perfect kernels out of crushed and broken shells, which filled the air with a thick, brown, suffocating dust; they sliced tobacco leaves in stogiemakers' stripping rooms at unsafe, breakneck speed. In New York, Philadelphia, Baltimore, and Boston they sewed shirts and work pants in unventilated sweatshops, made hats, and finished ladies' blouses by hand at $.60 to $1.10 a dozen. In Chicago, they scrubbed the floors of restaurants, hospitals, and hotels (and offices at night), and washed dishes for fifteen hours a day until the ten-hour law for women restored a semblance of sanity to their lives. In the farm fields, where onions and tobacco (worked by Polish farmers on abandoned lands) had revitalized New England's agriculture, the women worked from sunrise to sunset, along with their men. But when the day's work in the field or factory was done, the women would begin their labor for their households: its cooking, sewing, mending, cleaning, vegetable gardening, pickling and preserving, planning and accounting, and—all too often—part-time, piece-rate night work to earn the money that might send the family's brightest boy to school. Few families could afford to send more than one child to college until their second generation was born in America; and, invariably, that child would be a boy. Girls, like their overworked mothers in the male-oriented Polish peasant immigrant society, usually got short shrift where money for education was concerned. Worn and wasted when they were barely into their thirties, the Polish immigrant women were indomitable. They were both the heart and backbone of every family. Because they appeared to be strong and cheerful, American employers tended to assume that Polish girls could do far heavier work than any other women, that they would complain less and endure better. Thousands of them broke down under the strain of unremitting labor and the undermining of their expectations. Hundreds contracted tuberculosis in America and died or were deported. Sickness and unemployment were their greatest fears; avoiding one, they frequently fell victim to the other.

With an obsession for economic security that seemed to undermine reason, these thrifty Polish peasant women bought their homes in the cheapest districts of their towns, where dirt and disease had already ravaged earlier immigrants, then labored to turn these wretched dwellings into neighborhoods where thrift and cleanliness could give godliness an opportunity. Their homes grew upward, sideways, and forward as their families increased, sprawling in a haphazard fashion until every square foot of their neighborhoods was in use, but these homes were always clean, painted, and in good repair. It was a rare Polish section in an American city where front yards were not full of flowers, and where an apple or a pear tree did not grow behind the house among sweet peas, tomatoes, onions, cabbages, carrots, and potatoes. In time—twenty to thirty years, according to a variety of statistics—Polish home ownership in the United States would exceed that of any other ethnic minority. Struggling along on the margin of subsistence, Polish immigrant women created an American phenomenon: the clean, orderly, safe, and sacrosanct Polish neighborhood.

When this first generation of Polish peasant pioneers died—and most of them seemed to live to a surprisingly old age— the neighborhoods changed, their close-knit harmony disrupted by forces outside their control. Life in them had been deceptively simple and restrictive. The new American generations left them in droves, partly in flight from a "Polish" image, which seemed to deny them American opportunities, in part because they had evolved beyond their parents' simple absolutes. The neighborhoods' activities revolved around the church; the church hall; the church's elementary school (and often a high school, where Polish nuns taught obedience and conformity); a Polish-language political club and co-operative society; an educational or literary club and the Polish library; and the drill hall of the Falcons' Union (a paramilitary gymnastic society imported from Europe), where Saturday night dances offered a variety of physical encounters. The Polish National Home

of the nationwide Polish National Alliance provided cheap insurance and a meeting place for local organizations, along with an after-hours bar. There polka bands thumped their jittery little tunes, never heard in Poland, with little regard for what was really Polish or what Polish-Americans decided to call their own. A whole generation of young Americans would grow up believing that pinochle was a Polish card game and that the polka was a Polish dance. There, amid peasant cooking and uncertain folklore, the peasant immigrants founded the institutions of today's Polonia —the Latin name for Poland that the immigrants adopted for themselves, oblivious of yet another irony: Latin had been the ancient language of the Polish aristocracy whom they had feared the most.

Such neighborhoods were the first home of Polonia's huge national organizations: the Polish Roman Catholic Union (1873), the Polish National Alliance (1880), the Alliance of Poles (1895), the Polish Women's Alliance (1898), and the Association of the Sons of Poland (1903). Wars would add veterans' posts, commemorative tablets, streets named after Kosciuszko and Pulaski, and innumerable Polish-language newspapers which, however, were really American newspapers disguised under sonorous Polish mastheads like *Zgoda* (Harmony), *Ojczyzna* (Fatherland), or *Pielgrzym Polski* (The Polish Pilgrim). In their heyday, there were more than sixty newspapers, written in a version of the Polish language that could have been described as a parody. But they gave the people what the people needed: a consciousness of heritage and identity.

Most of the best-known Polish neighborhoods still exist in Brooklyn, Cleveland, Chicago, Boston, and Detroit, but in a manner that would have bewildered their humble, laboring founders. Working Polish-Americans still live there among the bars and bowling alleys, miniature golf courses, the clubs and churches; few of them can now speak any kind of Polish. Plastic flamingos have replaced the flowers in the tidy front yards, the family Chevy is garaged where the pear tree once stood, and a forest of TV antennas breaks the skyline where laundry used to sway. But there are books on the coffee tables, records on the stereo, and long-haired children live their leisurely American lives, free to plan whatever future their parents can afford. Their fathers, elder brothers, and uncles (but never their husbands, if the girls can help it) are skilled blue-collar workers who own their own homes, hardhats with sons (and daughters!) in college, mechanics who are never out of work, factory foremen, tool- and dyemakers, blueprint specialists, lathe and machine-tool operators, pressmen, lithographers and bookbinders who take vacations in Canada and retire to Fort Lauderdale, union secretaries and organizers, travel agents and insurance salesmen, rich butchers and owners of bakeries, minor-league baseball players, firemen and policemen, hauling contractors, and the normally impoverished American schoolteachers.

Other kinds and colors of Americans have penetrated these fastnesses of Polish immigrant labor, often to face the same resentment and suspicion met by the Polish peasant immigrants in another era. The unofficial but traditional name of the neighborhood may be "Warszawa" or "Poznan" (where a Pulaski Boulevard crosses Kosciuszko Street, near St. Stanislaus' Church, down by the PNA's "Dom Polski" and the editorial offices of the *Czas* and *Glos*), but the voices along the asphalt pavements call to each other in Hispanic dialects, and black children are taught by Polish nuns in schools built on scrimped Polish dollars.

Urban decay has devoured much of the work of the peasant toilers, time and its changes have altered their imperatives. Their children have retired to Florida, and their grandchildren commute from expensive suburbs, as likely as not, and high-rise apartments have soared skyward out of the rubble of their primitive dreams. The dreams themselves have been romanticized by image-conscious amateur historians, and they—the builders, the crude strugglers,

and the illiterate scrimpers—have vanished, unrecorded among the dusty bric-a-brac of American history.

But that is the America to which the Polish peasant pioneers came in the first place, and that more sophisticated "exiles" can seldom understand: a country of continuous change and built upon change, of constant motion upward and downward simultaneously, of sudden thrusts and churnings, of impermanence except as an ideal, where life itself is a process of planned obsolescence. In this huge country of promise and contradiction, those who would stand athwart the path of time and its progressive currents are swept away and forgotten, whether they are immigrants or Presidents who do not flow with change, and change with the country.

A later wave of educated Polish émigrés, thrown on America's shores by the tragic aftermath of the Second World War, fled from these Polish neighborhoods as though from a plague. They looked down their noses at the prosperous (and not so prosperous) American grandchildren of the toiling peasants, appalled by their lack of sophistication, their blue-collar humor and their manners. It never occurred to them to consider the sacrifices that had gone into the Polish-Americans' climb out of the pits, nor the miracle of their emergence in less than half a century. It had taken the Kennedys three generations to advance from English-speaking lace-curtain Irish to the election of John F. Kennedy as President of the United States: a record in immigrant achievement. U. S. Senator Edmund S. Muskie, son of a Polish immigrant in Maine, stood for election as Vice President after only one generation. That same generation was enough for Dr. John Gronouski, former United States Postmaster General and American ambassador to Poland, to bridge the gulfs of his immigrant origin.

Cultured and educated Poles continued to arrive in America in the peasants' time, each less an immigrant than a "temporary" exile whose energies would be expended in the cause of an independent Poland rather than on behalf of the leaderless and voiceless immigrants around them. Some did take note of the new Polish reality in America and struggled against peasant distrust to offer both the needed leadership and the voice. The great Polish fraternal institutions are largely their work, as are the newspapers, libraries, amateur theatrical groups, and patriotic associations in which the peasant immigrant could find, and then confirm, his identity.

Polish poet, dramatist, and amateur novelist Teofila Samolinska came to the United States immediately after the Civil War and dedicated herself, in a rather overpowering manner, to uplifting the quality of peasant immigrant lives. Like most well-born, educated Poles of her time, she had a sentimentally patronizing notion of peasant virtues and no suspicion of the depths of the distrust and resentment they felt toward members of her class (and to which they were quite entitled after centuries of exploitation, broken promises, and thwarted hopes). She was an indifferent but voluminous writer, one of those sentimentalizing "Ladies in Literature" in whom the era abounded, who filled the pages of Polonia's newspapers with appeals to nationalistic pride, wrote cloying melodramas for and about Polish peasants in America (her first dramatic effort, *Emancipation of Women*, was staged by the Polish Theatre in Chicago in February 1873), and, above all, had access to her own educated kind among the Americanized intellectuals of former immigration waves. Her pleas on behalf of the Polish peasant immigrants have the sound of sentimental American concern for the red Indian as "the Noble Savage," but that was just what the displaced educated gentry was ready to hear. Her blend of emotional nationalism also appealed to the peasants, perhaps even enough to assuage their distrust of the intelligentsia.

Homesickness and disappointment also tended to bridge the social and cultural chasm between immigrant and exile, and the Polish National Alliance, which today embraces some four hundred thousand members (the eighth largest fraternal organization in the United States), came into being. Its effects would totally revolutionize Polish-American lives for the next half century. The peasants' own attempts at political leadership—and their eventual "uprising" against gentry rule—came after 1889, when the dramatist Szczesny Zahajkiewicz settled in Chicago to organize the Parish Theatre—a nonelitist communal theatrical movement that combined education with amateur dramatics. Zahajkiewicz wrote more than sixty plays about peasant life which, sooner or later, entertained every Polish parish audience in America and gave the immigrant a measure of pride in himself. He was the first Polish intellectual who searched for community leadership in the common masses, organized a variety of circles and clubs to give the new leaders experience, and provided his own tireless guidance until his health collapsed in 1912.

By that time, a new generation of American-born Poles had come out of the neat, strangely named neighborhoods that had replaced the slums and shanties around mills and pitheads: some three million largely literate and organized workmen, tradesmen, small businessmen and priests, schoolteachers and librarians who wrote and edited sixty-seven newspapers, who built with their own hands and money more than eight hundred Roman Catholic parishes throughout the United States, and who would shortly man and send two complete armies to a European war. By 1912 they were in the midst of a traumatic rebellion of their own: an out-and-out confrontation with the Irish hierarchy of the Roman Catholic Church in the United States, a bitterly fratricidal conflict after which the Church in America was never the same.

In partitioned Poland, the Roman Catholic Church had become the haven and the source of national opposition to Prussian, Russian, and Austrian domination. It was the only great organization permitted to Poles that could unite, in some measure, all their classes, help to preserve their language and traditions, and keep alive the flame of their suppressed independence. In America, the priest was the peasant's natural leader, whenever the Church hierarchy permitted him to lead. Polish priests and teaching nuns, who followed the immigrants everywhere, tried to satisfy the emotional needs that had been brought from Europe, against the opposition of Irish Catholic bishops whose lack of understanding of Slavic immigrants expressed itself in a demand for instant "Americanization" of Polish parishes. That meant that parishes organized by the Polish clergy, and churches built with hard-earned Polish money, were to be turned over to Irish pastors. This meant that sermons would be preached in English, which the immigrants could seldom understand, and that all traces of Polish ceremonials, liturgical language, and discipline had to be abolished. This was too much even for the religious peasant immigrants: The community revolted.

With no help or guidance from the Church, they had built glorious basilicas and temples in the midst of desolation and poverty, in the gloomiest wastes of their industrial cities (in time there would be 899 Polish churches—each with its schools and convent, its societies and social programs), and their reward was to be "denationalization," loss of their language and their reborn sense of identity. To the Irish bishops, adherence to the Polish language for Church services was un-American, a sign of ingratitude for America's bounties to the immigrant and, above all, a threat to Irish domination of the Church. And the bishops were not about to relinquish control of anything without battle.

The battlelines were soon drawn. One out of every six American Catholics was Polish at that time. (Now it is one out of five.) More than two thousand Polish priests worked in urban parishes, Catholic universities, and missions, and two orders of teaching nuns had come from Poland

between 1874 and 1885: the Felician Sisters and the Sisters of the Holy Family of Nazareth, who were soon teaching Catholic children of all races from Chicago to Alabama. But the highest rank a Polish priest had held in the hierarchy was that of monsignor. Of the sixty-nine bishops of the American Church in 1886, thirty-five bishops, archbishops, and cardinals were Irish by birth or descent, fifteen were Germans, eleven were of French origin, five were of English stock, and the remaining three were of Dutch, Scots, and Spanish origin. Of these, the Irish and the Germans formed a solid front against Polish demands to liberalize the definition of the Church in America.

"We are American bishops," Archbishop Ireland was to write in 1891 to Cardinal Gibbons. "An effort is [being] made to dethrone us, and to foreignize our country in the name of religion." In a lecture urging restriction of immigration, Archbishop Ireland went even further on May 2, 1895: ". . . A due respect for American citizenship guards against a reckless extension of it to men coming from other lands. No encouragement might be given to social or political organizations which perpetuate in this country foreign ideas or customs." Shortly afterward, disturbed by a slackening of Irish immigration, Cardinal Gibbons published an article in Ireland in which he encouraged Irish immigration "because there are at stake more than economic considerations. There are at stake the interests of the Catholic religion, which in this land and age are largely bound up with the interests of the Irish people." The New York Times quoted the good cardinal as saying at the same time: "The country, it seems to me, is overrun with immigrants, and a word of caution should be spoken to them."

But by that time the embattled Polish Catholics were in no mood for words of caution, or even for paternal condescension. They demanded greater ecclesiastical autonomy in the American Church and their right to define themselves within it. But the truculent Irish bishops, noted for their ability to bear lasting grudges, were determined to deprive the Poles of their language and cultural traditions. The bishops enlisted the support of the popular American press in this "pacification and Americanization" campaign of what they termed "a rebellious and disloyal foreign minority."

Amid the flash and rumble of sacerdotal thunderbolts, with threats of excommunication raining like stale manna from the cardinal's throne in Baltimore (and slightly smaller thrones all over America), eighty thousand Poles left the American Church, either to seek spiritual solace in more liberal surroundings, or to turn their backs on organized religion, or to found a Catholic Church of their own. In September 1904,

twenty-four parishes claiming twenty thousand adherents formally united in a 'new denomination, the Polish National Catholic Church, and elected their first bishop, the Reverend Francis Hodur.

Ironically, when Bishop Hodur went to Rome, to appeal for a modernization of the American Church's attitudes, he was turned down by yet another Pole, Cardinal Ledochowski who, from 1892 to 1902, stood at the head of the Sacred Congregation of the Propagation of the Faith, which then guided the affairs of the Church in the United States. As much an Austrian nobleman as he was a Pole (and twice as much a Churchman as anything else), Cardinal Ledochowski refused to listen to Polish-American demands that at

An attempt by the Irish-dominated hierarchy of the Roman Catholic Church in America to force an "Americanization" of Polish immigrant parishes brought about a Church revolt in which a large segment of Polish-American Catholics broke away to organize a Church of their own. The Polish National Catholic Church, founded by Bishop Francis Hodur, now numbers more than 300,000 members and is headed by Prime Bishop Tadeusz F. Zielinski, who is shown here at the Church's Scranton, Pennsylvania, seminary under a plaque honoring the founder. PHOTO BY FRANK ALEKSANDROWICZ. COPYRIGHT © FRANK ALEKSANDROWICZ.

least two archbishops and 11 bishops should be selected from their community, in keeping with their numbers in the Church. The Poles pointed to their 800 parishes in America, in contrast to the Germans' 456, and asked why 14 bishops and 3 archbishops of *their* Church were of either Austrian or German descent. To some transplanted Polish peasants, with their folklore and their memories of genuine German tyranny in mind, that must have seemed like being led to heaven by the devil.

Defying excommunication and its attendant horrors, Bishop Hodur denounced the Gibbons-Ireland-John Spalding definition of American Catholicism, demanded the right for all Catholics to worship in their own languages, and stood his ground, come hell or papal bull, for he had ample support from his united people. Rome, which had been completely indifferent to the fate of Polish immigrants in America, was suddenly confronted with its first major defeat since the Reformation. The Pope sent a personal representative who made 350 speeches at 160 Polish parishes, and the emerald grip on American Catholicism was forced to relax just enough, so that, during the next 60 years, nine Polish priests could rise to the rank of bishop, and one, Archbishop John Krol of Philadelphia, could become a cardinal.

Cardinal Gibbons never forgot or forgave his defeat. Nor did the Irish hierarchy which, until 1963, had produced all but four of the seventeen American cardinals, incline toward charity and forgiveness. But Archbishop Messmer of Milwaukee was quoted as saying two years after Gibbons' death: "I know that Cardinal Gibbons and Archbishop Ireland understood that they had made a mistake." It was an error of judgment, in the matter of ethnic definitions of Catholicism, that the American Church never made again.

What had kept the hierarchy of the Church in America so adamantly opposed to Polish aspirations was, ironically, the extraordinary quality of the Polish priesthood. These were no indolent holders of parish sinecures or organization politicians. Polish priests, more than any liturgical deviations they may have represented, were a threat to mediocrity in religious service. They had brought from Poland a holy zeal for the cause of God, His Church, and their people, and they reminded comfortable ecclesiastics that God's service had once meant the care of the underprivileged. Nothing quite like them had been seen in America since the heroic French Jesuit missionaries of Colonial times. They antedated the worker-priests of Western Europe by three quarters of a century in the mines and factories. Brother Augustine Zeyts, a Franciscan exile from Russian-occupied Poland, arrived in the United States in 1872 to work among the Polish and Lithuanian pit folk in the Shenandoah; he went to work in the pits alongside his flock, causing a sacerdotal uproar in the hierarchy's chambers. In the pits, he celebrated Mass, gave consolation, instructed working children, encouraged the lapsed by his own example to return to the faith, and even provided medical assistance. He returned to Europe in 1880 to urge the creation of a Franciscan community in America so that the spiritual and social needs of Polish and Lithuanian immigrants could be met. Seven years later, he led the ground-breaking for the Franciscans' first great American monastery in a marshy plot of 129 acres, about 17 miles northwest of Green Bay, Wisconsin, near a tiny Polish community named Pulaski.

The Reverend Joseph Dabrowski, who had invited the Felician Sisters to America in 1874, had an equally broad and far-reaching vision of his calling. From his wide grasp of the immigrants' religious and social needs he was convinced that they could best be served by an American-born, American-educated priesthood of their own nationality who could immediately relate to the immigrants' problems. This conviction was unlikely to cause much enthusiasm among the Irish bishops, all the more irritated because they were helpless against the will of an apparently resourceless immigrant community that, somehow, was able to raise parishes and churches. Father Dabrowski built his SS. Cyril and Methodius Seminary in Detroit in 1885 with no encouragement from the hierarchy. His successors moved it to Orchard Lake, Michigan, where it is now part of an educational complex that includes a young men's preparatory school and a four-year college.

John Cardinal Krol, archbishop of Philadelphia, is the first Polish-American priest to reach the highest rank in the Roman Catholic hierarchy in the United States. Approximately one out of every five American Catholics is of Polish origin or descent. PHOTO BY FRANK ALEKSANDROWICZ. COPYRIGHT © FRANK ALEKSANDROWICZ.

CREDIT: LIBRARY OF CONGRESS.

Altar boys in the procession at the Easter High Mass, at the Corpus Christi Church in Buffalo, New York, April 1943. PHOTO BY MARJORIE COLLINS. CREDIT: LIBRARY OF CONGRESS.

The Roman Catholic Church has been the social and spiritual mainstay of several generations of working Polish-Americans. Built solely on the contributions of parishioners, with no help from the Irish-dominated Catholic hierarchy in America, nine hundred parishes such as this one in Buffalo, New York, observe ancient Polish religious rituals. Here a procession forms before the high altar during the Easter Sunday Mass. CREDIT: LIBRARY OF CONGRESS, PRINTS AND PHOTOGRAPHS DIVISION.

A rising national awareness helped to humanize the bitter determination of the evolving Polish-American civilization. America had threatened to deform them, in the way that a giant might be stunted by a lifetime of stooping littleness; they, in turn, armed themselves with pride—pride in the resurrected glories of a past in which none of them had ever played a part, and in the extraordinary renown of that time's Polish artists on the American concert, dramatic, and operatic stages.

The pages of the great American newspapers of the late nineteenth century were

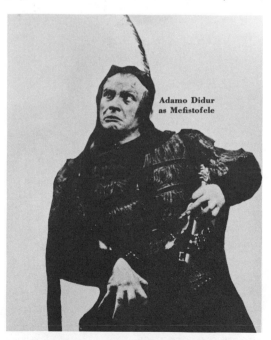

Adamo Didur as Mefistofele

Adam Didur, who brought the role of Mephisto in Gounod's Faust *to the stage of the Metropolitan Opera in New York.*
COURTESY OF TEATR WIELKI, WARSAW.

studded with glittering Polish names. Adam Didur and the brothers Jan and Edouard de Reszke, who would shortly begin their reign over the Metropolitan Opera in New York, were making their first American appearances to thunderous acclaim; Jozef Hofmann, soon to be musical director of the Curtis Institute, gave fifty-two concerts in his first, seventy-day American tour in 1887, and came to settle in America in 1898. Henryk Wieniawski, violinist and composer, toured the United States with Anton Rubinstein in 1872; Zygmunt Stojowski, a musical prodigy (like several others), made his American debut as a piano virtuoso at the turn of the century, and Leopold Stokowski, first in a long series of brilliant Polish conductors of American orchestras, had also reached America in that grim era of the peasant workers' trial by ordeal.

Stokowski was destined to become one of the few truly great conductors of symphonic orchestras in the twentieth century, who brought the contemporary music of Prokofief, Stravinsky, Berg, Schoenberg, and Varèse into the American orchestral repertoire, but he would be best remembered as the founder of the All-American Youth Orchestra which he created out of twenty girls and sixty boys chosen from ten thousand talented candidates from throughout the United States. His American orchestral career began with the Cincinnati Symphony in 1909. From 1912 to 1936 he would direct the internationally famous Philadelphia Orchestra, with which he'd introduce Berg's opera *Wozzeck* to American audiences.

Jan de Reszke, who earned the highest fees ever paid by the Metropolitan Opera, is shown here in the role that made him internationally famous, as Tristan.
COURTESY OF TEATR WIELKI, WARSAW.

Jozef Hofmann, child prodigy, piano virtuoso, and the future musical director of the Curtis Institute, played more than fifty concerts in his first appearance in the United States in 1887. CREDIT: NEW YORK PUBLIC LIBRARY, LINCOLN CENTER.

Elder of the two de Reszke brothers, Edouard de Reszke, is shown here as he appeared during the premiere of Wagner's Ring *at the Metropolitan Opera, New York.* COURTESY OF TEATR WIELKI, WARSAW.

Zygmunt Stojowski, conductor and composer, who was among the first of the internationally known Polish virtuosi to appear in the United States, and to settle here in the closing decades of the nineteenth century. CREDIT: NEW YORK PUBLIC LIBRARY, LINCOLN CENTER.

Born in Cracow in 1882 (although some encyclopedias list his birthplace as London), Stokowski was the son of a Polish father and an Irish mother, and he was brought up and educated in England, where he began his career as an organist. A musical innovator, fascinated by every experiment in sound and direction, he once conducted a symphonic concert in pitch darkness so as not to distract the listeners with the sight of the musicians and himself. Ironically, he spoke not one word of Polish, and yet it was Stokowski's Polish name (as well as his innumerable and stormy romantic entanglements) that inspired many struggling immigrants to take pride in their rising consciousness of their Polish heritage.

During one season in this remarkable period, just before the splendor of the Victorian Era ended with the First World War, seventeen Polish virtuosi were in concert throughout the United States, four were directing American symphonic orchestras, twelve held professorships in prestigious musical institutions, and stunning artistic successes had given fame and wealth to Helena Modrzejewska (Modjeska), the Metropolitan Opera Company's spectacular Marcella Sembrich-Kochanska, and the pianist and composer Ignacy Jan Paderewski.

A barren and inhuman wasteland seemed to stretch between Paderewski's private train and the stark reality of the pits and shanties. And miners' huts, precariously pitched on the slopes of arid Penn-

Helena Modrzejewska (Modjeska) was the reigning Shakespearean actress on the American stage at the break of the century. Her reputation as an artist added luster to the developing national consciousness of Poles in America. COURTESY OF BOWERS MUSEUM, SANTA ANA, CALIFORNIA.

*Modjeska's home, named "Arden," in the Santiago Canyon, California, was the
setting of one of the most unusual utopian communities in America, where
artists, intellectuals, and writers such as Henryk Sienkiewicz, Poland's first
Nobel Prize-winning novelist, lived and worked in the last decades of the 1800s.*
CREDIT: COURTESY OF BOWERS MUSEUM, SANTA ANA, CALIFORNIA.

sylvania slagheaps, seemed far more than
just a continent away from the arcadian
joys of Modjeska's private utopia in Paso
Robles, California. But to the struggling,
grasping, faceless mass of mute and artless
people, this passage of distant stars was almost religious: a glimpse of paradise,
where all the glorious denizens had names
as difficult to pronounce as their own.

The future first Polish Nobel Prize
laureate in literature, Henryk Sienkiewicz,
came to travel and write in the United
States and became a part of "Arden"—an
extraordinary Polish intellectual and artistic community in California where Helena
Modjeska, not yet the great Shakespearean
actress, romped through her sylvan acres at
Paso Robles. In an age of either dour or
hysterical utopian communities, the Paso
Robles "nut farm" was unique: a wholly

liberated, unreligious commune of artists
and writers whose principal crop was artistic talent. It was there that Sienkiewicz
wrote his *Letters from a Journey in
America* and found the prototypes of Polish literature's two most memorable characters: Zagloba and Longinus, both of
whom lived in Paso Robles under mortal
names. Sienkiewicz eventually returned to
Poland, but Modjeska launched herself on
the American stage at the age of thirty-
seven (on August 13, 1877, in San Francisco's California Theater), and for the next
quarter century played Shakespeare's and
Ibsen's most memorable women.

Marcella Sembrich-Kochanska was
twenty-five when she made her American
debut at the Metropolitan Opera House in
1883, having already been the coloratura
star of the Vienna, Berlin, Budapest, Ma-

drid, Lisbon, and London operas during nine triumphant years. Few of her first American listeners knew that she was also one of Europe's finest violinists and a pianist whose artistry had been admired by Liszt himself. The following spring, at a special benefit performance for Henry E. Abbey, then director of the Metropolitan, Sembrich-Kochanska displayed all her talents in voice, violin, and piano and stunned the New York critics.

When she made her last appearance at the Metropolitan in 1909, after a brilliant reign as that opera's lyric and coloratura soprano, she was given a two-hour ovation by such operatic luminaries as Farrar, Eames, Homer, Caruso, and Scotti, who joined a resplendent audience in lauding her for the friendship she had established between the American artist and the community. President Theodore Roosevelt

Marcella Sembrich-Kochanska, the reigning lyric and coloratura soprano of the Metropolitan Opera Company until her retirement in 1909, as she appeared in the role of Mimi in La Bohème. COURTESY OF TEATR WIELKI, WARSAW.

wrote to her: "I am glad to tell you that all those who know best say that your singing has meant very much indeed to the American people, and I especially thank you for the generous way in which you have used your great gift for every philanthropic and charitable undertaking."

She was made director of the vocal departments of both the Curtis Institute of Music (where her friend, Hofmann, was director of the music department) and the Juilliard Graduate School of Music in New York, and remained America's living link to the era of great singing until her death in New York City in 1935. In her last fifteen years, her position in the world of music was like that of Liszt during his Weimar days: artists of all nationalities came to her summer home on Lake George, New York, seeking guidance in the most demanding of all the musical arts. Out of hundreds who came to her for training, she selected and guided only a few, but among them were such future operatic legends as Alma Gluck, Dusalina Giannini, and Marion Talley.

Of all the Polish artists in America, on the eve of the First World War, none had a deeper and more far-reaching effect on the evolving Polish-American community— with its new leadership, national consciousness, and soaring sense of worth— than the slim, very nervous young pianist with the colorless face and tawny-red hair whose first American concert, on the evening of November 17, 1891, grossed an unpromising $500 and netted mixed reviews. Within two months, Madison Square Garden proved too small for the audiences that flocked to hear Ignacy Paderewski's 18 New York recitals on his first American tour—a 6-month musical odyssey in which he played 117 concerts in every major American town and city. His next 3 concert tours launched the Paderewski legend as he crossed and recrossed the United States in his private train, practicing on his Steinway Grand as his traveling studio thundered across the country, and people

Marcella Sembrich-Kochanska with two of the orphans she befriended and supported in the American Deep South. Her many charities brought her the thanks of President Theodore Roosevelt. COURTESY OF TEATR WIELKI, WARSAW.

came to wayside stations just to watch his train go by. His legend seemed never brighter than the afternoon of March 8, 1902, when Paderewski filled both Carnegie Hall and the Metropolitan Opera House in two separate concerts. His name and face were familiar from one end of the United States to another. He played before the largest audience in musical history (until the modern times of the counterculture) when 16,000 persons came to hear him at Madison Square Garden in a benefit for unemployed musicians that yielded $50,000—while Paderewski paid for his own tickets to his own performance.

Paderewski was one of those unusual artists for whom art was not the reason for existence, as it has been and will be for all truly great artists of all times. Perhaps that is why he was an exponent and a virtuoso rather than a creator, better known for the perfectionist's lucidity he gave to the works of others than for his own inspired compositions. His credo was: *La Patrie avant tout; l'art ensuite.* He was a Polish patriot who used himself and his genius as instruments in the service of an idea that he considered greater than art itself: the cause of Polish independence in an era when such independence appeared less substantial than a visionary's dream.

Poland, partitioned among her relentless neighbors, had been without an insurrection for so long that most Poles living at the turn of the century had never known the horrors of war, nor the intoxicating feeling of being free in their own independent country. The desperation of 1863 had strewn the fields and woods of Poland with its gallant dead, towns and countryside were ravaged, and the flower of Polish youth had been massacred or driven to Siberia. Despite all their efforts, the Russians and the Germans continued to rule the Poles, and so they turned their backs on romantic suffering, violence, and death and sought a bloodless liberation through work and education. Every school built, every diploma won, every factory completed, every book written, every aria sung, every discovery made were seen as steps to-

ward eventual independence, as these are seen in Poland today. Every artistic or scientific triumph was to remind the world that Poland was alive although invisible on maps. Peace and progress breathed over the country, but this peace was deceptive. Behind the magnificent façade of Poland's stately homes, in the fashionable boulevards of Warsaw, in the confidently bubbling cafe life of Cracow and Lwow, outside the lecture halls of universities and in the artists' studios, independence was the reason for living; and, in the meantime, talented Poles scattered throughout the world.

Paderewski had been three years old in 1863 when his father was dragged from the family's country home by Russian gendarmes (for storing insurrectionists' arms), while their village of Kurylowka, in Russian-held Podolia Province, was burned to the ground and its inhabitants slaughtered. Reared in the ancient tradition of Polish-Russian conflict, Paderewski never lost touch with the various Polish independence movements and worked to spread their reach among the Polish masses settled in America. They listened to him as though to an oracle, dazzled by his legend as much as by their need.

He became an orator, an organizer, and a propagandist, working through the educated émigré leadership of the Polish National Alliance to turn the direction of the American Polonia's evolution into an extension of the Polish cause. On May 11, 1910, a monument to Kosciuszko was unveiled with great solemnities in Washington, and later another to Pulaski, as much to remind Americans of Poland's contribution to their independence as to revitalize the Polish immigrants' pride in ancestry. In Cracow, Poland, on the five hundredth anniversary of the Battle of Grunwald (where, in 1410, the Polish-Lithuanian forces of King Wladyslaw Jagiello toppled the power of the Teutonic knights), Paderewski dedicated another monument, which he had commissioned as "a work of deep love for my homeland."

Other accomplished Poles were doing

Marie Curie-Sklodowska, discoverer of radium, shown here in her French laboratory, came to the United States before the First World War to open educational institutions and to help win American sympathy for the cause of an independent Poland. COURTESY OF THE NEW YORK ACADEMY OF MEDICINE.

the same. Marie Sklodowska, who, with her physicist husband, Pierre Curie, broke the ground for nuclear research in chemistry and physics, named the two elements she had discovered radium and polonium, the last for her native country. In America, another Polish expatriate, Albert Michelson, had already become the first American scientist to win the Nobel Prize in physics for his discovery of instrumentation to measure the speed of light.

The national solemnities in Washington and Poland were part of a worldwide movement to draw together the scattered fragments of the Polish nation, and, for the first time in Polish history, all the classes of Polish society, at home and abroad, united in optimistic confidence about their country's future. Thus a Polish historian could say: "In 1800 we prayed to be allowed to live; in 1900 we knew that we would live." And the Polish masses in America were viewed as a vital source of influence and manpower for the coming liberation.

Dr. Albert A. Michelson came to the United States from a small town in Poland and became the first American to win the Nobel Prize in physics. He is shown here in his Irvine, California, laboratory with the instruments he developed for measuring the speed of light. CREDIT: NATIONAL ARCHIVES (USIA PHOTO).

And still the Poles continued to come to the United States. The total number of ethnic Poles who reached America in the twentieth century, before the outbreak of the First World War, has been computed by Polish Government statisticians at 2,122,504, but where that figure could have come from is a mystery. Poles landing in America were most often registered as Russians, Prussians, or Austrians, depending on which part of partitioned Poland had contained their homes. The Polish Government figure presumably excludes an equal mass of Polish Jews, who had been loyal Polish citizens while there had been a Poland to which they could be loyal, and whose emigrant hegira forms no part of this book.

The final migratory rush, which took place just before Europe exploded into what would be the first global conflict, brought an additional mass of 174,365 Poles to the United States, according to U. S. Immigration and Naturalization Service statistics. Among them came a seventeen-year-old tailor's apprentice, sent out of Poland by his parents to avoid conscription into the Russian armies, whose American-born son, Edmund Sixtus Muskie, would be the first American of Polish lineage to be elected governor of an American state, then United States senator, and then become a candidate for the Vice Presidency of the United States.

In 1914, a Polish National Committee had sprung into being, to assist Poland in regaining independence. Led by John Smulski of Chicago, the committee worked through 500 lesser Polish organizations to raise more than $50 million in money and goods, and helped to recruit a volunteer corps of 26,000 Polish-Americans to fight in France, on the Allies' side, as the famed "Blue Army" of General Joseph Haller. That force would grow to more than 100,000 before the war's end.

War was a signal of hope, as well as desperate sorrow, for Poles everywhere. Paderewski was in Switzerland when the guns of August boomed across Europe in 1914. As he surveyed the broad sweep of Poland's history, he could sense the import of onrushing events, convinced that the moment of Poland's final liberation was at hand. The price that Poles everywhere would pay for that freedom would be staggering. While the attention of the Western world was on Western Europe, Poland was in flames as the gigantic armies of Russia and the Central Powers rolled back and forth across the country, leaving devastation in their wake. Sensing that the United States would play a leading role in the world's affairs before the European tragedy was over, Paderewski returned to the United States to become the spokesman of his people. Again his famous private train thundered across the country but, this time, he gave his audiences eloquent words as well as brilliant music. "I have to speak about a country which is not yours, in a language which is not mine," he said, beginning his final American tour in San Francisco in 1915. "My errand is not of hatred but of love," he told another audience. "I do not intend to incite passion but to awaken compassion." Under his inspiration a complete official thesis was prepared

Famed piano virtuoso Ignacy Paderewski, with his wife and leaders of the Polish National Alliance, posed on the steps of the PNA's Alliance College in 1915 when he arrived in the United States to raise funds for the Polish War Relief Committee. The college, which would become an officers' school for the army that Polish-Americans sent to France in 1917, was the last great educational venture of American Poles before the First World War swept away their leadership. CREDIT: ALLIANCE COLLEGE LIBRARY, CAMBRIDGE SPRINGS, PENNSYLVANIA.

for those Poles who needed direction to channel their emotions, and all the various Polish national relief committees were forged into one.

For the majority of Americans, for whom Poland was a faraway place that produced either superb artists or illiterate labor, Poland's name became synonymous with that of Paderewski. The Congress passed resolutions expressing sympathy with devastated Poland, and New Year's Day 1916,

was proclaimed "Polish Day" by President Wilson, who invited popular subscriptions to Paderewski's relief fund.

Never before had the name of Poland been so widely and sympathetically acknowledged in the United States—as it has never been again. But this American response to Poland's plight was only a beginning for the impassioned virtuoso. He wanted Poland's cause tied to America's name, as so many Polish lives had become tied to America's substance. He used all his personal and professional friendships in Poland's behalf, and won influential new friends, such as President Wilson's enigmatic alter ego and trusted adviser, Colonel House—the first of a long line of powerful, unelected American "assistant Presidents" whose unacknowledged presence would have such grave results on future American policies.

Josephus Daniels, Secretary of the Navy from 1913 to 1921, thus described his first meeting with the Polish pianist: "I never saw Ignace Paderewski until he called at my office in the Navy Department during the World War to request cooperation to help his suffering countrymen in Poland. With eloquent words on his tongue and tears in his eyes, he related the story of the dismemberment of his country as if it were a fresh tragedy, and the present hopes and needs of his countrymen. With an audience of one, he was as much moved as if he were speaking to a multitude. He opened his heart to me and from that moment I was an ardent advocate of the ambition of the Poles. Again I saw him at the White House when he was entertained by the President and Mrs. Wilson. His playing moved Wilson—he played nothing but Chopin—and his presentation of his hopes for his native land converted Wilson to the cause of Poland."

Paderewski's influence on Colonel House was equally complete. In a biography of the mysterious colonel (*Intimate Papers of Colonel House* [Boston, 1926]), Charles Seymour was to write of Paderewski: "[He] came as a spokesman of an ancient people whose wrongs and sorrows had stirred the sympathies of an entire world. The artist, patriot and statesman awakened the Congress to do justice to his native land and sought its help to make a great dream come true. . . ."

The first result of Paderewski's efforts came in President Wilson's "Peace Without Victory" address on January 22, 1917, when the President made his first declaration of what should follow the close of the war: "I take it for granted that statesmen every-

where are agreed that there shall be a united, independent and autonomous Poland."

Two days before the United States entered the war, Paderewski moved to consolidate his nation's position as a potential ally of the Western powers. This nation had no government or state, but it had its people. Under the sweep of his impassioned vision, the Union of Polish Falcons, in convention in Pittsburgh, voted to raise a 100,000-man "Army of Kosciuszko to fight by the side of the United States," and offered such an army to the United States. Newton D. Baker, the Secretary of War (whose own constituency in Cleveland, Ohio, was overwhelmingly Polish), regretfully refused this astounding offer on constitutional grounds, but the American Poles went on, anyway, by opening two huge training camps on the Niagara frontier, where men of overdraft age could enlist in "Paderewski's Army." Thirty-eight thousand of them entered the United States Army, 22,000 more went to join Haller's forces in France, and in some American communities the male Polish population simply vanished from the civilian scene. When Wilson finally called for volunteers for the American armed forces, 40,000 of the first 100,000 Americans reporting for service proved to be Poles.

All Polish newspapers in America called for 100 per cent registration of their readers for military service; all Polish priests spoke to their flocks on "Registration Sunday" with a similar appeal. In Milwaukee, Lieutenant Colonel Peter F. Piasecki was placed in charge of recruiting Polish-born Americans in the 1st Wisconsin Infantry and, in one day, found himself commanding a battalion. In South Bend, Indiana, 100 men enlisted on the first day of recruiting: 96 of them were Polish laborers from the steel mills. In New York's Union Square, 5,000 Polish men and women rallied to thank President Wilson for his interest in the Polish cause, laid a wreath at the Washington monument, and then all the men of military age marched to enlist in the American Army. Graham

Paderewski, and members of the Polish military mission in the First World War, appeared with New York Mayor Hylan on the steps of New York's City Hall to urge all Poles residing in the United States to join the American Army. Of the first hundred thousand volunteers for the American armed forces, forty thousand were Polish immigrants. Another thirty thousand went to France to join a Polish army fighting on the side of the Allies. CREDIT: NATIONAL ARCHIVES (U. S. SIGNAL CORPS PHOTO).

Taylor, reporting on *Pioneering on Social Frontiers* (Chicago, 1930) has described the scene in the windswept capital of Polish settlement in America, which was duplicated throughout the continent: "[In Chicago] over 8,000 of the 12,000 or more men who registered with the draft board . . . were Poles from Austria, and over 2,000 more of them came from Russia. When asked where they were born, they replied *Poland.* . . . Most of them said that they did not want to be soldiers, as they left Poland partly to escape an oc-

cupying power's military service. But many who were exempt because they were aliens quickly added, *I go if you need me.* Scores of them proceeded at once to file their intention to become American citizens. Returning from the City Hall with their first papers to be registered as subjects of the draft, not a few of them exclaimed *I may meet my father or brother in the Austrian trench.* All of them might have added that, if captured by Austrians or Germans, they would have been shot as traitors. Of no American lad's patriotism was such an acid test extracted as these young Polish men so bravely stood."

Hard-earned Polish dollars went by the millions to Red Cross and Liberty Bond campaigns. In proportion to their numbers in America, the Polish workingmen and -women subscribed more to the Third Liberty Loan than any other community—including native-born Americans themselves. In one mining district of Pennsylvania, Polish miners subscribed $11,000,000 to the loan, as Paderewski reported to the Polish General Convention in 1917, while one Polish bank in Chicago received 15,000 subscriptions from their laboring depositors, exceeding $1,500,000. No other community in America would give so much in men and treasure to their new country in the opening stages of America's first global conflict—which is all the more astonishing in view of their pitiful resources, their struggle, and the treatment they had received. No American could have been surprised when, on January 8, 1918, Wilson proclaimed before the Congress his program for world peace, in the ringing periods of his "Fourteen Points," which flew like lightning to the remotest corners of the world. His Thirteenth Point was: an independent Poland guaranteed by all nations. To the embattled Poles in Poland and in France, this declaration seemed to sound the death-knell of their enslavement, and seemed to make the freedom of their country an accomplished fact. No matter what the Poles did for themselves in Europe— and they performed miracles of sacrifice and valor on both sides of the lines—it was the weight of the Polish worker's calloused hand in the United States, guided by Paderewski's visionary passion, that tipped the delicate balances of international recognition to Polish aspirations. By a terrible historical irony, the Polish-Americans who had done so much to restore Poland's independence found themselves most cruelly deprived by Poland's resurrection: At one unwitting stroke, free Poland reclaimed from them whatever leadership they had managed to develop in America.

Paderewski left the United States in De-cember 1918 to work with other Polish exile-statesmen in the Versailles Conference, where the erstwhile Allies' political jealousies threatened to emasculate the struggling new Polish Republic. The English were doing all they could to weaken France's natural ally, and the French themselves—prostrate in their victory—could be of little help. Once more the Polish community in America stepped into the breach with money for the devastated country; Hoover's relief commission in Poland represented the last flicker of their influence. Theirs was a moral power, based on demonstrated devotion to the United States, and not—as Polish historians are fond of arguing—the result of any great American appreciation for Poland and her role in Europe.

Most of the leaders of the Polish National Alliance—that painfully and laboriously constructed citadel of ethnic self-esteem and unification—left America, and few of them would return. Paderewski would shortly become Prime Minister and then Foreign Minister of Poland. The "Blue Army" marched to Warsaw to help in repelling a new Bolshevik invasion, and all but a few of Polonia's schoolteachers, editors, writers, ideologues, social activists, idealistic priests, youthful professional persons, promising political leaders, public speakers, historians, and exponents of cultural traditions marched right along with it. All but a minuscule fraction of this exodus of leaders were "gentry," as opposed to the peasant masses, which they had organized and led. Most would remain in Poland, where their hearts had always been. They left behind them in America a huge and agitated, undirected national organism, its growth stunted by a single decapitating blow, its intellectual evolution effectively destroyed for nearly two decades.

Leaderless at a point of crisis, when a sense of unity and a firm direction were more essential than ever, the Polish community in America faced overwhelming problems. Returning veterans found themselves crowded out of a constricting peacetime labor market. The first intimations of a national economic disaster were making their spectral appearances among the poor and needy. New immigrants (no better trained for life in America than their peasant predecessors) were crowding into the bulging Polish neighborhoods, in flight from Poland's wrecked economy and unenlightened agrarian policies. And, finally, the American labor movement itself—battling an artificial Bolshevist image and ruthless capitalist exploitation simultaneously—was moving toward its own violent eruption.

Polonia's major segments could turn for guidance only to its priests, and the results of that well-intentioned but frequently naïve clerical leadership were sometimes disastrous.

It took the advent of the Great Depression before all Polish immigrants (the toilers of the 1880s, their American descendants, the wave of 1900 to 1914, and the new arrivals of the 1920s) could realize what had happened to their aspirations. Their sudden fall from grace had embittered many, as they watched Polonia's hard-won sense of worth slipping from their grasp. Even before the First World War, a bitter schism had split them between the priest-led Roman Catholic Union and the secular PNA, whose European slogans now failed them entirely. They felt themselves exploited and betrayed by the departed "gentry" and never forgot it. Factions fragmented into smaller fractions, each with its own priorities and programs, and the community's energies flowed out in wasteful internecine bickering.

Legend has turned this period into a time of unrestrained joy and enthusiasm, an inspiration for uninhibited Polish identification everywhere, "when laughter and excitement filled the American Polish communities . . . a time for civic outbursts." The truth is somewhat less elating.

There *were* parades and mass meetings in New York, Chicago, Cleveland, Buffalo,

Pittsburgh, Milwaukee, and Detroit, and many Polish Americans *did* come to stand outside the new Polish consulate-general in New York, just to look at its crowned white eagle on a plaque, but time's perspective tells a different story. Except for a few individual egos, an independent Poland did not enhance the prestige of Polish settlements in America. It is one of the sad ironies of Polish-American history that the Old Country had seldom been of any help to the immigrants' evolution and was, too often, a liability—as it is today in its Soviet-directed totalitarian form. When they had most needed cultural and educational guidance, there had been no Polish state to supply it, and the reconstituted Polish Republic of the 1920s was wracked by such immense internal problems of its own that it could spare no thought to the plight of its American brethren. If reverent crowds did come, for a time, to touch the consulate's plaque as though it were a relic, it was surely more an expression of bewildered loss than of jubilation. Poland was free, and all the best energies of Polish-Americans had gone to that accomplishment. Now they were, once more, alone in an American reality, painted with the same uncomplimentary brush that was erasing American sympathies for Poland. A bitterly vocal mass of impoverished immigrant Polish Jews was beginning to proclaim its own version of Polish history in America, as the harassed and inexperienced Polish governments wrestled with the partition's terrible legacies: a virulent nationalism contemptuous of minorities, an abysmal economic poverty, and sectional jealousies. Polish-Americans had neither voice nor knowledge for effective protest. In any event, all they could have done in their own defense would have been to offer lists of reasons for the existence of unpalatable facts—such as manifestations of antisemitism in independent Poland—and reasons can merely explain why certain facts may be logical, they do not justify an immorality. Paderewski himself was shunted aside as "out-of-touch" with Polish nationalist realities in Europe, and the United

States hastened to put up shutters of isolationist oblivion against any further European involvements.

It was in this climate of helplessness to cope with movements and events beyond their control, and in the midst of an accelerating collapse of the American economy, that the descendants of the peasant immigration finally became American in name as well as in fact.

At one stroke they severed their dependence on leadership by "gentlemen from Europe." They recognized their future lives and goals to be American and sought American means. Gone from their ears was the messianic fervor of Polish nationalist exiles; never again would they willingly surrender control of their institutions to European intellectuals. Henceforth, their links with Poland were to be merely sentimental. An American-born leadership began to emerge "from the block" in the American manner, and Polish-American organizations became rooted in the lives of the workingpeople from whom they had sprung. They recognized instinctively what social science would not dare to label for two more generations: Hyphenated Americans are necessarily schizophrenic since no man can live with total commitment in two worlds simultaneously. If culture is the total of a people's values, then, at this stage in their evolution, Polish-Americans could measure their culture only in dollars and cents—a recourse to materialism that was the antithesis of Polish cultural traditions. It would repel a later wave of Polish political exiles who would attempt, once again, to dominate Polonia.

Yet they remained attached through symbols to Polish origins that still continued, in those years of transformation, to dominate their wholly American lives. Tens of thousands of them marched on New York's Fifth Avenue on October 10, 1937, in the first of the massive annual Pulaski Day parades, but this was a parade of *Americans of Polish descent*, rather than one of *Poles who live in America*.

The PNA founded American educational establishments for the children of their worker-members—the greatest of them at Alliance College in Cambridge Springs, Pennsylvania, an accredited liberal-arts institution that had been an officers' school for the Falcon armies. New York's Kosciuszko Foundation also stems from this period of new directions for American Poles. It was founded in 1924 by Dr. Stephan Mizwa, the son of a Polish peasant, who came to the United States in 1912, rose to a university professorship, and induced a group of American educators to sponsor a scholarship facility for Polish-Americans.

The labor wars that exploded upon this continent in the 1920s further hastened the pace of Americanization of Polish working-people's consciousness and ideals, as the Polish neighborhoods of Hamtramck in Michigan, Homestead in Pennsylvania, Lowell in Massachusetts, Gary in Indiana, and in Pennsylvania's Shenandoah, became the great historic battlefields of the American labor movement's fight for recognition. The Lattimer Massacre of 1897 had never been forgotten by Polish coalminers, and 47,000 of them battled to secure the rights of the United Mineworkers to organize the anthracite coalfields.

One of the reasons why mine owners were unable to break Polish miners, as they had done the Irish and the Germans, was the near-pathological thrift of the Polish miners' women. Laboring Poles purposely kept to a low standard of living in order to save money, and these savings provided the cushion that served them in strikes. They were also willing to take almost any chance to be sure of work in the future, including violent confrontations inside and outside their unions. The most recent of their leaders to die while fighting the corruption of his union was "Jock" Yablonski, who was murdered in 1969 during his reform campaign for the presidency of the UMW, which Polish labor had helped to organize. Wyndham Martin, vice president of the United Auto Workers in the 1930s, singled out the 300,000 Polish workers of

Detroit for special praise in their fight against the entrenched auto industry.

More than 500,000 Polish workers fought as part of American labor's war on social injustice in the 9,223 strikes that erupted in America between 1919 and 1921. More than 9,000 striking workers went to prison in those desperate years, more than 200 were killed by owners' private armies, imported strikebreakers, sheriffs' deputies, and regular regiments of the United States Army, which had been called out to the aid of the manufacturers. The gathered wealth of the Polish community practically disappeared as the Depression sent more than 6,700,000 workmen into the streets. Many Polish working families sailed once more for Europe, but an overwhelming majority remained to help in the creation of the UMW, the UAW, the United Steelworkers, and of the International Ladies' Garment Workers' Union under the fiery leadership

David Dubinsky, a graduate of the old Polish Social-Democratic party, which gave leaders to many European labor and independence movements, emerged as one of the most fiery American leaders in the labor movement's battle for social justice in the 1930s. PHOTO BY HARRY RUBINSTEIN. COURTESY OF INTERNATIONAL LADIES' GARMENT WORKERS' UNION.

of David Dubinsky, a graduate of the old Polish Social Democrats who had given leaders to all European workers' movements since 1905. This is a vital part of the history of Poles in America that ethnic historians will seldom acknowledge, considering it insufficiently conservative for the docile "respectable" image they wish to project. The preferred image of orderly humility denies the enormous contribution of Polish-American workingmen and -women to the development of social justice in the United States.

Distinguished Poles continued to come to the United States in those deceptively settled years between the World Wars, when isolationist xenophobia, and an attempt to keep America Protestant and white, designed immigration quotas against them. The Polish quota, practically pre-empted by Jewish emigrants, was a meager six thousand a year.

Count Alfred Korzybski, the founder of the science of semantics, came to the United States in the 1920s and applied his new science to an experimental system of understanding human behavior, possibly even the discriminatory behavior of American lawmakers. (In 1938, he founded the Institute of General Semantics, now located in Lakeville, Connecticut.) The internationally renowned sociologist, Florian Znaniecki, one of the original pioneers in his field, also arrived to teach in the United States at that time, while Polish-born Casimir Funk, a specialist in the field of nutrition as it concerns disease, first isolated a substance that he named "vitamins." Marie Curie-Sklodowska came back to the United States to accept a gift of radium, which she needed for research, and to dedicate the Hepburn Hall of Chemistry in 1929. Bronislaw Malinowski, who revolutionized the study of anthropology (by emphasizing the functional interrelationships of all cultural phenomena in the structure of society) also arrived in America in 1933.

These brilliant Polish scientists would leave indelible imprints on American

Count Alfred Korzybski, who originated the science of semantics, and founded the Institute of General Semantics in the United States, as he appeared in this 1950 photograph by Lotte Jacobi. COURTESY OF MRS. CHARLOTTE REED, INSTITUTE OF GENERAL SEMANTICS, LAKEVILLE, CONNECTICUT.

Dr. Casimir Funk, a pioneer in the field of nutrition as it concerns disease, first discovered, isolated, and named a substance that is known today as vitamins. CREDIT: NATIONAL LIBRARY OF MEDICINE, BETHESDA, MARYLAND.

scientific systems, but their own lives would seldom touch upon that of the Polish-American community, which—it must be admitted—was often unaware of the scientists' existence. Along with the rest of America, the new American Poles were far more aware of Stanislaw "Zbyszko" Cyganiewicz, who became world wrestling champion in 1921 and 1922 and was one of the most popular persons in American athletics. What few of his admirers suspected was that Cyganiewicz was a graduate in philosophy at the University of Vienna and spoke eleven foreign languages. He was the last undefeated American world champion in the classic Greco-Roman wrestling style and won his final contest at the age of fifty-nine. Shortly before his death he was also featured in *Night and the City*, which was meant to have been the beginning of his acting career.

Few American boxing enthusiasts in the first quarter of the twentieth century didn't know and revere the name of Stanley Ketchel (Stanislaw Kiecal), middleweight boxing champion of the world in 1908, who defeated Mike Sullivan (then champion) in the first round of the championship bout, and then outfought Mike's twin brother, Jack. In a bid for the light-heavyweight championship of the world, Ketchel knocked out champion "Philadelphia Jack" O'Brien in the twelfth round of a memorable battle, and was preparing for the heavyweight challenge when he was shot to death by a jealous rival in quite another field of athletic endeavor. *Ring* magazine recently listed Ketchel as the best American professional boxer of all time, above Mohammed Ali and Sugar Ray Robinson. In the sixth place in that boxing lexicon was Tony Zale (Antoni Zaleski), who won the middleweight championship of the

Bronislaw Malinowski, originator of the functional theory in anthropology, and internationally renowned analyst of primitive social behavior, talks to a native sorcerer in this early photograph dated about 1916. COURTESY OF HELENA MALINOWSKA WAYNE.

CREDIT: LIBRARY OF CONGRESS, PRINTS AND PHOTOGRAPHS DIVISION.

The last great undefeated American world champion of wrestling in the classic Greco-Roman style was Stanislaw "Zbyszko" Cyganiewicz, one of a large family of Polish athletes settled in America. What few of his admirers knew was that Dr. Cyganiewicz was a graduate of philosophy from the University of Vienna and spoke eleven foreign languages. In the early 1920s he was the most popular sports figure in the United States. CREDIT: LIBRARY OF CONGRESS, PRINTS AND PHOTOGRAPHS DIVISION.

Stanley Ketchel (Stanislaw Kiecal), the darling of the American fight fans in the first quarter of the twentieth century, was in training for the world heavyweight championship challenge when he was shot and killed by a jealous rival in a love triangle. CREDIT: CULVER PICTURES, INC., NEW YORK.

world in 1940 and is remembered to this day by boxing professionals as a fighter of great courtesy and skill.

Paderewski returned to Carnegie Hall in 1922. At sixty-two, the reddish-blond mane had turned to silver-white, a neat beard and mustache concealed the lines of pain and disappointment, and the weary eyes reflected a deep inner sorrow. His performance had a nostalgic and old-fashioned air, a crystalline quality of great power under absolute control, as though he were restat-

ing the past *as the past* and naming it Prologue, as though he were attempting to put to rest his own impassioned dream. Those who were there have written that almost all his audience were in tears: A certain dream had ended for them, as it had for him. When the audience rose to cheer Paderewski, hour after hour, it was to acknowledge their own new directions as much as to pay tribute to the music and the man.

During the remainder of the 1930s until the outbreak of the Second World War, an entirely different breed of professional Polish intellectuals, scientists, and artists began to arrive in the upper reaches of American life. Artur Rubinstein, considered by many of his peers as the greatest living pianist, returned to Carnegie Hall in 1937 "to leave his audience cheering and his piano limp," as Louis Biancolli put it the day after Rubinstein's first bravura recital. Rubinstein had been Paderewski's favorite protégé, and an impassioned Polish patriot who had been among the first to at-

Jan Kiepura, the celebrated tenor of the Warsaw Opera, joined the Metropolitan Opera Company, New York, in 1938. COURTESY OF TEATR WIELKI, WARSAW.

tempt enlistment in the Falcons' "Blue Army"; he also represented the new Polish artist whose dedication to his art took precedence over other commitments. A soaring young tenor named Jan Kiepura came from the Warsaw Opera to join the Metropolitan Opera Company in New York in 1938, and Artur Rodzinski, one of the most disciplined symphony conductors of his time, arrived to gain a measure of musical fame as a repairer and builder of American orchestras. In 1933, he developed the Cleveland Orchestra into an outstanding musical organization, then organized and trained the NBC Symphony for Arturo Toscanini and, in 1943, he became conductor of the New York Philharmonic.

The work of Boleslaw Cybis, a distinguished painter of frescos and designer of ornamental artifacts, was known in the United States for six years before his arrival in 1939. In these final years of European peace, American critics were acknowledging Zygmunt Jozef Menkes, a graduate of the Cracow Academy of Fine

years would also bring allegorical cartoonist Artur Szyk to the United States, where he would paint decorative renderings of fragments of Polish-American history.

It is yet another irony of biographical history, as taught by historians, that it is largely a tale of flamboyant creatures moved, here and there, on restless historical currents: mad Kings, compulsive voyagers, and patriots blinded to all truths but their own. The men who actually alter the course of history, the great creative scientists and mathematicians, are hardly mentioned at all. And so no ethnic historian cared to note the arrival in America, in the 1930s, of an extraordinary group of Polish mathematicians whose apocalyptic scribbles on the backs of menus would change the course of human affairs.

Stanislaw Ulam, a member of the famous Lwow mathematical school, founded in Ulam's native city by the near-legendary Waclaw Sierpinski, arrived at the Institute for Advanced Study at Princeton in 1936. He is an originator of ideas for nuclear pro-

Artur Rodzinski gained musical fame as a repairer and builder of American symphonic orchestras. CREDIT: NEW YORK PUBLIC LIBRARY, LINCOLN CENTER.

Dr. Stanislaw Ulam, creator of an "iterative scheme" that made possible the practical development of the hydrogen bomb, and an originator of ideas for nuclear propulsion of space vehicles, was one of the brilliant school of Polish mathematicians who came to America shortly before the outbreak of the Second World War. COURTESY OF S. M. ULAM.

Arts, as one of ten most distinguished painters working in America, along with Eliasz Kanarek, who had been sent by the Polish Government to paint the murals in the New York World's Fair Polish pavilion, and who would make a brilliant career as an American portrait painter. The war

pulsion of space vehicles, one of the first to use and advocate computers for scientific research, and he has now been acknowledged by his mathematical peers as the American scientist whose genius made possible the invention of the hydrogen bomb.

What Dr. Ulam did to modify a previous and unworkable plan of Dr. Edward Teller, the self-styled "Father of the Hydrogen Bomb," will probably remain a secret in our lifetimes. In Dr. Ulam's recent autobiography (*Adventures of a Mathematician* [New York, Scribner's, 1976]), he merely mentions an "iterative scheme" that apparently appeared in his remarkable head in much the same manner as the leaps that his mind seems to be able to take to generate new branches of his science. One such leap was the invention of the Monte Carlo Method, a technique too complex for definition and explained only by a complete system of equations; it occurred at Los Alamos, during World War II, when Dr. Ulam was working on the first atomic bomb and found a way to simulate chain reactions by using a computer to generate random numbers.

Invisible to all but a few of their own extraordinary kind at Princeton, Cambridge, and in Warsaw were other Lwow mathematicians who developed much of the twentieth century's mathematics and who landed in the United States during the last decade of Poland's brief existence as an independent country. Mathematician Witold Hurewicz joined the faculty of the Massachusetts Institute of Technology and remained there until his accidental death in 1956; statistician Jerzy Neyman left Poland in 1934, spent four years in London, then joined the University of California at Los Angeles, where he remained until his retirement; statistician William Birnbaum came to New York University during the last three years of European peace, as did Dr. Mark Kac, a widely known developer of mathematical analysis and probability theories, who is now a member of the National Academy of Sciences and a Professor of Rockefeller University. The eminent logician Alfred Tarski, author of many books

Professor Mark Kac is a widely known developer of mathematical analysis and probability theories, and a member of the National Academy of Sciences. COURTESY OF PROFESSOR MARK KAC, THE ROCKEFELLER UNIVERSITY, NEW YORK.

that have advanced the knowledge of mathematical logic in the United States and that set the foundation for semantics as a branch of logic, also made his unremarked appearance in America, where he is now acknowledged as a leading philosopher of science.

Far more visible to pragmatic Americans was the work of Ralph Modjeski, son of the former century's great Shakespearean actress, who had become America's leading construction engineer, and whose Philadelphia–Camden bridge over the Delaware River was the world's longest single-span suspension bridge when it was opened in 1926.

Even more visible (far too visible, according to the moralists of her time) were the work and person of Gilda Grey, whose name had been Maryanna Michalska before she quivered to glory in the Ziegfeld *Follies* and in George White's *Scandals* as

Ralph Modjeski, son of the Shakespearean actress, became a foremost bridge builder and construction engineer in the United States. Among his projects is the Oakland Bridge, Oakland, California, and the Philadelphia–Camden bridge across the Delaware River, which was the world's longest single-span suspension bridge when it was opened in 1926. HISTORICAL SOCIETY OF PENNSYLVANIA.

the supposed creator of the "shimmy." Another creative first that boggles the mind was the painted toenail, apparently brought to Hollywood by yet another Pol-

ish temptress of the silent screen, the sultry Pola Negri (the great love of Rudolph Valentino) whose name had been Apolonia Chalupiec before the obligatory change.

Among the other Polish stars, moons, and planets that floated, glittered, and occasionally fell from the skies of Hollywood in the 1930s were Gloria Swanson, a genuine first lady of the screen; Estelle Clark (Stasia Zwolinska); the durable Mike Mazurki (Mazurkiewicz); the veteran Stanley Clements; Jean Wallace (Janina Wałasek); Lydia Roberti; Kathy Marlowe; and the beautiful and tragic Carole Landis, who had often starred in Hollywood's better pieces of illusion. Film producer and director Joseph L. Mankiewicz, and composer and musical director Bronislaw Kaper began their long cinematographic careers in that eye-glazing era and have continued into the times of serious actresses and actors like Jack Palance (of partly Polish parentage); Carroll Baker (Karolina Piekarska), who raised blood temperatures in the erotic *Baby Doll;* and the enormously talented Loretta Swit of Broadway and television's M.A.S.H. And then there is Stephanie Powers, who was once named Stefania Federkiewicz; her former husband, actor Gary Lockwood; Michael Landon (Orowicz); and scowling movie muscleman Charles Bronson, who is said to earn his studio a million dollars each time he takes off his shirt on the screen. There are other distinguished actors and actresses who do not care to advertise their Polish descent, and yet others who do the Polish-American community a service by concealing theirs.

Maryanna Michalska, better known on Broadway as Gilda Grey, danced her way into the story of her times with the invention of the shimmy and the black bottom. Sheer energy made the feathers fall. CREDIT: CULVER PICTURES, INC., NEW YORK.

In what is far from her most flattering photograph, the beautiful and talented Gloria Swanson, a genuine first lady of the screen, posed for publicity in her early Her Gilded Cage. *Swanson's parents, belonging to Poland's affluent landed gentry, were born in an Austrian province of partitioned Poland.* CREDIT: CULVER PICTURES, INC., NEW YORK.

Estelle Clark (Stasia Zwolinska) made a pert addition to the MGM troop of actresses. She was given her first big film role in Rupert Hughes' production of Don't. CREDIT: CULVER PICTURES, INC., NEW YORK.

Pola Negri, beloved of Rudolph Valentino, glittered in Hollywood and is supposed to have introduced the painted toenail to America. Her name, before the obligatory change, was Apolonia Chalupiec. CREDIT: LIBRARY OF CONGRESS, PRINTS AND PHOTOGRAPHS DIVISION.

Jean Wallace (Mrs. Franchot Tone, née Janina Walasek) was a Paramount actress and one of the studio's thirteen Louisiana belles in Louisiana Purchase. Here some of her talents are shrouded in film strips as she is elected a "Celluloid Queen." CREDIT: CULVER PICTURES, INC., NEW YORK.

The beautiful Carole Landis was a young Polish actress who won Hollywood stardom in such films as One Million B.C., with Victor Mature. CREDIT: CULVER PICTURES, INC., NEW YORK.

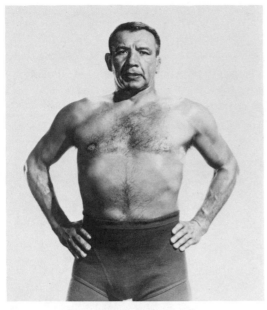

Mike Mazurki (Mazurkiewicz) has been acknowledged as the greatest American film "heavy" of all time, the epitome of mindless brutality and physical terror. In point of fact, he was a gentle and retiring man and a voluminous reader of the classics. CREDIT: CULVER PICTURES, INC., NEW YORK.

Bronislaw Kaper wrote some of the most memorable musical scores in Hollywood and created original music that has lasted into the present in the light-classical fields. COURTESY OF ASCAP.

Shown in his Hollywood office, young Joseph Mankiewicz became one of the most talented American motion-picture producers, whose work has gone well into modern times. CREDIT: CULVER PICTURES, INC., NEW YORK.

Stephanie Powers (Stefania Federkiewicz) is shown here on location near Windsor, Ontario. She is one of the most professionally competent young actresses of today's stage, motion pictures, and television. PHOTO BY FRANK ALEKSANDROWICZ. COPYRIGHT © FRANK ALEKSANDROWICZ.

Loretta Swit, who reached national prominence as the star of television's M.A.S.H., is considered one of the most brilliant and versatile actresses on the American stage, according to her contemporary peers in the theater. PHOTO BY FRANK ALEKSANDROWICZ. COPYRIGHT © FRANK ALEKSANDROWICZ.

Charles Bronson (Buchinski), one of the most successful American screen actors, has become a cult hero to a large segment of the television public. COURTESY OF THEATRE ARTS LIBRARY, UCLA.

Jack Palance (Walter Palaniuk) is a veteran screen, stage, and television actor of partly Polish parentage. COURTESY OF THEATRE ARTS LIBRARY, UCLA.

Show business, as opposed to acting and music, has always had its share of widely promoted, temporarily notorious personalities of no artistic merit, who have a dubious place in their community's evolution and none in their history. But athletes of Olympic stature or national importance are part of that history, as a legitimate focus of ethnic consciousness and pride.

Few Polish-Americans had not heard of the extraordinary Stella Walsh who, as a seventeen-year-old girl, was to have represented the United States in Los Angeles, during the first Olympic Games in which women athletes were permitted to compete. She was the pride of their community, and all their hopes for recognition seemed to ride on her predicted triumph. But shortly before the Games, it was discovered that the record-breaking American

Janet Lynn (Nowicki), women's world figure-skating champion, skates as a guest star at the Ice Follies. PHOTO BY FRANK ALEKSANDROWICZ. COPYRIGHT ⓒ FRANK ALEKSANDROWICZ.

Stella Walsh autographs her track shoes on being elected to the Polish Sports Hall of Fame at Orchard Lake, Michigan. PHOTO BY FRANK ALEKSANDROWICZ. COPYRIGHT ⓒ FRANK ALEKSANDROWICZ.

track star, whose real name was Stanislawa Walasiewicz, had not been born in the United States but had been brought here, as an infant, by parents who had never become American citizens. She could not compete for the United States. Her Gold Medal in the Games (a record-breaking hundred-meter dash) was won by her under Polish colors. Eventually, she was to become women's track champion of the United States, Europe, Poland, and even Japan but she was never to represent the United States in international Olympics. Today, at an age when her girlhood friends are playing with grandchildren, Stella Walsh still runs the eight hundred meters in near-record time. Far more recently, American-born Janet Lynn (Nowicki) had become an Olympic figure-skating gold medalist, five times United States figure-skating champion, and the professional skating star of various Ice Follies.

Not far from the factories of celluloid dreams, in Glendale, California, almost prophetically placed in Forest Lawn Memorial Park, is the largest and most dramatic religious painting in America, Jan Styka's "The Crucifixion" (named by the artist "Golgotha"), which he painted at the instigation of Ignacy Paderewski—and which almost did not get to the United States at all.

Styka was driven by a monumental passion to impress upon mankind once and forever the lessons of freedom through sacrifice, and life within death—the age-long Polish ethic that seemed to exemplify the peasant immigration in America more than any other. "The Crucifixion" was his biggest and most demanding painting, 195 feet long and 45 feet deep. With painstaking care he sketched, verified, and added to his work, plotted its mobile composition, and journeyed to the Holy Land to see and experience the shades and half tones of its light, the texture of its lives. When he finally unrolled his completed canvas, it was rich in humanity and of unparalleled historic authenticity (although, then as now, hair-splitting Polish critics and envious academics moved mountains of words to discredit the artist). This was art that informed, that caused scholars to say: "This is how it was, and how it always will be." "The Crucifixion" was first shown in Warsaw in 1895 as one of the greatest European artistic and religious events of the century; then the huge canvas was rolled up and shipped, in a steerage hold full of immigrants, to America, where it was never shown because no building could be found for its exhibition. Then the painting vanished. It was bought for a pittance to settle the artist's debts, and lay rolled up in storage for more than a generation until an American entrepreneur, Dr. Hubert Eaton, stumbled across it and built his Hall of the Crucifixion, where Styka's monumental work now hangs and is seen by tens of thousands of visitors each year.

But as the 1930s ended with the New York World's Fair (in a year that began with an unnoticed announcement that scientists had succeeded is splitting an atom of uranium by means of a bombardment of neutrons) Europe was on its way to its own multiple crucifixions.

On September 1, 1939, the Second World War began with Nazi Germany's invasion of Poland, and the civilized world would never be the same again.

The history of the Second World War is well enough known to form no part of this book, except as it concerns Americans of Polish origin or descent. Its aftermath spilled a new wave of exiles on American shores, fragmented the community, and has created something of a crisis in group identity from which will come whatever definite new directions Polonia will take.

Poland went down in five bloody and chaotic weeks of hopeless and catastrophic battle—its flat, dry terrain a perfect testing ground for Hitler's new panzer-and-air "lightning war"—while its French and English allies stood inactive in the West, and while its other age-long enemy, Russia, joined the Germans in Poland's fourth par-

The largest religious painting in the United States, Jan Styka's "Golgotha" or "Crucifixion," hangs in the Hall of the Crucifixion-Resurrection, Forest Lawn Memorial Park, Glendale, California. CREDIT: FOREST LAWN MEMORIAL PARKS.

tition. In six years of horror unmatched elsewhere in Europe, more than a quarter of a million Polish soldiers would be killed, nearly five and a half million Polish citizens would die at German hands, more than one and a half million others would vanish in the frozen hells of Stalin's labor camps—among them 15,000 Polish officers, doctors, professors, journalists, and other intellectual leaders, some of whose bodies would be uncovered in 1943 in the Katyn Forest.

Two hundred thousand Polish-Americans, most of them in tears, marched up New York's Fifth Avenue in the October 1939 Pulaski Day parade, profoundly mov-

ing the vast crowds that watched them in silence. Neither the marchers nor the watchers knew it, but on that very day, on the marshy plains of eastern Poland, the last surviving regiments of the Polish army were beaten to the ground. Polish-Americans entered the war with a grief and anger found in no other American ethnic community, although to most of them, immigrants' grandchildren born and bred in the United States, Poland was just a place that the old folks used to talk about. More than one million of them—or 12 per cent of the entire armed forces of the United States in that struggle—went into uniform. From their numbers would come

**KOŚCIUSZKO
PULAWSKI**

walczyli o wolność w Ameryce.
Czy ty pomożesz Ameryce walczyć
o wolność w Polsce?

Jedz Mniej

Pszenicy-mięsa-tłuszczy-cukru
abyśmy mogli pomodz naszym
braciom walczacym w Armiach
Alianckich

ZARZAD SPOŻYWCZY STANÓW ZJEDNOCZONYCH

*As the United States prepared to go to war once more, the magic
names of Kosciuszko and Pulaski (misspelled on this poster)
were resurrected to call Polish-Americans into service. Here they
are being asked to "eat less" on the home front.* NATIONAL
ARCHIVES.

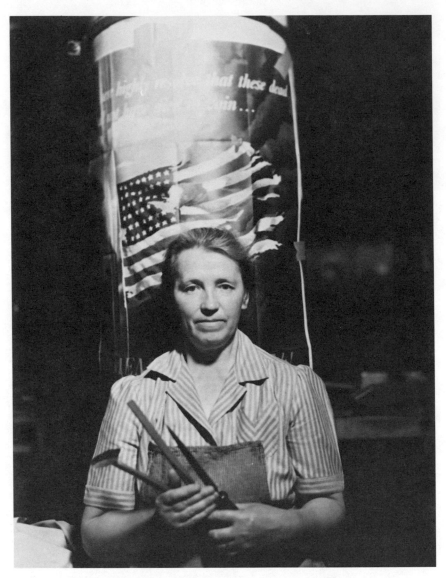

More than one million Polish-Americans went into uniform during the Second World War; their places at the factory benches were taken by their wives and mothers. This Office of War Information photograph shows a Polish-American wife and mother of men in the Army, going to war work in New Britain, Connecticut. LIBRARY OF CONGRESS, PRINTS AND PHOTOGRAPHS DIVISION.

"Home on Leave" was the title of this photograph, taken by Marjorie Collins in 1943. It contains all the basic elements of evolving Polish-American life: *devoutness, patriotism, and family.* CREDIT: LIBRARY OF CONGRESS, PRINTS AND PHOTOGRAPHS DIVISION.

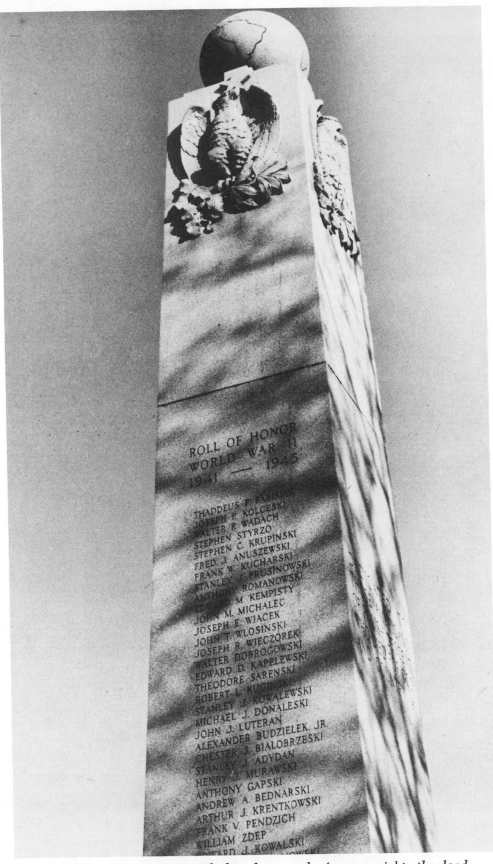

ROLL OF HONOR
WORLD WAR II
1941 — 1945

THADDEUS F. PABISIAK
JOSEPH P. KOLCESKI
WALTER P. WADACH
STEPHEN STYRZO
STEPHEN C. KRUPINSKI
FRED J. ANUSZEWSKI
FRANK W. KUCHARSKI
STANLEY J. PRUSINOWSKI
ANTHONY ROMANOWSKI
EDWARD M. KEMPISTY
JOHN M. MICHALEC
JOSEPH E. WJACEK
JOHN T. WLOSINSKI
JOSEPH R. WIECZOREK
WALTER DOBROGOWSKI
EDWARD D. KAPELEWSKI
THEODORE SARENSKI
ROBERT L. KUCINSKI
STANLEY J. KOWALEWSKI
MICHAEL J. DONALESKI
JOHN J. LUTERAN
ALEXANDER BUDZIELEK, JR.
CHESTER J. BIALOBRZESKI
STANLEY J. ADYDAN
HENRY J. MURAWSKI
ANTHONY GAPSKI
ANDREW A. BEDNARSKI
ARTHUR J. KRENTKOWSKI
FRANK V. PENDZICH
WILLIAM ZDEP
EDWARD J. KOWALSKI

*No comment seems necessary with this photograph of a memorial to the dead
of the Second World War in Syracuse, New York. All the names are Polish.*
COURTESY OF ALINA ROBACZYNSKA.

such American commanders as Admiral William Maxwell (Dzwoniecki), Generals Barzynski, Rataj, Wisniewski, Matyka, and Krygier, and Major General Maurice Rose, who was killed in March 1945 at the head of his famous 3rd Armored Division. Marine Lieutenant General Leo J. Dulacki also began his rise from the ranks in the Second World War, as did Army General Edward L. Rowny. Their professional skills and courage helped to undermine the walls of bigotry that had made the upper echelons of rank in the American services into a private Anglo-Saxon club after the Civil War. Captain (later Colonel) Francis S.

Colonel (then Captain) Francis Gabreski of Oil City, Pennsylvania, became America's air ace of aces in the Second World War. Here he meets General Wladyslaw Sikorski, Polish Prime Minister and commander in chief of the Polish armed forces in the West, to receive a Polish decoration on the occasion of his twenty-eighth air victory. COURTESY OF POLISH MUSEUM OF AMERICA, CHICAGO.

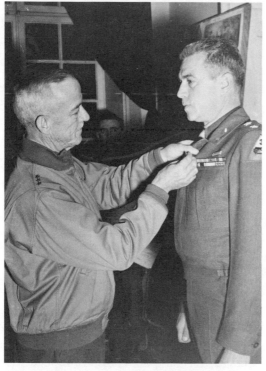

The Second World War abolished some of the social barriers that had turned the higher echelons of American military rank into an Anglo-Saxon preserve. Among several Polish-Americans who reached star rank in the armed services was Major General Maurice Rose, commander of the 3rd Armored Division in the assault on Germany, who is shown here receiving the Distinguished Service Cross from Lieutenant General Courtney Hodges. CREDIT: UNITED STATES ARMY PHOTO.

Gabreski emerged from that war (and, later, from Korea) as the leading American air ace, with 12 Distinguished Flying Crosses and 37½ confirmed victories to his credit. Military service to the United States had seemed to many Poles the simplest and most direct way of showing their devotion to their country; Army and Navy records indicate that 20 per cent of the United States Armed Forces, on the eve of war, consisted of men of Polish extraction. They were among the first to die at Bataan and Corregidor, and in the gutted hulks of the American fleet at Pearl Harbor.

Few Polish-American mothers could hang eleven stars in their windows, one for each son in uniform, like Mrs. Rose Radziminska of California, or Chicago's Mrs. Frances Dyka. But five or six men in the services were a rather common occurrence in Polish-American families, who also invested their savings in U. S. War Bonds as a measure of their American patriotism, and took part in the various activities of the civilian war effort.

In this world war, unlike its forerunner,

few Polish-Americans hurried into Polish uniform (only about 2,000 enlisted, through Canada, in the reconstituted Polish army in Great Britain) and after President Franklin Delano Roosevelt's obligatory political rhetoric (Poland, he said, was "the inspiration of the nations"), Americans turned to the business of winning their own war—the Polish-Americans very much among them. The Polish state had fallen once again, its government and institutions reconvened in England, and that was just about all that most Americans cared to know about Poland in the Second World War. But the war's aftermath would be tragically reminiscent of the Polish service in the Napoleonic wars and would have a lasting effect on Polonia's existence.

The Polish armed forces and people fought at home and abroad and suffered staggering losses in the Allied cause, then found themselves dismissed to the tender mercies of their enemies, becoming, in effect, the only Allied nation that lost the war that everyone else won. While the war still raged, President Roosevelt and Britain's Winston Churchill confirmed Stalin's seizure of Polish territories in 1939, and agreed to hand over the rest of Poland to a Communist puppet government hastily created in the Soviet Union from a few expatriate Polish communists and Soviet citizens. At one bitter stroke, the Western Allies rendered homeless the fourth largest Allied army in the West (third largest until the liberation of France in 1945), the fifth largest Allied navy, and a brilliant air force which, with fifteen squadrons of its own, had accounted for more than 20 per cent of German aircraft destroyed in the immortal Battle of Britain, which had saved the British in 1940. How these valiant men and women managed to reach the West is an untold epic that includes, by a horrible irony, mass imprisonment in the Soviet Union. There could be no return for them to Soviet control. Almost a hundred thousand of them came to America after the Second World War—shocked and bitter political emigrants forced to accept shelter among people who (they felt) had sold their hopes as well as their country to its enemies.

There was no question of their appreciation of American culture (which few of them would ever bother to explore) nor of their acceptance of their homeless status as anything but a detour on their way to an independent Poland—a Poland in which they, and their highly cultured and educated kind, could continue to control a national destiny. They would become the most fanatical of America's Cold Warriors of the Eisenhower era, overwhelming Polonia's embryonic native leadership, and doing their best to wrench Polish-Americans back into a European orientation.

More than thirty years later, many of them remain embittered *émigrés* (a term they prefer to the American Polonia) for whom the currents of contemporary American life represent nothing of interest or value. Their various European skills particularly their mastery of literary Polish, have allowed them to seize control of the best of the Polish-language press and those Polish-American organizations that claim some kinship with culture and the arts. (New York's Kosciuszko Foundation is a besieged exception.) They tend to look with condescension on native-born Polish-Americans who have not developed a European-style intellectual elite, and who have not bowed without resistance to the émigrés' superior qualities.

Many of these unwilling arrivals in America were officers in the Polish armies in the West; many are academic intellectuals, former politicians, European-style polemical journalists and writers, and members of a professional intelligentsia who could not return to a Communist-dominated Poland in 1945 for reasons of personal safety. The force of their formidable collective personality, their militant conservatism, and their exorbitant awareness of their own cultural worth have virtually driven all but the best-entrenched of Polonia's American-born leaders out of Polish-American public life. For Polonia's evolving native-born political and intel-

The Second World War ended in Europe in 1945, but there was no going home for the Polish soldiers who had fought in every Allied campaign in the West after the fall of Poland in 1939. Several thousand came to America. For some of them the war had never ended, and they remain uneasily poised between two cultures, remembering their past with a greater urgency than their present. In these three photographs, a veteran of the storming of Monte Cassino in Italy peers from a stand of American banners, as though not quite able to believe his American reality, while other Poles, in their British-style uniforms, organize a patriotic parade. PHOTOS BY FRANK ALEKSANDROWICZ. COPYRIGHT © FRANK ALEKSANDROWICZ.

The show begins as young Polish-Americans of the Galicja group in Detroit dance Polish folk themes in regional costumes, under the guidance of Michael Krolewski (center). Krolewski's group is part of a young persons' movement to maintain Polish pride in the United States. PHOTO BY FRANK ALEKSANDROWICZ. COPYRIGHT © FRANK ALEKSANDROWICZ.

A touch of Poland in America is the city of Warsaw, county seat of Kosciuszko County, Indiana—which has never had anything to do with Warsaw or Poland. No Poles live there. More than one hundred American towns are named for Polish heroes or locations. PHOTO BY FRANK ALEKSANDROWICZ. COPYRIGHT © FRANK ALEKSANDROWICZ.

Young girls in regional dress carry a statue of the Holy Mother and the infant Jesus in a Polish religious observance of Corpus Christi in Erie, Pennsylvania, while their elders come out of their homes in the neat and orderly Polish neighborhood to kneel in the streets. © FRANK ALEKSANDROWICZ.

Children dance in Polish peasant dress, and bands play, as one hundred thousand Polish-Americans march up Fifth Avenue, New York, in one of the annual Pulaski Day parades. The parades serve as a link between the marchers' Polish past and their American present. PHOTO BY FRANK ALEKSANDROWICZ. COPYRIGHT © FRANK ALEKSANDROWICZ.

Pokoj (*Peace*) *is the name of the newspaper published by a group of young Polish-Americans in Detroit, and read here by an elderly woman as she waits for a Polish folk-theater troupe to begin its concert.* © FRANK ALEKSANDROWICZ.

lectual leadership, the émigrés' arrival has been a disaster comparable to the disappearance of the nationalist "gentry" after the First World War. Through them, Polonia has acquired a powerful and educated voice, but its tones have little to do with American currents and directions. What had begun to grow from American soil, concerned with American problems in the context of an evolving American civilization, is withering before it could flower; and the currents of Polish life in America have begun to turn once again from an American future to a new preoccupation with a Polish past. In effect, all Americans of Polish origin or descent, are being asked to choose between being Polish *or* American—in America—without a middle way. It is a question of identity that the next generation of Polish-Americans will be obliged to answer.

But talented Polish refugees had begun to arrive in the United States even before the war had come to an end and were swiftly absorbed by American science, in-

Mathematician Antoni Zygmunt came to the United States during the Second World War. He has been elected to the National Academy of Sciences. COURTESY OF ANTONI ZYGMUND.

dustry, and education which welcomed their talents. The scholars among them reconstituted the Warsaw Academy of Learning in the Polish Institute of Arts and Sciences in New York to provide a focus for Polish academic traditions. Mathematician Antoni Zygmund arrived in 1943 to join his brilliant brethren at the University of Chicago and was soon elected to the National Academy of Sciences; Professor Znaniecki, who had been visiting professor of sociology at Columbia University before the war, returned to settle in America and was elected president of the American Sociological Society, in recognition of his pioneering work in that new branch of the humanities; and two remarkable medical scientists, Drs. Ludwik Gross and Hilary Koprowski, came to continue their work in cancer research and virology. Both would be elected to the National Academy of Sciences, and occupy other prestigious positions.

Among the principal contributions made by Dr. Gross, in American cancer research, was the first isolation of the leukemia virus in mice (1951), then the isolation of an oncogenic virus (later named polyoma) from leukemic tissue, and finally the isolation of a transmissible leukemogenic virus from radiation-induced leukemia in mice (1958). Dr. Gross has advanced the concept that cancer and its related killer diseases, such as leukemia and lymphomas, are caused by oncogenic viruses that remain latent in their carriers and that are transmitted from one generation to another. His studies of tumor viruses, and the concept of "vertical" transmission of oncogenic viruses between the generations, has revolutionized the modern experimental approaches to American cancer research, suggesting the important role of viruses in leukemia and malignant tumors. Among his many honors and appointments, Dr. Gross has headed the cancer research unit at the Bronx Veterans Administration Hospital since 1946; he has been the hospital's senior medical investigator since 1960, an associate scientist at the Sloan-Kettering Institute and research professor of medicine at the Mount Sinai School of Medicine, City University of New York. He is also a director of the American Association for Cancer Research. His brother, Dr. Felix Gross is president of the Polish Institute of Arts and Sciences in America.

Dr. Koprowski, who came to the United States in 1944, after four years of yellow fever research in Brazil, work on the Vitamin B complex at the Lister Institute in England, and other studies in virology and biochemistry, is director of the prestigious Wistar Institute in Philadelphia, Pennsylvania. He is Wistar professor of research medicine at the University of Pennsylvania and a member of the National Research Council of the National Academy of Sciences. He was also chairman, in 1964, of a U. S. Public Health Service mission to the Soviet Union, and the U.S. representative to the international committee of virus

Dr. Hilary Koprowski, the leading American specialist on the biology of cells, is Wistar professor of research medicine at the University of Pennsylvania, and a member of the National Research Council of the National Academy of Sciences. CREDIT: THE WISTAR INSTITUTE, PHILADELPHIA.

Dr. Ludwik Gross is a distinguished medical scientist whose studies of tumor viruses have revolutionized the modern experimental approaches to American cancer research. CREDIT: NATIONAL LIBRARY OF MEDICINE, BETHESDA, MARYLAND.

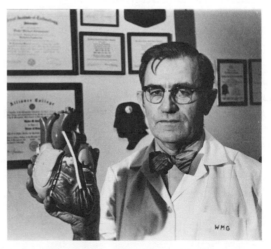

Dr. Walter M. Golaski, currently chairman of the board of the Kosciuszko Foundation, is shown in his laboratory with one of the vascular prostheses he had developed. PHOTO BY FRANK ALEKSANDROWICZ. COPYRIGHT © FRANK ALEKSANDROWICZ.

identification. He is the leading American specialist in biological research, with emphasis on the biology of cells.

Of comparable importance to the mechanically oriented American society were the inventions in medical equipment made by Dr. Walter M. Golaski, who developed the most successful vascular prostheses to date used in heart surgery throughout the world, and Zbyslaw M. Roehr, inventor of the disposable hypodermic needle and syringe, whose work was hailed by the American Medical Association in 1964 as among the five most significant medical advances in the preceding quarter century.

A Polish inventor whom American metallurgical engineers have placed on a par with Bessemer, Thomas, and Siemens in the lexicon of their industry's history is Dr. Tadeusz Sendzimir, who has been responsible for three striking technical developments that have totally revolutioned the steel industry's principal operations in galvanizing, annealing, and continuous rolling of steel. Of more than 50 patents in Dr. Sendzimir's name, these 3 have been enough to turn a brilliant engineer into a millionaire-philanthropist who is totally involved in Polish-American cultural and educational life. More than 140 steel plants throughout the world now use one or more of Dr. Sendzimir's inventions. His quite unostentatious headquarters in Connecticut (he has been an American citizen since 1947) are something of a mecca for young Polish engineers who come to study the Sendzimir techniques, then enter American industry with their own ideas. Another Polish wartime engineer-immigrant is Mieczyslaw Bekker, creator of the Moon Rover vehicle, which the American nation watched on television as it trundled about the lunar surface in man's first conquests of a planetary body outside his own natural living space.

The Second World War which, among pain and horror, also produced an aerospace industry, harnessed and then released the energies and talents of two other engineer-inventors (of partly Polish parentage): Aleksander de Seversky, who

Dr. Tadeusz Sendzimir, a Polish inventor, whose striking technical developments have revolutionized three of the steel industry's principal operations, holds more than 50 patents used by 140 steel concerns throughout the world. PHOTO BY FRANK ALEKSANDROWICZ. COPYRIGHT © FRANK ALEKSANDROWICZ.

founded the Republic Aircraft Corporation, and Igor Sikorsky, a pioneer in the helicopter industry. Sikorsky's work with the ungainly, spidery vehicles—which were to alter American military tactics in two later wars—found a talented successor in Frank N. Piasecki, founder of the Piasecki Aircraft Corporation and inventor of the flying Jeep.

These discoveries and inventions have all been a part of normal human enterprise, no matter how much specialized talent is involved. They are a product of conventional values, education, and a socially acceptable definition of accomplishment, against the background of America's material demands. But each age has its rare individuals of genius whose work becomes a monument for the ages and moves humanity itself; they possess an inspired creativity that makes them more than ordinarily human. One such wartime immigrant to America

The Moon Rover vehicle, shown here during the successful Apollo 15 exploratory flight in July 1971, was the brainchild of Mieczyslaw Bekker, another Polish scientist-immigrant. COURTESY OF NASA.

was Wanda Landowska, who began to study the piano at the age of four, in a self-contained world of the imagination where she could contemplate the gulfs between her vision of musical perfection and a musician's reality.

By the time she was fourteen, Landowska was a graduate of the Warsaw Conservatory of Music. In her performances as a concert pianist, her greatest triumph was her interpretation of Bach's intricate *English Suite in E Minor*. By the time she was twenty-one, she was well on her way to being Bach's pianist laureate, but this was not enough. She decided to revive Bach's favorite instrument, the concert harpsichord, as well as his work. Few more difficult instruments exist than the

eighteenth-century harpsichord—half a harp, half a piano with its double keyboard and deep, plunky tones, and nothing quite like either of those instruments. With her husband, folklorist Henri Lew, who died in 1919, she journeyed through European museums in search of harpsichords, and finally asked Paris's famed Pleyel to build for her a replica of the instrument on which Bach had played. Under Landowska's hands, the harpsichord took on a rare brilliance; through her, the works of Bach, Handel, and Mozart became a revelation to European concertgoers. In 1907 she carried her harpsichord by train and sleigh to Leo Tolstoy's home in Yasnaya Polyana and played for him while he talked to her.

From 1913 to 1919 she was a professor at

This early photograph of Wanda Landowska, the world's foremost exponent of the classical harpsichord, shows her in practice for her American debut with conductor Leopold Stokowski. Landowska did not come to settle in the United States until after the Second World War, but her international fame did much to bolster ethnic pride among Polish immigrants of an earlier era. CREDIT: NEW YORK PUBLIC LIBRARY, LINCOLN CENTER.

the musical Hochschule in Berlin, then settled in Paris. So many music-lovers made the pilgrimage to her suburban home that Paris station guards called the 2 P.M. Sunday run to Saint-Leu-la-Forêt "Mme. Landowska's train." In 1923 she shipped her harpsichord to Philadelphia for her American debut under conductor Leopold Stokowski—a musical genius in his own right who organized her visit to America. "Anyone who has heard Wanda Landowska play Bach's *Italian Concerto* on the harpsichord," wrote Albert Schweitzer, "finds it hard to understand how it could ever again be played on the piano." Her art caused Manuel de Falla to compose his *Harpsichord Concerto* especially for her.

The Second World War brought Landowska permanently to the United States. Her recording of the forty-eight labyrinthine preludes and fugues of Bach's *Well-tempered Clavier* is a modern classic. At seventy-six, she turned once more to the piano and the works of Mozart, working no less than five hours each day on her recordings of Mozart's sonatas, the *Rondo in A Minor,* and the *Country Dances.* In the autumn season of her life she recorded an album of Haydn sonatas and, in a final tribute to her own interpretation of her art, she made arrangements to record Bach's difficult *Three-part Inventions;* but on an August morning in 1959, she suffered a stroke and died at the age of eighty.

The war ended with the evil blossom of mushroom clouds over two cities in Japan. President Harry Truman put a small sign on his desk that stated that the buck stopped there. The American citizen-Army was dismantled, the citizen-Navy vanished under mothballs. Sixty million jobs, once a dream, barely accommodated returning servicemen. The colleges were jammed with veterans of all ages, studying under the G. I. Bill. Americans moved into suburban developments under a forest of television antennas; neighborhood movie theaters closed like banks in the Great Depression. Jet transportation shrunk the air spaces. The supermarket and the filter cigarette were born. Men scaled Mount Everest, and rocket scientists were looking at the moon.

In Europe, twelve million persons had no homes to which they might return; among them were more than two million Polish servicemen and women, survivors of Nazi concentration camps and Soviet slave labor, the lost and the wandering. They had been the first to stand against the Nazis, now they were herded into resettlement camps in England and into detention camps in Germany, resisting every Anglo-American pressure to return them to Communist-run Poland. In October 1948 they began arriving in America.

The first ship to bring some of them to New York, under the Displaced Persons Act that opened America's doors to the homeless, was the *General Black*, which sailed from Bremerhaven, Germany, in mid-October 1948. That weary old troopship's name would be adopted, in fond

irony, by a whole generation of eager young Polish student immigrants in the last half of the 1940s and the first half of the 1950s. Among the 831 "black generals" on board were several hundred of these youthful veterans whose childhood had taught them more of man's inhumanity to man than most persons witness in a lifetime. They had been wandering about the brutal face of Europe since Hitler's armies wrecked and scorched their country nine years earlier; they were anxious that all the "black generals" on this Polish *Mayflower* should finally find stability in a country of their own. Many children who stepped on American soil off that well-remembered ship had never seen fruit, and few of them

Three young Polish refugees, and their mother, arrive in New York aboard the General Black *in October 1948.* CREDIT: ACME PHOTO.

This twenty-eight-year-old Polish farmer, coming ashore off a troop transport in Boston in 1949, was the fifty thousandth refugee admitted to the United States under the Displaced Persons Act. He and his wife met in a German slave-labor camp. Their daughter was born there. CREDIT: NATIONAL ARCHIVES (USIA PHOTO).

knew what it was to sleep in a house (or a bed!) of their own. Scores of scientists, writers, and teachers were among them, brought to America by the Polish Institute of Arts and Sciences. The PNA and the Polish-American Congress stood as sponsors for several thousand others—and then allowed their talents to be wasted in manual labor until they could struggle up, on their own, into some level of security.

The young Poles who came to the United States in those postwar years were a distinct element that should not be confused with the older (émigré) arrivals. Most had been born in Poland but were brought up in countries other than their own, frequently in England and the English dominions; they were well-educated, poised, intelligent, and quite sure that America would be their country and their home. If Dr. Zbigniew Brzezinski is not en-

tirely representative of that remarkable group of immigrants, it's only because he is unique in any ethnic group and because he didn't have to cross the Atlantic to come to the United States.

The end of the war had found Zbigniew Brzezinski in Canada, where his father was serving as a member of the Polish diplomatic corps and where he completed his education and began his academic career. It was to be a step that would take him higher toward the seats of power than any Polish-American has ever approached.

As of this writing, Dr. Brzezinski is chairman of President Jimmy Carter's National Security Council, an advisory body that does not make policy but that creates those conditions under which policy may be made. As such, Dr. Brzezinski is the only Polish-American in the upper reaches of government today, the second to reach

Dr. Zbigniew Brzezinski, chairman of President Carter's National Security Council, is the second Polish-American to reach Cabinet-level rank in the U. S. Government. He is the first Polish-born American to do so. COURTESY OF ZBIGNIEW BRZEZINSKI.

Cabinet-level rank (although the NSC chairmanship is not a Cabinet position).

He came to the U. S. Government from Columbia University where he had been director of the prestigious Research Institute on Communist Affairs (renamed the Research Institute of International Change) and where he had proved himself a remarkable analyst of political behavior and a socio-political thinker of rare perception. As chairman of the recent (1973) Trilateral Commission, Dr. Brzezinski has established a reputation as one of the foremost American experts on Soviet policies and plans, and on the political, economic, and security problems of America's allies. As a foreign-policy adviser to three Presidents, Dr. Brzezinski was the author of President Johnson's "peaceful engagement policy" toward the Soviet Union and its satellites—a phrase taken by the President from one of Dr. Brzezinski's eight published books.

Another remarkable Polish social philosopher, who came to the United States after the Second World War, was Dr. Jacob Bronowski, who had been raised and educated in England, where he is best remembered for his eleven books, among them *Science and Human Values, The Face of Violence, William Blake and the Age of Revolution, The Identity of Man, Nature and Knowledge: The Philosophy of Contemporary Science,* and his last great work, *The Ascent of Man,* which was nothing less than a full-scale history of science developed from a BBC television series that Dr. Bronowski had written. Mathematician and statistician, poet, historian, inventor, and leader in the modern movement of scientific humanism, Dr. Bronowski was senior fellow of the Salk Institute for Biological Studies in San Diego, California, when he died in 1974.

Dr. Bronowski could not be called a member of the irreverent but determined "black generals" generation of new Americans (his evolution had taken a gentler path) but he shared their enthusiasm for America and their contempt for some of the insular-minded émigrés who had made

Dr. Jacob Bronowski—mathematician, historian, inventor, and poet—was a leader in the modern movement of scientific humanism and the author of eleven books, among them The Ascent of Man. PHOTO BY FRANK ALEKSANDROWICZ. COPYRIGHT © FRANK ALEKSANDROWICZ.

a patriotic virtue out of ignorance of American literature, history, and culture.

The student-immigrants of the postwar years had all been raised within the Polish cultural heritage, but they had seen quite enough of Europe. Virtually all of them worked their way through American colleges and universities (aided, when possible, by the Kosciuszko Foundation) and entered the American professions—mostly in medicine, the law, engineering, and the pure sciences. A few brave souls among them tried the dizzy, competitive world of American journalism, where the Poles are woefully unrepresented and frequently misrepresented. More than five thousand are now on the faculties of American universities, bringing the total of Polish-born, or -descended, American educators to well above twelve thousand. Their children, born in the 1950s and the 1960s, have truly inherited the best of both worlds: the rich humanist traditions of their parents' country, and all the opportunities and energy of their own America.

Joining this new American-born generation is one of the most extraordinary waves of all: the young creative artists, brought up in Marxist Poland, who have been coming to the United States in a steady flow since the 1960s. About two thousand Polish painters, sculptors, designers, musicians, conductors and actors, have landed in the United States in the last fifteen years, seeking that freedom of expression that is impossible in a more regimented society. Some —like the internationally renowned avant-garde theater director Jerzy Grotowski— come only to see America, touch the surfaces of the American arts, drink from the currents of Western literary and dramatic expression, demonstrate their skills, teach and return to Poland or go elsewhere to work. Most of them are young and they come to stay. No matter what America is, or may have been to others, it does provide a creative artist with the conditions that enable him to live in and for his art, developing in his own way, in his own time, and

not according to a Five-year Plan for social reconstruction. Their best work is still ahead of them, to America's profit.

Just as in former times it was Modjeska, Sembrich, Styka, Paderewski, Rubinstein, and Landowska who brought a distinctively Polish genius to the American arts, so today it is Skrowaczewski, Kosinski, Anuszkiewicz, Cybis, Polanski, Menkes, and Kuhr. A score of others, among them talented newcomers like the poet-novelist Jacek Gulla (forced out of Poland only five years ago and now writing in English) and Michal Urbaniak, a musical entrepreneur whose jazz Fusion group plays to full houses in New York's Greenwich Village, have not yet achieved international notice. But what is most encouraging to any student of Polish-American history, is the final emergence of young Polish artists, born in the United States since the Second World War, whose presence spells the end of Polish-American cultural and intellectual isolation. Elzbieta Szczygielska, born in 1950 of refugee parents in Detroit, and now completing her operatic training in Warsaw, may serve as an advance example of Polonia's future evolution.

Avant-garde director Jerzy Grotowski comes each year to the United States to teach his techniques to young American professionals in the performing arts. Here he is seen (seated, right) while conducting a technical seminar for actors and directors at Yale University. PHOTO BY PETER MOORE. COURTESY OF THE DRAMA REVIEW.

Stanislaw Skrowaczewski was only 38 when he was chosen from among 250 internationally famous candidates to become the conductor of the Minneapolis Symphony Orchestra—exactly 99 years after another Pole, Edward Sobolewski, organized the first symphonic orchestra in that city. As the young director of the National Philharmonic Orchestra in Warsaw, Skrowaczewski had come to the United States as guest conductor of the Cleveland and Pittsburgh orchestras in the 1950s, a period of seething intellectual and artistic discontent in Marxist Poland. These same tumultuous years would bring Jerzy Kosinski and Czeslaw Milosz to the United States. Kosinski would create brilliant novels of terrifying impact that would earn him the National Book Award in 1969 and the deserved reputation of a formidable literary artist. He is the only

Artur Rubinstein, considered the greatest living pianist, has been a lifelong Polish patriot. Asked to play at the opening session of the new United Nations in San Francisco—at which Poland had not been represented—he brought a highly embarrassed diplomatic audience to its feet by choosing for his concert the Polish National Anthem. PHOTO BY FRANK ALEKSANDROWICZ. © FRANK ALEKSANDROWICZ.

Stanislaw Skrowaczewski conducts a summer concert of the Milwaukee Symphony Orchestra. © FRANK ALEKSANDROWICZ.

Jerzy Kosinski is a distinguished American. novelist of international acclaim. PHOTO BY SCIENTIA.

foreign-born American literary figure to be awarded the coveted NBA—which is the *only* prize for contemporary literature honored by literate Americans; and he remains the only Pole to win the Award in Literature from the National Institute of Arts and Letters and the American Academy of Arts and Letters (1970). Kosinski is also the first foreign-born and -educated writer to be elected president of the American Center of PEN, the leading international association of poets, playwrights, essayists, editors, and novelists.

Milosz, the brilliant author of *The Captive Mind,* and the most widely translated contemporary Polish poet, sought political asylum in the West in 1951, in protest of the unenlightened policies of Poland's present rulers. He is currently professor of Slavic languages at the University of California, Berkeley. Among his books in English are *Native Realm: A Search for Self-definition,* and the monumental *History of Polish Literature,* which is the first such work written by a man whose creativity stands among the very small body of truly important poetry written in English today.

The 1960s would bring into maturity the work of Richard Anuszkiewicz, regarded as an important contemporary American op-art painter; while the world's most gigantic and ambitious sculpture, a monument to the Sioux Indian Chief Crazy Horse, began

to emerge under the hands of Janusz Korczak-Ziolkowski out of the cliff-face of Thunderhead Mountain in South Dakota. Planned for completion in 1981, Korczak-Ziolkowski's tribute to the conqueror of Custer will be 560 feet tall and 625 feet wide; the Polish sculptor expects the project to take him 30 years. A wholly different kind of sculptor, who arrived in the United States in the 1970s, is Yan Khur, founder of Ero-Art, in which human biological structures are used to express mankind's contemporary commitments and problems. In much the same manner, filmmaker Roman Polanski (*Knife in the Water, Cul-de-sac, Rosemary's Baby,* etc.) uses vivid erotic imagery in his exploration of twentieth-century human possibilities.

Their presence here may be said to complete the spectrum of Polish immigration. Through them, through the wholly Ameri-

Czeslaw Milosz, the leading contemporary Polish poet, essayist, and critic, is an exponent of modern literary humanism in three languages and the author of The Captive Mind. COURTESY OF CZESLAW MILOSZ. PHOTO BY G. PAUL BISHOP.

Janusz Korczak-Ziolkowski with the model of his monumental "Crazy Horse," which is to be the world's largest sculpture upon completion in the 1980s. CREDIT: SOUTH DAKOTA STATE HISTORICAL SOCIETY.

Richard Anuszkiewicz, American-born Polish painter of the optical artists group, with his "Apex" (rear) and "Mauve Plus" in the foreground. PHOTO BY FRANK ALEKSANDROWICZ. COPYRIGHT © FRANK ALEKSANDROWICZ.

Sculptor Yan Khur (Jan Kuracinski) explains the dynamics of his work, which uses biological structures to express contemporary human commitments and problems. COURTESY OF BARBARA LOJKOWNA.

American-born Elzbieta Szczygielska, who is completing her operatic training in Europe, represents a new generation of young artists who are finally beginning to emerge from the Polish-American community.

can children of the young postwar student-immigrants, and through the fourth generation descended from the peasant workers (who are beginning to reach into the arts beyond the limits of middle-class achievement), Poland's traditionally finest gift—the imagination of its creative artists—is

Urszula Dudziak sings at the Village Gate, while her husband, Michael Urbaniak (right), leads his jazz group Fusion.

PHOTO BY FRANK ALEKSANDROWICZ.

COPYRIGHT © FRANK ALEKSANDROWICZ.

joining the cultivated idealism of the aristocracy, the blood of the soldiers, the sweat of the peasants, and the inventive talents of the middle class among us.

The true figure for Polish-Americans stands at 10 million to 12 million today. Fewer than 500,000 are fluent in Polish. Most of them are Americans who are removed by three or four generations from European origins. They form about 10,000 fraternal, dramatic, musical, literary, religious, athletic, and social organizations, most of which are affiliated with national associations that number more than 800,000 members. With no assistance from an unconcerned American Roman Catholic hierarchy, they have built 899 Roman Catholic parishes, 553 elementary schools, 71 high schools, 8 colleges, 4 seminaries, 34 hospitals, and 146 other institutions connected with education or social services.

The Polish National Catholic Church, founded by Bishop Hodur, now has 140 parishes, with more than 300,000 members.

Today there are three major daily newspapers published in the Polish language in the United States, including the influential *Nowy Dziennik,* which serves the New York metropolitan area's million Polish-Americans. The weekly and biweekly Polish-language and English-language press for Poles numbers about 30 publications, including the PNA's *Zgoda,* with a circulation of more than 320,000. Among some three dozen quarterlies that operate on a variety of cultural and intellectual levels, the most prestigious is the *Polish Review* of the Polish Institute of Arts and Sciences, edited by Professor Ludwik Krzyzanowski, one of the original founders of the Institute in the United States.

As in the purely American communications media, the Roman Catholic hierarchy, and the creative (rather than performing) arts, native-born Polish-Americans are virtually unrepresented in U. S. Government and high political office—a cause of growing anger and frustration for Polonia's emerging younger leadership. Senator Edmund Muskie, a respected leader of the Democratic party, and a former governor of Maine, is an exception to this impoverishing rule, as are 10 members of the House of Representatives, each of whom either heads or serves on a critical committee. Among the most influential of these American legislators is Rep. Klenent Zablocki, chairman of the powerful House Foreign Relations Committee.

Senator Muskie's rise in Washington has not been typical of the Polish-American political experience, either in style or substance, nor has he ever been that most appalling of ethnic creations: the professional ethnic politician. His Polish background, a matter of quiet pride devoid of rhetoric, has not been a help to his greater political ambitions, but it may have helped to shape his understated political personality. He has never used the Polish-American community to his ends, nor has he ever allowed any community to use him; in this he has dismayed some lesser Polish-American leaders who insist on manipulating their unwilling symbols.

In his eighteen years in the Senate (he was re-elected to his fourth term in 1976), he has built a reputation as a competent American politician—a man who works hard, tends to his business, does his homework, and speaks only when he has something to say. His skills as a legislator and his capacity for hard work caused the Democratic party to nominate him for Vice President in 1968, and he was a serious contender for the presidency four years later. Because he refused to bend to pressure that would commit his vote to a proposed rules change, he did not win the Senate committee assignments he had sought. But over the years he has become a Senate expert in government and environmental affairs (his home state of Maine has much to do with that), in national and international economics, and in the structure of American finance and business.

Senator Muskie is chairman of the Senate Committee on the Budget, which has become a most important position in the era of continuing economic problems, and he has been the leader in two of the most imaginative approaches enacted in the past

United States Senator Edmund S. Muskie is the first Polish-American to have been elected governor of his state and U.S. senator. PHOTO BY JACK PUTNAM. COURTESY OF EDMUND MUSKIE.

decade to stimulating jobs and business activity across the country. The first, passed in 1965, was the Public Works and Economic Development Act, landmark legislation that attacked unemployment on regional, state, and local levels and that created the Economic Development Administration to aid small businesses and communities. The second, finally passed in 1976 after two presidential vetoes, was the Countercyclical Assistance Amendment, the only truly new antirecession idea considered in the Administrations of Presidents Nixon and Ford. Senator Muskie authored the provision, then guided its passage in the Senate and the House of Representatives, despite White House hostility and the opposition of a key House chairman.

Remarkably little oratory has come from this man, the second of six children of a Polish tailor (Stefan Marciszewski) who came to the United States in 1903, in flight from Russian conscription, and settled in

Mary Ann Krupsak, seen here talking with a delegation of young Polish nuns, is the first woman to be elected lieutenant governor of New York, and the first Polish-American woman to hold high public office in the United States. PHOTO BY FRANK ALEKSANDROWICZ. COPYRIGHT ©️ FRANK ALEKSANDROWICZ.

Dr. John Gronouski, former U. S. Postmaster-General and American ambassador to Poland, was the first Polish-American to become a member of the Cabinet in Washington, D.C. He is shown here outside his offices at the Lyndon B. Johnson School of Public Affairs, University of Texas, where he served as dean. He now heads U.S. information broadcast services to Iron Curtain countries. PHOTO BY FRANK ALEKSANDROWICZ.

Rumford, Maine, where the future senator was born. In his good-humored, brief campaign biography, written while he was a contender for the presidency (*Journeys* [New York: Doubleday, 1972]), Senator Muskie wrote warmly of his father's influence—an indication of respect for his Polish past that has never been allowed to intrude into his American present.

On state government level, Mary Ann Krupsak has been elected as the first woman to hold the office of lieutenant governor in New York, and the younger generations of Polish-Americans view this event with considerable hope for their own overdue participation in American public life.

In the federal government, Dr. John Gronouski, formerly dean of the Lyndon Johnson School for Public Affairs, had been

Mitchell Kobelinski, of Chicago, was appointed head of the U. S. Small Business Administration by President Gerald Ford. PHOTO BY FRANK ALEKSANDROWICZ. COPYRIGHT ©️ FRANK ALEKSANDROWICZ.

U. S. Postmaster-General and U.S. ambassador to Poland—the first Polish-American to hold a Cabinet post. More recently, Chicago finance expert Mitchell Kobelinski had been appointed head of the Small Business Administration.

Tradition has it that the only way that immigrant miners' sons could get into an American college was by trading their brawn for athletic scholarships. Certainly, no other kinds of scholarships were available to them until the G. I. Bill of Rights of the Second World War. Whatever the truth about that may be, Polish-American football stars have become an institution in college and professional leagues ever since Bronislaw "Bronco" Nagurski led the University of Notre Dame's immortal "Four Horsemen" in the 1920s—causing Coach Knute Rockne of the Fighting Irish to say: "If I can't pronounce their names, I know they are good."

Frank Piekarski was the first Polish-American to be named to the All-American football squad in 1904. Since then, among the most valuable gridiron stars have been John Matuszak (the Washington Redskins and the Oakland Raiders), Walt Patulski (Notre Dame and the St. Louis Cardinals), the brothers Dick and Ed Modzelewski (the latter of the New York Giants), the Kansas City Chiefs' iron-willed coach Hank Stram (lately with the New Orleans Saints), Steve Bartkowski (University of California), Steve Pisarkiewicz (University of Missouri), Greg Landry (Detroit Lions), Ron Jaworski (Los Angeles Rams), Mark Olejniczak (New York Giants), Mike Boryla (Philadelphia Eagles), Bob Bobrowski (Baltimore Colts), and Steve Okoniewski and Chester Marcol, both of the Green Bay Packers.

In baseball, the great Stan Musial of the St. Louis Cardinals and Carl "Yaz" Yastrzemski of the Boston Red Sox have won their own niches in the history of the oldest

John Matuszak plays as the star defensive lineman of the Oakland Raiders, the 1977 National Football League champions. PHOTO BY FRANK ALEKSANDROWICZ. COPYRIGHT © FRANK ALEKSANDROWICZ.

Carl "Yaz" Yastrzemski, Boston Red Sox outfielder and first baseman, holds many American League baseball records. PHOTO BY FRANK ALEKSANDROWICZ. COPYRIGHT © FRANK ALEKSANDROWICZ.

Stan "The Man" Musial, a baseball immortal, leads the "Polonaise" at the Kosciuszko Foundation's annual debutante ball in the Waldorf-Astoria. PHOTO BY FRANK ALEKSANDROWICZ. COPYRIGHT © FRANK ALEKSANDROWICZ.

Danny Abramowicz was a record pass-receiver when he played football with the San Francisco Forty-niners. PHOTO BY FRANK ALEKSANDROWICZ. COPYRIGHT © FRANK ALEKSANDROWICZ.

Walt Patulski played football for Notre Dame, then became a star defensive end for the Buffalo Bills. He is now with the St. Louis Cardinals. PHOTO BY FRANK ALEKSANDROWICZ. COPYRIGHT © FRANK ALEKSANDROWICZ.

Dick Modzelewski, formerly a star defensive player with the New York Giants and the Cleveland Browns, is shown here during a recent Browns' game, where he is the defensive coach. PHOTO BY FRANK ALEKSANDROWICZ. COPYRIGHT © FRANK ALEKSANDROWICZ.

Hank Stram, former coach of the legendary Kansas City Chiefs, now coaches the New Orleans Saints. © FRANK ALEKSANDROWICZ.

American team sport. Others whose names have become synonyms for endurance and skill are Al Simmons, Pete Rose, Tony Kubek, Greg Luzinski, Richie Zisk, Ted Kluszewski, Ed Lopat, Jim Konstanty, Ray Jablonski, Hank Majeski, George Shuba, Bill Skowron, Ted Kazanski, Bob Kuzava, Steve Gromek, Chet Laske, Cass Michaels, Eddie Lubanski, and Stan Lopata.

These, then, are some of the distinguished Americans of Polish origin or descent, and this has been their story in the United States. American historians have virtually ignored them, no history of their three hundred years in America has ever been written outside the narrow reach of Polish academic circles, and amateur ethnic apologists have only managed to compound the confusion.

There have been no significant movements in American history in which the Poles have not played a part, no area of American life in which they have not left an imprint of their own. They are today a vital and energetic community of Americans, of many talents and considerable material resources, whose voice is only now beginning to be heard. The swift and swelling tides of a changing world wash against their values and traditions; their former goals of middle-class security no longer seem sufficient in their evolution.

Old Europe knew them well as a fearsomely proud and independent people who seldom could be led and never controlled. Rapacious neighbors could swallow their country but never digest them. A German philosopher has described them as an authoritarian's despair.

Their humor is full of stories of shipwrecked Poles who first thank God for dry land and then immediately organize as many warring political camps (and twice as many newspapers) as there are survivors. Their ruinous history has taught them the value of thinking for themselves. Having been led to near disaster so often in their thousand years of recorded history, they distrust leadership, each thinking himself at least the equal of anyone who would presume to lead him, but once committed to a course, they cannot be turned. One national characteristic that all Poles seem to share, no matter what their era, social origin, or intellectual level, is a spirit of curiosity and restlessness that makes them unable to accept any limitations on their possibilities that they do not voluntarily impose upon themselves. This quality, a source of tireless energy and frequent inspiration, gave the New World a special meaning to early Polish settlers and has particular relevance to the Poles in America today.

There are many dreams left to all Americans, we have not yet evolved into what we shall be; and dreams of the future are at least as good as dreams of the past. They are alive, they beckon.